I0006026

START WITH AZURE: LEARN IT FAST, BUILD IT RIGHT.

FIRST EDITION

Preface

Welcome to *Start with Azure: Learn It Fast, Build It Right*. This book is designed to provide a practical and approachable introduction to Microsoft Azure for those who are just stepping into the world of cloud computing. Whether you're a student, a developer, a business professional, or someone simply curious about cloud platforms, this book aims to break down Azure in a straightforward, easy-to-understand way—without all the unnecessary jargon.

The journey begins with Chapter 1, where we explore the fundamental concepts of Azure and the evolution of cloud computing. You'll learn why Azure has become one of the leading platforms in the industry and how it compares to other major cloud providers.

In Chapter 2, you'll get hands-on with setting up your Azure environment. From creating your first Azure account to understanding the layout of the Azure Portal and essential tools like Azure CLI and PowerShell, this chapter sets the stage for everything that follows.

Chapter 3 is where the core services of Azure come into play. You'll gain a solid foundation in compute, storage, networking, and database services—key pillars that form the infrastructure of virtually every Azure-based solution.

By the time you reach Chapter 4, you'll be ready to build and deploy your first app on Azure. We walk you through service selection, development environment setup, deployment strategies, and how to integrate DevOps practices to streamline your workflows.

Security is crucial in the cloud, and Chapter 5 dives into identity management and protection strategies using tools like Azure Active Directory, Key Vault, and network security groups.

Monitoring and diagnostics are essential for keeping your applications running smoothly. Chapter 6 teaches you how to use Azure Monitor, Application Insights, and other tools to track performance and troubleshoot issues effectively.

Chapter 7 focuses on scalability and performance optimization. You'll explore how to design systems that not only handle growth but do so cost-effectively, leveraging autoscaling and Azure's pricing tools.

As you become more comfortable with Azure basics, Chapter 8 takes things to the next level with advanced services and real-world scenarios. Learn about serverless computing, container orchestration with Kubernetes, AI-powered services, and hybrid deployments with Azure Arc.

In Chapter 9, we bring it all together with practical use cases and project ideas. These examples are designed to show how Azure is used in real-world environments—from serverless APIs to scalable e-commerce platforms.

For those interested in certification, Chapter 10 is your guide. It provides insights into Microsoft's certification tracks, effective study resources, and tips to pass your exams with confidence.

Finally, Chapter 11 serves as your reference toolkit with glossaries, links for further learning, sample code, and frequently asked questions.

This book isn't just a guide—it's a launchpad. By the time you reach the end, you'll be equipped with both the knowledge and the confidence to start building your future in the cloud.

Table of Contents

Preface 0

Chapter 1: Introduction to Microsoft Azure...19

  What is Azure? 19

    The Cloud Explained 19

    Azure at a Glance..19

    Azure's Global Infrastructure 20

    Azure's Value Proposition 20

    Azure Service Models..20

    Example: Creating a Virtual Machine...20

    Use Cases for Azure 21

    Azure Pricing and Cost Management 21

    Getting Started with Azure 22

  The Evolution of Cloud Computing 22

    From Mainframes to Virtualization 22

    The Emergence of Cloud Computing 23

    Key Milestones in Cloud Computing History...23

    Cloud Service Models 23

    Technological Shifts Driving Cloud Growth 24

    Benefits Realized Over Time 25

    The Hybrid and Multi-Cloud Era 25

    Cloud-Native and Serverless Computing 25

    Cloud's Role in Digital Transformation 26

    Real-World Example: A Retail Company 26

    Future Trends in Cloud Computing 26

    Conclusion 27

  Core Benefits of Using Azure..27

    Global Reach and Availability 27

    Unparalleled Scalability 28

    Flexible Pricing and Cost Management...28

    Robust Security and Compliance 29

    Hybrid Capabilities 30

    Integrated Development and DevOps Tools 30

    Rich AI and Analytics Capabilities..31

    High Availability and Disaster Recovery 32

Continuous Innovation...32

Ecosystem Integration 33

Community and Support..33

Azure vs. Other Cloud Providers 34

Market Position and Adoption 34

Service Offerings: Breadth and Depth...34

Pricing Models and Cost Management...35

Developer and DevOps Tooling 36

Hybrid and On-Prem Integration 37

Identity, Security, and Governance..37

Compliance and Certifications 38

AI, Machine Learning, and Big Data..38

User Experience and Management Tools...39

Support and Documentation 39

Summary Comparison Table 40

Conclusion 40

Chapter 2: Setting Up Your Azure Environment 42

Creating an Azure Account 42

Why You Need an Azure Account 42

Step-by-Step: Creating a Free Azure Account...42

Navigating the Azure Account Hierarchy 43

Choosing a Subscription Plan..44

Securing Your Azure Account...44

Exploring the Azure Portal..45

Using Azure Cloud Shell 45

CLI Authentication Options 46

Setting Up Billing Alerts..47

Common Issues and Troubleshooting 47

Summary 47

Navigating the Azure Portal 48

What is the Azure Portal? 48

Logging In and First-Time Experience 49

Key Interface Areas 49

Customizing Your Dashboard 50

Managing Resources via the Portal 51

Using Azure Marketplace 52

Monitoring and Alerts 53

Portal Shortcuts and Productivity Tips 53

Integrating Azure CLI and Cloud Shell 53

Troubleshooting Common Issues 54

Summary 54

Understanding Azure Subscriptions and Resource Groups 55

What is an Azure Subscription? 55

Why Use Multiple Subscriptions? 56

Creating and Managing Subscriptions 56

Role-Based Access Control (RBAC) at Subscription Level 57

What is a Resource Group? 57

Best Practices for Structuring Resource Groups 58

Creating a Resource Group 58

Moving Resources Between Groups 59

Deleting a Resource Group 59

Tagging Resource Groups 60

Policies and Locks 60

Viewing and Auditing Activity 61

Summary 61

Essential Tools: Azure CLI, PowerShell, and Cloud Shell 62

Overview of Azure Command-Line Tools 62

Azure CLI 63

Azure PowerShell 64

Azure Cloud Shell 66

Choosing the Right Tool 67

Integrating Tools with DevOps Workflows 67

Troubleshooting Common Issues 68

Summary 68

Chapter 3: Core Azure Services Explained 70

Compute Services (VMs, App Services, Functions) 70

Virtual Machines (VMs) 70

Azure App Services 71

Azure Functions 72

Choosing the Right Compute Service 74

Summary 74

Storage Solutions (Blob, Table, File, Queue) 75

Azure Storage Overview 75

Blob Storage 75

Table Storage 77

File Storage 78

Queue Storage 80

Security and Access...81

Monitoring and Management..81

Summary 82

Networking Basics (VNets, Load Balancers, DNS) 82

Azure Virtual Networks (VNets)..82

Network Security Groups (NSGs) 84

Azure Load Balancer..84

Azure DNS 86

Application Gateway 87

Private Endpoints and Service Endpoints 87

Traffic Manager and Front Door 88

Best Practices for Azure Networking..88

Summary 89

Databases on Azure (SQL Database, Cosmos DB, MySQL) 90

Azure SQL Database 90

Azure Cosmos DB 91

Azure Database for MySQL...93

Security and Compliance...94

Backup and Disaster Recovery 95

Monitoring and Performance Tuning...95

Cost Optimization Tips...96

Choosing the Right Azure Database..96

Summary 97

Chapter 4: Building and Deploying Your First Azure App 98

Choosing the Right Azure Services 98

Understanding Your Application Requirements...98

Selecting the Compute Service 98

Choosing the Right Database...100

Storing Application Files and Assets 101

Networking and Access Control 101

CI/CD and DevOps Integration 102

Logging, Monitoring, and Alerting 103

Security Considerations 104

Sample Architecture Scenarios..104

Summary 105

Setting Up a Development Environment 105

Choosing Your Development Machine Setup 106

Installing Azure CLI and PowerShell 106

Setting Up Visual Studio Code (VS Code) 107

Configuring SDKs and Runtime Environments 108

Setting Up Docker and Kubernetes 109

Using Azure Dev CLI (azd) 109

Version Control and GitHub Integration 110

Emulators and Local Services...110

Environment Variables and Configuration...111

Setting Up CI/CD with Azure DevOps or GitHub Actions 111

Debugging and Live Testing...112

Summary 113

Deploying via Azure App Services 113

Why Use Azure App Services?..113

Creating an App Service Plan...114

Creating the Web App 114

Deploying Code 114

Setting Environment Variables...115

Using Deployment Slots 116

Managing Application Configuration...116

Monitoring and Logging...117

Scaling the App...118

Secure Your App...118

Common Deployment Scenarios 118

Troubleshooting Deployments...119

Summary 120

Continuous Integration and Delivery with Azure DevOps...120

Overview of Azure DevOps Services 120

Setting Up a CI/CD Pipeline 121

Configuring a Build Pipeline (CI)...121

Setting Up a Release Pipeline (CD)..122

Environments and Approvals 123

Running Tests Automatically 123

Managing Secrets with Azure Key Vault 124

Parallel Jobs and Matrix Builds..125

Notifications and Integration 125

Deploying to Kubernetes (AKS) 126

Best Practices for CI/CD 126

Summary 127

Chapter 5: Security and Identity Management in Azure.......................................128

Introduction to Azure Active Directory 128

What is Azure Active Directory? 128

Azure AD Editions 128

Authentication and SSO...129

☐Multi-Factor Authentication (MFA) 129

☐Conditional Access...130

Azure AD B2B and B2C 131

Integration with On-Premises Active Directory 132

☐Privileged Identity Management (PIM) 132

Best Practices for Azure AD 133

Conclusion 133

Managing Users, Groups, and Roles...133

User Management in Azure AD 134

Managing Groups 135

Assigning Users to Groups 136

Role-Based Access Control (RBAC)...136

Custom Roles...138

Group-Based Access Management 138

Directory Roles (Azure AD Roles)...138

Lifecycle Management 139

Best Practices 139

Conclusion 140

Azure Key Vault and Secrets Management...140

Overview of Azure Key Vault 140

Creating a Key Vault..141

Storing and Retrieving Secrets 141

Access Control 142

Keys and Cryptographic Operations 143

Managing Certificates 144

Soft Delete and Purge Protection..144

Audit Logging 145

Integration with Azure Services 146

Programmatic Access via SDKs 146

Best Practices 147

Conclusion 147

Network Security Groups and Firewalls 147

What Are Network Security Groups?...148

NSG Security Rule Structure 148

Creating an NSG 149

Associating NSGs..150

Application Security Groups (ASGs) 150

Azure Firewall 151

Deploying Azure Firewall 151

Firewall vs. NSG...152

Using Route Tables (UDRs) 153

Threat Intelligence 153

Logging and Monitoring...154

Best Practices 154

Conclusion 155

Chapter 6: Monitoring, Logging, and Diagnostics...............................156

Azure Monitor and Log Analytics 156

Overview of Azure Monitor 156

Data Sources for Azure Monitor...157

Log Analytics Workspaces 157

Writing KQL Queries 158

Metrics in Azure Monitor...158

Dashboards and Workbooks 159

Alerts and Actions 160

Action Groups...161

Monitoring Non-Azure Resources...161

Integration with Other Services..161

Best Practices 162

Conclusion 162

Setting Up Alerts and Dashboards 162

Types of Alerts in Azure..163

Metric Alerts 163

Log Alerts 164

Activity Log Alerts 165

Action Groups...165

Suppression and Alert Rules..166

Alert Severity Levels 166

Dashboards in Azure..167

Workbooks vs Dashboards 169

Best Practices for Alerts and Dashboards 169

Conclusion 170

Diagnosing Issues with Application Insights 170

Core Concepts of Application Insights 170

Enabling Application Insights 171

Real-Time Monitoring Dashboard 172

Investigating Failures...173

Diagnosing Performance Issues 173

Distributed Tracing with Application Map 174

Availability Tests 174

Live Metrics Stream..175

Custom Events and Metrics..176

Smart Detection and Anomaly Detection 176

Integration with DevOps and Incident Response 177

Exporting Data 177

Best Practices 177

Conclusion 178

Leveraging Azure Advisor..178

What is Azure Advisor? 178

Accessing Azure Advisor 179

Understanding Advisor Categories 179

Implementing Advisor Recommendations 182

Integrating Advisor into DevOps..183

Programmatic Filtering 183

Tagging and Governance...184

Best Practices 184

Conclusion 185
Chapter 7: Scaling and Performance Optimization 186
Autoscaling Strategies 186
Why Autoscaling Matters...186
Azure Autoscale Options..186
Virtual Machine Scale Sets (VMSS)...186
App Service Autoscaling 188
Azure Kubernetes Service (AKS) Autoscaling..188
Serverless Autoscaling 189
Best Practices for Autoscaling...190
Real-World Scenario: E-Commerce Application...190
Summary 191
Load Balancing Techniques...191
Why Load Balancing Is Essential..191
Azure Load Balancing Solutions Overview...192
Azure Load Balancer 192
Azure Application Gateway 193
Azure Front Door 194
Azure Traffic Manager 195
Comparing Azure Load Balancing Solutions...196
Load Balancing in Real Architectures 196
Best Practices for Load Balancing 197
Summary 198
Cost Management and Optimization 198
Understanding Azure Pricing 198
Core Cost Optimization Principles..199
Azure Cost Management + Billing...199
Cost-Saving Features by Service..200
Tagging for Cost Visibility 201
Governance Through Azure Policy and Blueprints......................................202
Real-World Optimization Scenario..203
Cost Forecasting and Trend Analysis 203
Leveraging Azure Advisor 204
Summary 205
Designing for High Availability 205
Core Principles of High Availability 205

Azure Regions and Availability Zones...206
High Availability for Compute Resources 206
High Availability for Data and Storage 207
Networking for High Availability 208
Automation and Recovery 209
HA for Serverless and Containers 210
Multi-Region High Availability 210
Monitoring and Health Checks 211
Real-World Architecture Example...211
Summary 212
Chapter 8: Advanced Azure Services and Scenarios..214
Serverless Architectures with Azure Functions..214
What is Serverless Computing?..214
Azure Functions: Overview and Use Cases...214
Hosting Plans for Azure Functions...215
Anatomy of an Azure Function..216
Triggers and Bindings..216
Deploying Azure Functions 217
Monitoring and Troubleshooting 218
Durable Functions: Serverless Orchestration 219
Best Practices for Serverless Architectures...219
Real-World Example: Image Processing Pipeline 220
Summary 221
Containers and Kubernetes on Azure 221
Why Containers? 221
Azure Container Services Overview 222
Azure Container Instances (ACI)...222
Azure Kubernetes Service (AKS) 223
Creating an AKS Cluster 224
Deploying to AKS: Basic YAML Example...224
Helm: Kubernetes Package Management 225
Container Registries...225
Networking and Ingress Controllers 226
Security and Identity 227
Monitoring and Logging..227
Best Practices for Containers and AKS 228

Real-World Scenario: Microservices on AKS 228

Summary 229

AI and Machine Learning with Azure Cognitive Services 230

What is Azure Cognitive Services? 230

Setting Up Cognitive Services in Azure 231

Computer Vision 231

Speech Services 232

Language Services 233

Decision Services 233

Deployment and Customization Options 234

Integrating AI into Applications 235

Monitoring, Governance, and Compliance 235

Best Practices 236

Summary 236

Hybrid Cloud with Azure Arc 237

What is Azure Arc? 237

Key Benefits of Azure Arc 238

Onboarding Machines to Azure Arc 238

Azure Arc for Kubernetes 239

Azure Arc-Enabled Data Services 240

Governance and Policy Management with Arc 241

Security Integration 242

DevOps and Automation with GitOps 242

Real-World Scenario: Hybrid Retail Infrastructure 243

Best Practices 244

Summary 244

Chapter 9: Real-World Projects and Use Cases 246

Building a Serverless Web API 246

Project Overview 246

Architecture 247

Step 1: Environment Setup 247

Step 2: Create the Azure Function App 248

Step 3: Build Function Endpoints 248

Step 4: Test Locally and Deploy 251

Step 5: Secure the API 251

Step 6: Monitor and Optimize 252

Step 7: CI/CD with GitHub Actions...253
Summary and Learnings..254
Migrating a Legacy App to Azure 255
Legacy App Overview 255
Step 1: Assessment and Planning 255
Step 2: Choosing a Migration Strategy...256
Step 3: Migrating the Web Application 257
Step 4: Migrating the Database 258
Step 5: Handling File Storage...259
Step 6: Securing the Application 260
Step 7: Observability and Optimization..261
Step 8: CI/CD Pipeline Integration...261
Step 9: Post-Migration Enhancements 262
Summary and Lessons Learned 263
Setting Up a Secure Multi-Region App...263
Objectives...264
High-Level Architecture 264
Step 1: Create Resource Groups in Both Regions 264
Step 2: Deploy Web Apps 265
Step 3: Configure Azure SQL Geo-Replication 265
Step 4: Setup Azure Front Door 266
Step 5: Secure with Key Vault and Managed Identity 268
Step 6: Monitoring and Alerts..269
Step 7: Automate with GitHub Actions 269
Step 8: Enhancements 271
Summary 271
Hosting a Scalable E-commerce Platform 271
Key Requirements 272
Architecture Overview..272
Step 1: Create the Frontend...273
Step 2: Set Up Authentication 274
Step 3: Deploy Backend Microservices...274
Step 4: Database Design and Setup 275
Step 5: Integrate Queueing for Resilient Workflows 276
Step 6: Enable Caching...276
Step 7: Add Search Capability...276

Step 8: Secure the Platform 277
Step 9: Monitoring and Observability 277
Step 10: Automate CI/CD with GitHub Actions 278
Step 11: Scaling and Global Distribution 279
Summary 280
Chapter 10: Preparing for Azure Certification.................................281
Overview of Azure Certification Tracks 281
Certification Levels and Roles 281
Azure Fundamentals (Beginner Level) 282
Role-Based Associate Certifications 282
Expert-Level Certifications 284
Specialized Certifications 286
Certification Benefits..286
Choosing the Right Path 286
Summary 287
Study Resources and Practice Exams 287
Microsoft Learn: The Official Starting Point 288
Microsoft Documentation and Exam Guides 288
Hands-On Labs and Sandboxes..289
Video Courses and Bootcamps...290
Books and Study Guides 290
Practice Exams and Simulators 291
Building a Study Plan..292
Learning Communities and Forums 293
Summary 293
Tips for Exam Success 294
Understand the Exam Format..294
Pre-Exam Preparation Tips 294
Memory and Study Techniques...296
Practice Tests: Use Wisely 296
Exam Day Tips 297
During the Exam: Mindset and Focus 298
After the Exam: Review and Reflect 298
Common Mistakes to Avoid...299
Summary 299
Continuing Your Azure Learning Path 300

Embrace Lifelong Learning in Cloud 300

Create a Personalized Learning Map 300

Use Microsoft Learn for Continued Growth 301

Join Cloud Communities and Stay Engaged 302

Build and Share Real-World Projects 302

Maintain and Renew Certifications 303

Explore Advanced Topics and Emerging Tech 303

Build Toward Expert Roles and Multi-Cloud Skills 304

Give Back: Teach, Mentor, and Lead 304

Summary 305

Chapter 11: Appendices 306

Glossary of Terms...306

A 306

B 306

C 307

D 307

E 307

F...308

G 308

H 308

I..308

J...309

K 309

L...309

M..309

N 310

O 310

P 310

Q..310

R 311

S 311

T...311

U 311

V 312

W 312

X 312

Y 312

Z..312

Summary 313

Resources for Further Learning 313

Microsoft Learn...313

Microsoft Documentation 314

GitHub Repositories 314

YouTube Channels 315

Books...315

Blogs and Newsletters 316

Learning Platforms 317

Events and Conferences...317

Certification Support and Communities...318

Developer and Architecture Tools 318

Long-Term Learning Plans 319

Summary 319

Sample Projects and Code Snippets..319

Project 1: Azure Web App with Continuous Deployment 320

Project 2: Serverless API with Azure Functions and Cosmos DB 321

Project 3: Static Website Hosting with Blob Storage and CDN............323

Project 4: Securing a Web App with Azure AD Authentication............324

Project 5: Infrastructure as Code with Bicep 325

Project 6: Real-Time Notification System with SignalR 326

Project 7: CI/CD Pipeline with Azure DevOps 327

Summary of Learning Outcomes 328

API Reference Guide..329

Azure REST API Basics...329

Authentication with Azure APIs 329

Common Azure Management APIs 330

Using SDKs Instead of Raw HTTP 332

Monitoring and Logging APIs...333

Azure Graph API vs Azure REST API...334

Rate Limiting and Throttling 334

Automation with REST APIs 335

API Best Practices 335

Summary 336

Frequently Asked Questions 336

    General Azure Questions 337

    Services and Usage 337

    Cost and Pricing 337

    Identity and Security 338

    Development and Deployment 338

    Monitoring and Troubleshooting 339

    Networking and Access 339

    Governance and Policy 340

    Certification and Learning 340

    Miscellaneous 340

    Summary 341

Chapter 1: Introduction to Microsoft Azure

What is Azure?

Microsoft Azure is a cloud computing platform and service created by Microsoft, offering a broad set of global cloud services to help organizations meet their business challenges. These services include computing power, analytics, storage, networking, databases, machine learning, IoT, and much more. Azure provides developers and IT professionals with the tools and capabilities to build, deploy, and manage applications through Microsoft-managed data centers.

The Cloud Explained

To understand Azure, we first need to grasp the broader concept of the cloud. The cloud refers to the delivery of computing services—such as servers, storage, databases, networking, software, analytics, and intelligence—over the internet. Instead of buying and maintaining physical hardware or software, you access these services on-demand from a provider like Microsoft.

This paradigm shift allows businesses and developers to scale their infrastructure up or down rapidly, pay only for what they use, and avoid the complexities of traditional IT setups.

Azure at a Glance

Azure is one of the "big three" public cloud providers, alongside Amazon Web Services (AWS) and Google Cloud Platform (GCP). Launched in 2010, Azure has grown to encompass over 200 services and is available in more regions globally than any other cloud provider. Azure's services are divided into several broad categories:

- **Compute**: Services that allow you to run applications in the cloud using virtual machines, containers, or serverless functions.

- **Storage**: Reliable and scalable cloud storage for structured and unstructured data.

- **Networking**: Tools to manage secure connections between Azure services, your on-premises environment, and the internet.

- **Databases**: Managed services for relational, NoSQL, and in-memory databases.

- **AI and Machine Learning**: APIs and frameworks to build intelligent apps.

- **DevOps**: CI/CD pipelines, project tracking, and collaboration tools.

Azure's Global Infrastructure

Azure's infrastructure is built around **regions** and **availability zones**. A region is a set of datacenters deployed within a specific geographic area. Availability zones within a region are physically separated datacenters with their own power, cooling, and networking to ensure resilience and high availability.

Azure currently operates in over 60 regions around the world, giving customers the flexibility to deploy resources where it makes the most business sense or meets compliance needs.

Azure's Value Proposition

Azure is designed to cater to a broad spectrum of users—from startups and independent developers to Fortune 500 companies and government organizations. Its value proposition includes:

- **Scalability**: Easily scale applications vertically or horizontally depending on demand.

- **Security**: Industry-leading compliance and identity protection with Azure Active Directory and built-in governance tools.

- **Hybrid Capabilities**: With services like Azure Stack and Azure Arc, organizations can run Azure services on-premises or across multiple clouds.

- **Integrated Ecosystem**: Seamless integration with Microsoft tools like Windows Server, Active Directory, Office 365, and Visual Studio.

- **Innovation**: Rapid access to emerging technologies like quantum computing, blockchain, and cognitive services.

Azure Service Models

Azure supports the three primary cloud service models:

- **Infrastructure as a Service (IaaS)**: Provides raw computing resources like virtual machines, networks, and storage.

- **Platform as a Service (PaaS)**: Offers a platform for developers to build, deploy, and manage apps without worrying about infrastructure.

- **Software as a Service (SaaS)**: Delivers software applications over the internet, such as Microsoft 365, Dynamics 365, and Power BI.

Example: Creating a Virtual Machine

Let's look at a quick example of how you might use Azure to create a virtual machine using the Azure CLI:

```
az login
az group create --name MyResourceGroup --location eastus
az vm create \
  --resource-group MyResourceGroup \
  --name MyFirstVM \
  --image UbuntuLTS \
  --admin-username azureuser \
  --generate-ssh-keys
```

This script does the following:

1. Authenticates your session (`az login`)

2. Creates a resource group named "MyResourceGroup" in the East US region

3. Creates a new VM called "MyFirstVM" with an Ubuntu image and SSH authentication

Use Cases for Azure

Azure is used in countless ways across industries:

- **Web and Mobile Apps**: Host backends, APIs, and web applications with scalability in mind.

- **Big Data and Analytics**: Analyze massive datasets with services like Azure Synapse Analytics.

- **Disaster Recovery**: Ensure business continuity with geo-redundant backups and recovery tools.

- **AI-Driven Apps**: Integrate speech, vision, and language APIs with minimal effort.

- **IoT**: Connect, monitor, and manage IoT assets with Azure IoT Hub.

Azure Pricing and Cost Management

One of Azure's key advantages is its flexible pricing. You pay for what you use, and Azure offers a **cost calculator** and **pricing tiers** to help estimate and manage costs.

You can choose between:

- **Pay-as-you-go**: No upfront commitment.

- **Reserved instances**: Commit for 1 or 3 years in exchange for significant discounts.

- **Spot pricing**: Bid on unused capacity for non-critical workloads.

Getting Started with Azure

To get started, you'll need to create an Azure account. Microsoft often provides free credits (e.g., $200 for the first 30 days) and a free tier that includes access to a limited set of services.

Visit: https://azure.microsoft.com/free

Once registered, you can start exploring via the **Azure Portal**, use **Azure CLI** for command-line management, or script deployments with **PowerShell** and **ARM templates**.

Azure is not just a platform—it's an ecosystem that empowers you to innovate, build, and grow with confidence. In the next section, we'll explore how cloud computing has evolved and why Azure has emerged as a leader in this space.

The Evolution of Cloud Computing

Cloud computing didn't emerge overnight—it is the product of decades of innovation, driven by the need for more efficient, scalable, and cost-effective computing solutions. To understand Microsoft Azure and where it fits in the modern tech ecosystem, it's important to trace the evolution of cloud computing, from its conceptual origins to its widespread adoption today.

From Mainframes to Virtualization

The earliest form of centralized computing dates back to the 1950s and 1960s, with **mainframe computing**. Organizations housed large, powerful machines in data centers, which users accessed via dumb terminals. This model was expensive, required specialized knowledge, and was inherently centralized.

As technology progressed, **minicomputers** and **microcomputers** emerged, giving businesses more localized computing power. By the 1980s and 1990s, **client-server architecture** became the dominant model, with desktop computers (clients) connecting to more powerful servers for resource-intensive tasks. Though more flexible, it still required substantial investments in hardware, software licenses, and IT management.

The next leap came with **virtualization**. This technology allowed multiple virtual machines to run on a single physical server. Tools like VMware and Hyper-V let companies maximize their hardware utilization, reduce physical server sprawl, and improve redundancy. But managing infrastructure still required capital investment, physical space, and ongoing maintenance.

The Emergence of Cloud Computing

The term **"cloud computing"** began gaining traction in the early 2000s. Its core idea was to offer computing resources over the internet—on-demand and at scale. This concept became increasingly feasible as internet speeds increased, data centers became more sophisticated, and global infrastructure matured.

One of the earliest and most influential milestones was Amazon's launch of **Amazon Web Services (AWS)** in 2006. AWS introduced services like **EC2 (Elastic Compute Cloud)** and **S3 (Simple Storage Service)**, allowing developers to provision servers and store data without owning any hardware.

Microsoft joined the race with **Azure**, officially launched in 2010. Initially focused on PaaS offerings for developers, Azure rapidly expanded its catalog to include IaaS, SaaS, and hybrid solutions. Google, IBM, and other tech giants followed, making cloud computing a highly competitive, rapidly evolving space.

Key Milestones in Cloud Computing History

- **1960s** – John McCarthy suggests that computing might someday be organized as a public utility.

- **1990s** – Virtualization technologies emerge, enabling multiple OS instances on a single machine.

- **1999** – Salesforce pioneers SaaS with its CRM platform delivered via the internet.

- **2006** – Amazon introduces AWS, kickstarting the public cloud revolution.

- **2010** – Microsoft launches Azure, bringing enterprise-focused cloud services to the market.

- **2014–2020** – Widespread adoption of containers, serverless, and hybrid cloud strategies.

Cloud Service Models

The evolution of cloud computing also introduced **three primary service models**, each addressing different needs:

Infrastructure as a Service (IaaS): Provides virtualized computing resources over the internet. Users manage the OS, applications, and data while the cloud provider manages the infrastructure.

Example:
Provisioning a virtual machine in Azure using the CLI:

```
az vm create \
  --resource-group MyGroup \
  --name MyVM \
  --image UbuntuLTS \
  --admin-username user \
  --generate-ssh-keys
```

•

Platform as a Service (PaaS): Offers a platform allowing developers to build and deploy applications without managing infrastructure.

Example:
Deploying a web app in Azure App Service:

```
az webapp up --name myWebApp --resource-group MyGroup --plan MyPlan
```

•

- **Software as a Service (SaaS)**: Delivers fully functional applications to end users via the internet.

  Example: Microsoft 365, Power BI, Dynamics 365.

Technological Shifts Driving Cloud Growth

Several innovations and market shifts have fueled the explosive growth of cloud computing:

- **Broadband Internet**: The proliferation of high-speed internet has made cloud access seamless and reliable.

- **Commodity Hardware**: Cloud providers use cost-effective, standardized hardware to build scalable infrastructure.

- **Open Source Software**: Tools like Kubernetes, Docker, and Linux have become foundational to cloud environments.

- **Automation and DevOps**: Infrastructure as code (IaC), CI/CD pipelines, and monitoring tools enable faster development and deployment.

- **Global Data Centers**: Cloud providers operate massive networks of data centers, offering low-latency access and redundancy worldwide.

Benefits Realized Over Time

As the cloud matured, its benefits became clearer:

- **Elasticity**: Instantly scale resources to meet demand—whether handling 100 or 1 million users.

- **Cost Efficiency**: Replace capital expenses with predictable operating expenses. Pay only for what you use.

- **Speed and Agility**: Rapidly provision environments, iterate quickly, and reduce time-to-market.

- **Reliability**: Cloud providers offer high SLAs (Service Level Agreements) with built-in redundancy and disaster recovery.

- **Security and Compliance**: Providers implement rigorous security standards, often exceeding what organizations could manage independently.

The Hybrid and Multi-Cloud Era

Not all workloads are suitable for the public cloud. Concerns around data sovereignty, latency, and legacy systems have given rise to **hybrid cloud** strategies, where on-premises and cloud environments are integrated. Azure has been a leader in this space, offering tools like **Azure Arc**, **Azure Stack**, and **ExpressRoute** to bridge these environments.

At the same time, many organizations opt for **multi-cloud architectures**—leveraging services from multiple providers (e.g., AWS + Azure + GCP) to avoid vendor lock-in and optimize for cost, performance, or geographic availability.

Cloud-Native and Serverless Computing

Modern cloud applications are often built using **cloud-native** principles. These include:

- **Microservices Architecture**: Applications are broken into smaller, independently deployable services.

- **Containers**: Lightweight, portable environments that simplify deployment across systems.

- **Serverless Functions**: Event-driven functions that run on-demand and scale automatically.

Azure supports these paradigms with services like **Azure Kubernetes Service (AKS)** and **Azure Functions**, making it easier than ever to build applications that are scalable, resilient, and maintainable.

Cloud's Role in Digital Transformation

Cloud computing is no longer just a technology shift—it is a **business transformation enabler**. Organizations are using the cloud to:

- Launch new digital products quickly

- Support remote and distributed workforces

- Enable real-time analytics and AI

- Enhance cybersecurity

- Improve customer engagement through intelligent applications

Real-World Example: A Retail Company

Consider a mid-sized retail company looking to modernize its operations. Traditionally, they hosted their e-commerce website, inventory system, and analytics tools on-premises. The system was expensive to maintain, suffered from downtime during peak shopping seasons, and lacked flexibility.

By migrating to Azure, the company achieved:

- **Elastic web app hosting** with Azure App Services

- **Centralized identity management** with Azure Active Directory

- **Secure data storage** in Azure SQL and Blob Storage

- **Real-time analytics** with Azure Synapse and Power BI

- **Improved performance** through global CDN and Azure Front Door

- **Automated deployments** using Azure DevOps

The result? A more responsive, scalable, and cost-effective IT infrastructure that supported business growth and improved customer satisfaction.

Future Trends in Cloud Computing

The evolution of cloud computing continues. Key trends on the horizon include:

- **Edge Computing**: Bringing computation closer to the data source to reduce latency and improve performance.

- **Quantum Computing**: Azure Quantum provides early access to quantum tools and algorithms.

- **AI-First Cloud Platforms**: Deep integration of machine learning and AI in application workflows.

- **Sustainability**: Green cloud initiatives and carbon-aware computing.

- **Regulatory Cloud Models**: Region-specific offerings to meet compliance and data sovereignty laws.

Conclusion

The journey from centralized mainframes to globally distributed cloud platforms like Azure has revolutionized how we build, deliver, and scale technology. This evolution is driven by both technological advancements and shifting business needs.

Understanding this historical context not only helps you appreciate the value of Azure but also positions you to make informed decisions when designing, deploying, and managing solutions in the cloud.

In the next section, we'll explore the core benefits that Azure brings to developers, organizations, and IT professionals alike. Whether it's flexibility, scalability, or innovation, Azure continues to set the standard for what's possible in the cloud.

Core Benefits of Using Azure

Microsoft Azure has rapidly grown to become one of the leading cloud platforms globally. While the technology and tools offered by Azure are extensive and diverse, it's the tangible benefits that have made it a cornerstone for organizations across every industry. Whether you're a startup, an enterprise, or an individual developer, Azure delivers significant advantages that extend beyond infrastructure provisioning.

This section explores the **core benefits** of using Azure—covering everything from scalability and cost-efficiency to security, innovation, and beyond.

Global Reach and Availability

Azure boasts a **massive global footprint**, with data centers in over 60 regions and available in more countries than any other cloud provider. This geographic diversity enables you to:

- **Deploy applications close to users** to reduce latency

- **Meet local compliance requirements** for data residency

- **Implement disaster recovery** strategies with multi-region replication

Each Azure region typically includes multiple **availability zones**, which are isolated locations within a region designed for high availability and fault tolerance. If one zone experiences an outage, services in other zones can continue without disruption.

Example: Deploying a web app in a specific region

```
az webapp create \
  --resource-group MyResourceGroup \
  --plan MyAppServicePlan \
  --name mywebapp123 \
  --runtime "NODE|14-lts" \
  --location "westeurope"
```

Unparalleled Scalability

One of the most touted advantages of Azure is its **on-demand scalability**. Whether you're dealing with a small development environment or a globally-used application, Azure scales both vertically and horizontally to match usage patterns and business needs.

- **Vertical Scaling**: Increase the size of resources (e.g., CPU, memory) for compute instances.

- **Horizontal Scaling**: Add more instances to distribute load and improve performance.

Azure offers tools like **Azure Autoscale** to automatically adjust resource allocation based on defined rules and metrics, such as CPU usage, memory utilization, or incoming request rate.

Example: Configuring autoscale for an App Service plan

```
az monitor autoscale create \
  --resource-group MyResourceGroup \
  --resource MyAppServicePlan \
  --resource-type Microsoft.Web/serverfarms \
  --name autoscale-rule \
  --min-count 1 \
  --max-count 10 \
  --count 2
```

Flexible Pricing and Cost Management

Azure supports a wide range of **pricing models** to suit different workloads and budgets:

- **Pay-as-you-go**: No upfront costs—pay only for what you use.

- **Reserved Instances**: Commit to 1- or 3-year terms for VMs at reduced rates.

- **Spot Pricing**: Purchase unused compute capacity at a discount, ideal for non-critical tasks.

- **Free Tier**: Access to limited Azure services free of charge, forever.

To help track and control spending, Azure offers **Cost Management and Billing** tools that allow you to:

- Set **budgets and alerts**

- Analyze **spending trends**

- Allocate costs by **tags** or **departments**

You can also use the **Azure Pricing Calculator** to estimate expenses before provisioning resources: https://azure.microsoft.com/en-us/pricing/calculator

Robust Security and Compliance

Microsoft invests over **$1 billion annually in security** and employs thousands of security experts. Azure offers **built-in, enterprise-grade security features**, including:

- **Identity and Access Management (IAM)** with Azure Active Directory

- **Encryption at rest and in transit**

- **Role-Based Access Control (RBAC)** for fine-grained permissions

- **Network security** with firewalls, private endpoints, and virtual networks

Azure is also highly compliant with **global, regional, and industry standards**, including:

- ISO 27001

- SOC 1, 2, and 3

- GDPR

- HIPAA

- FedRAMP

- UK G-Cloud

Example: Assigning a role to a user using RBAC

```
az role assignment create \
  --assignee user@example.com \
  --role "Contributor" \
  --scope /subscriptions/{subscription-
id}/resourceGroups/MyResourceGroup
```

Hybrid Capabilities

Unlike many cloud providers, Azure embraces hybrid cloud as a **first-class architecture**. With services like **Azure Arc**, **Azure Stack**, and **ExpressRoute**, organizations can bridge on-premises infrastructure with the cloud seamlessly.

- **Azure Arc**: Manage resources across on-premises, multi-cloud, and edge environments.

- **Azure Stack**: Run Azure services in your own data center.

- **ExpressRoute**: Establish private connections between your data center and Azure for higher security and lower latency.

This is particularly valuable for industries with **legacy systems**, **compliance constraints**, or **data sovereignty requirements**.

Integrated Development and DevOps Tools

Azure offers comprehensive tooling support for developers, DevOps engineers, and system administrators. Tools include:

- **Azure DevOps**: CI/CD pipelines, boards, repos, test plans, and artifact management.

- **GitHub Integration**: Direct integration with GitHub Actions for automation.

- **Visual Studio Integration**: One-click deployments from Visual Studio to Azure.

- **Infrastructure as Code (IaC)**: Native support for ARM templates, Bicep, Terraform, and Ansible.

Example: Creating a CI/CD pipeline with Azure DevOps YAML

```
trigger:
  branches:
    include:
```

```
  - main

pool:
  vmImage: 'ubuntu-latest'

steps:
- task: NodeTool@0
  inputs:
    versionSpec: '14.x'
- script: npm install
- script: npm run build
- task: AzureWebApp@1
  inputs:
    azureSubscription: 'MyServiceConnection'
    appType: 'webApp'
    appName: 'mywebapp123'
    package: '$(System.DefaultWorkingDirectory)/build'
```

Rich AI and Analytics Capabilities

Azure includes powerful **AI and analytics** services to build intelligent, data-driven applications. Key offerings include:

- **Azure Cognitive Services**: Prebuilt APIs for speech, vision, language, and decision-making.

- **Azure Machine Learning**: Build, train, and deploy ML models at scale.

- **Azure Synapse Analytics**: End-to-end analytics from ingestion to visualization.

- **Power BI**: Business intelligence dashboards and data visualization.

These tools allow organizations to derive actionable insights from data without needing a large in-house data science team.

Example: Analyzing sentiment using Azure Cognitive Services (Python SDK)

```
from azure.ai.textanalytics import TextAnalyticsClient
from azure.core.credentials import AzureKeyCredential

credential = AzureKeyCredential("<your-key>")
client = TextAnalyticsClient(endpoint="<your-endpoint>",
credential=credential)
```

```
response = client.analyze_sentiment(documents=["I love working with
Azure!"])
for doc in response:
    print("Sentiment:", doc.sentiment)
```

High Availability and Disaster Recovery

Azure's architecture is designed for **resilience and uptime**, supporting **99.95%+ SLA guarantees** for many services. Tools for high availability include:

- **Availability Sets and Zones**

- **Geo-redundant storage (GRS)**

- **Automatic failover for managed databases**

- **Backup and Site Recovery services**

Example: Configuring Azure Backup for a virtual machine

```
az backup protection enable-for-vm \
  --resource-group MyResourceGroup \
  --vault-name MyRecoveryServicesVault \
  --vm MyVM \
  --policy-name DefaultPolicy
```

Disaster recovery solutions with **Azure Site Recovery** allow replication of on-premises VMs and applications to Azure, enabling rapid failover and failback.

Continuous Innovation

Microsoft is committed to **rapid, ongoing innovation** in the Azure ecosystem. New services and improvements are released frequently, often based on customer feedback. Azure also leads in emerging technologies such as:

- **Quantum computing** (Azure Quantum)

- **Blockchain as a Service**

- **Augmented Reality** (via HoloLens integration)

- **5G and edge computing**

This continual enhancement ensures that developers and businesses are never left behind, but instead have access to the tools needed to compete and innovate.

Ecosystem Integration

Azure integrates seamlessly with Microsoft's broader ecosystem, which includes:

- **Microsoft 365**

- **Windows Server**

- **SQL Server**

- **Power Platform**

- **Active Directory**

- **Visual Studio Code and GitHub**

This integration means faster setup, easier identity management, and unified support, especially for organizations already using Microsoft tools.

Community and Support

Azure has a vast and active **global community**, including developers, MVPs, and solution architects. Microsoft provides robust documentation, tutorials, and learning paths via:

- **Microsoft Learn**

- **Azure Docs**

- **Certification programs**

- **Tech community forums**

- **Azure Marketplace** with prebuilt solutions and templates

For more complex needs, Azure support plans offer 24/7 access to cloud engineers.

Azure's strength lies in its **comprehensive offerings, enterprise-grade security**, and **developer-first approach**. Whether you're migrating legacy systems, launching a new SaaS product, or analyzing petabytes of data, Azure delivers the tools, scalability, and reliability needed to succeed in today's digital economy.

Next, we'll compare Azure with other cloud providers to help you understand where it stands and how it might fit your unique needs.

Azure vs. Other Cloud Providers

In the modern cloud ecosystem, several major players dominate the market—each with its own strengths, weaknesses, and unique features. Microsoft Azure, Amazon Web Services (AWS), and Google Cloud Platform (GCP) are the "Big Three," but they aren't the only options. Providers like IBM Cloud, Oracle Cloud, and Alibaba Cloud also serve niche and regional markets.

Understanding how Azure compares to these providers is critical for making informed architectural, operational, and financial decisions. This section dives deep into comparing Azure with other cloud platforms across various dimensions, including services, pricing, ease of use, developer tools, hybrid capabilities, compliance, and support.

Market Position and Adoption

Azure is currently the second-largest cloud platform globally, just behind AWS and ahead of GCP. According to various industry reports:

- **AWS**: First mover advantage, largest market share (approx. 30–35%)

- **Azure**: Strong enterprise adoption, particularly among existing Microsoft customers (approx. 20–25%)

- **GCP**: Gaining traction among data scientists, ML/AI projects, and startups (approx. 10–15%)

Other providers like IBM Cloud and Oracle Cloud appeal to organizations already invested in their proprietary technologies (e.g., IBM Mainframes or Oracle Databases), while Alibaba Cloud is dominant in the Asia-Pacific region.

Azure's edge comes largely from its **tight integration with Microsoft's enterprise tools**, strong hybrid capabilities, and robust global infrastructure.

Service Offerings: Breadth and Depth

All three major platforms offer a similar core set of services: compute, storage, networking, databases, AI/ML, analytics, and IoT. However, the depth, maturity, and naming conventions of these services can vary significantly.

Compute

- **Azure**: Offers VMs (Virtual Machines), App Services, Container Instances, and Azure Kubernetes Service (AKS). Strong PaaS and serverless options.

- **AWS**: EC2 for virtual machines, Elastic Beanstalk for PaaS, and Lambda for serverless.

- **GCP**: Compute Engine for VMs, App Engine for PaaS, and Cloud Functions for serverless.

Azure and AWS offer the widest variety of VM sizes, including options tailored for memory-intensive, compute-heavy, and GPU-based workloads. Azure's serverless computing is highly integrated with other services (e.g., Logic Apps, Event Grid).

Storage

- **Azure**: Blob Storage, Table Storage, Queue Storage, File Storage. Supports hot/cool/archive tiers.

- **AWS**: S3 (Simple Storage Service), EBS, Glacier, EFS.

- **GCP**: Cloud Storage, Persistent Disks, Nearline/Coldline/Archive tiers.

Azure's Blob Storage is a direct counterpart to AWS S3, but with different tiers and access policies. GCP is strong in performance for object storage but less feature-rich in file and archival services.

Databases

- **Azure**: Azure SQL Database, Cosmos DB (globally distributed NoSQL), PostgreSQL/MySQL managed instances, and Data Lake.

- **AWS**: RDS (PostgreSQL, MySQL, Oracle, SQL Server), DynamoDB, Aurora.

- **GCP**: Cloud SQL, BigQuery, Firestore, Spanner.

Azure's strength lies in hybrid scenarios (SQL Server on-prem + Azure SQL) and multi-model databases via Cosmos DB. AWS offers more mature managed services with Aurora, while GCP excels in analytical workloads with BigQuery.

Pricing Models and Cost Management

Cost comparison between providers is complex due to differences in instance types, pricing tiers, and discounts. However, the overall principles are similar:

- **Pay-as-you-go**

- **Reserved Instances (1–3 years)**

- **Spot/Preemptible instances**

- **Free tiers for basic usage**

Azure stands out with its **cost management tools**:

- **Azure Cost Management + Billing**: Built-in dashboards, budgets, forecasting.

- **Azure Pricing Calculator**: Transparent, easy-to-use tool for estimating costs.

AWS also offers detailed billing and a cost explorer but lacks the native integration with enterprise tools that Azure offers. GCP is typically praised for its simplicity and sustained usage discounts (e.g., automatic discounts for long-running workloads).

Example: Estimating VM cost in Azure CLI

```
az vm list-sizes --location "eastus"
```

This command lists all available VM sizes and can be cross-referenced with the pricing calculator to determine cost implications.

Developer and DevOps Tooling

Azure

- Deep integration with Visual Studio, GitHub, and Azure DevOps

- First-class support for .NET, JavaScript, Python, and more

- Azure Resource Manager (ARM), Bicep, and Terraform support

- GitHub Actions and Azure Pipelines for CI/CD

AWS

- Broad support for languages and IDEs

- CloudFormation for infrastructure as code (steeper learning curve)

- CodePipeline, CodeBuild, and CodeDeploy for DevOps

GCP

- Emphasis on containers and microservices

- Cloud Build, Cloud Source Repositories, and Deployment Manager

- Firebase support for mobile and web developers

Azure shines for organizations already using **GitHub**, **Visual Studio**, or **Azure DevOps**, offering seamless deployment pipelines and collaboration. GCP is strong in CI/CD and quick project setup, ideal for developers and data scientists.

Hybrid and On-Prem Integration

Azure is often considered the **most hybrid-friendly** platform:

- **Azure Arc**: Manage non-Azure servers and Kubernetes clusters from Azure

- **Azure Stack**: Run Azure services in your own data center

- **Azure Site Recovery**: Seamless disaster recovery across on-prem and cloud

AWS offers **Outposts**, a comparable solution for hybrid cloud, but it's more hardware-dependent and less flexible in management layers.

GCP lags behind in this area, though its **Anthos** platform provides multi-cloud Kubernetes management.

Identity, Security, and Governance

Azure leads in **identity management** due to its deep integration with **Azure Active Directory (AAD)**:

- Single Sign-On (SSO) across Azure, Microsoft 365, and third-party apps

- Conditional Access Policies, MFA, and Identity Protection

- Privileged Identity Management and Role-Based Access Control (RBAC)

AWS offers **IAM (Identity and Access Management)** with fine-grained policies and roles, but lacks the breadth of integration outside its own ecosystem.

GCP uses **Cloud Identity** and **IAM**, offering good management but less enterprise-level integration compared to Azure.

Azure also offers:

- **Azure Security Center**

- **Microsoft Defender for Cloud**

- **Key Vault** for secure secrets management

These tools combine security insights, automated remediation, and threat intelligence across hybrid environments.

Compliance and Certifications

Azure has a comprehensive list of **compliance offerings**, more than most providers:

- Over 90 compliance certifications (global, regional, industry-specific)

- Azure Blueprints for automating governance

- Region-specific clouds (e.g., Azure Government, Azure China)

AWS and GCP also meet most major compliance standards, but Azure's integration with **policy-driven automation** gives it an edge for regulated industries such as healthcare, finance, and government.

AI, Machine Learning, and Big Data

GCP is often seen as the **AI and data analytics leader**, thanks to:

- **BigQuery** for massive-scale data analysis

- **TensorFlow** and AI Platform

- **Vertex AI** for model management

Azure counters with:

- **Azure Machine Learning Studio** (drag-and-drop model builder)

- **Cognitive Services** (pre-built AI APIs for vision, speech, language)

- **Synapse Analytics** (big data + SQL integration)

- **Power BI** (industry-leading business intelligence)

AWS offers SageMaker and Redshift, which are mature and flexible but require more setup and expertise.

User Experience and Management Tools

Azure's **portal experience** is highly visual and customizable, allowing users to:

- Create dashboards

- Set up guided walkthroughs

- Deploy resources via forms or templates

AWS's console is powerful but often considered overwhelming, especially for newcomers. GCP's UI is clean and developer-centric, though occasionally limited in terms of enterprise-level visibility.

Azure also supports:

- **Azure CLI**

- **Azure PowerShell**

- **Cloud Shell** (browser-based terminal with pre-installed tools)

These tools make management accessible whether you're a sysadmin, DevOps engineer, or developer.

Support and Documentation

All three providers offer multiple support tiers, with 24/7 options and dedicated account managers for enterprise customers. However, Azure provides:

- **Microsoft Learn**: Interactive modules and learning paths

- **Docs.Microsoft.com**: Rich technical documentation with examples

- **Tech Community and MVPs**: Active forums and industry experts

AWS and GCP have similar support structures, but Azure's ecosystem often resonates better with enterprise teams already using Microsoft technologies.

Summary Comparison Table

Feature	Azure	AWS	GCP
Global Reach	60+ regions	30+ regions	35+ regions
Hybrid Cloud	Strong (Arc, Stack)	Moderate (Outposts)	Developing (Anthos)
Identity Management	Azure AD integration	IAM	Cloud Identity
Developer Tools	Visual Studio, GitHub	Broad SDKs	Firebase, GCP SDKs
AI/ML Capabilities	Cognitive Services, AML	SageMaker	TensorFlow, Vertex AI
Compliance Certifications	90+	80+	60+
Cost Management	Azure Cost Management	Cost Explorer	Billing Reports
PaaS Maturity	High	Moderate	High
Documentation & Community	Strong (MS Learn, Docs)	Rich but dense	Concise, developer-focused

Conclusion

Azure holds a **unique position** among cloud providers due to its enterprise alignment, hybrid capabilities, and seamless Microsoft integration. While AWS leads in service breadth and first-mover advantage, Azure is often preferred for organizations already embedded in the Microsoft ecosystem. GCP, meanwhile, excels in AI, machine learning, and data analytics, making it ideal for research-heavy or startup environments.

Choosing the right cloud provider often comes down to **use case, team expertise, budget, and existing tech stack**. However, Azure's consistent innovation, hybrid edge, and strong support for both startups and enterprises make it a compelling choice for a wide variety of cloud solutions.

In the next chapter, we'll move from theory to practice by setting up your Azure environment, creating your first account, and navigating the portal like a pro.

Chapter 2: Setting Up Your Azure Environment

Creating an Azure Account

Before diving into the world of Azure's powerful cloud services, you need to create and configure your Azure account. This is your entry point into the Azure ecosystem and forms the foundation of everything you'll do—from deploying your first virtual machine to building full-scale, production-ready applications.

This section walks you through every step of creating an Azure account, configuring the initial environment, understanding account structure, selecting a subscription plan, and ensuring your account is ready for development and deployment.

Why You Need an Azure Account

An Azure account serves as your digital identity in the Microsoft Cloud. It allows you to:

- Access and manage cloud services through the Azure Portal

- Track usage and billing

- Set up identity and access control

- Deploy applications and infrastructure globally

- Integrate with development, monitoring, and security tools

Every user of Azure—whether an individual developer or a global enterprise—starts with an account that connects to one or more **Azure subscriptions**, which in turn contain all your deployed resources.

Step-by-Step: Creating a Free Azure Account

Microsoft offers a **free tier** for new users, which includes:

- $200 in credits for the first 30 days

- Access to 55+ services free for 12 months

- Always-free access to core services like Azure App Services, Functions, and Blob Storage

Follow these steps to set up your account:

1. **Visit the Azure Free Trial Page**
   Go to: https://azure.microsoft.com/free

2. **Click "Start Free"**
   This will redirect you to a Microsoft sign-in page.

3. **Sign In or Create a Microsoft Account**
   If you don't already have a Microsoft account, click "Create one!" and follow the steps. You'll need to provide:

   - A valid email address

   - A secure password

   - Country or region

4. **Provide Identity Verification**
   Microsoft requires phone number verification via SMS or call. This step prevents fraud and ensures authenticity.

5. **Enter Credit/Debit Card Information**
   This is used for identity verification. You will *not* be charged unless you explicitly upgrade to a paid subscription.

6. **Agree to Terms and Complete Setup**
   Accept Microsoft's terms and conditions, then submit the form to finish creating your account.

You will then be taken to the **Azure Portal**, your central management dashboard.

Navigating the Azure Account Hierarchy

Understanding the structure of an Azure account helps you better organize, secure, and manage resources. Here's how the basic hierarchy looks:

- **Microsoft Account** (your identity, e.g., user@example.com)

- **Azure Subscription** (the billing container)

- **Resource Groups** (logical grouping of resources)

- **Resources** (VMs, storage accounts, web apps, databases, etc.)

Each **subscription** acts as a boundary for billing, quotas, and access controls. You can have multiple subscriptions under the same account for isolating projects, teams, or environments.

Choosing a Subscription Plan

When creating an Azure account, you start with a **Free Trial Subscription**. After the free period ends, you have the option to:

- **Upgrade to Pay-As-You-Go**: Keep your resources and pay only for what you use.

- **Activate a Visual Studio Subscription**: Includes monthly Azure credits (great for developers).

- **Use a Sponsorship or Enterprise Agreement**: Common for large organizations and academic institutions.

You can check and manage your subscription using the portal or the CLI:

```
az account show
az account list --output table
```

Securing Your Azure Account

Security is foundational. Before deploying any resources, take the following steps to secure your Azure account:

1. Enable Multi-Factor Authentication (MFA)

Use the Microsoft Authenticator app or SMS verification to protect your account against unauthorized access.

- Sign in to the Azure Portal

- Navigate to **Azure Active Directory > Users**

- Select your user, then click **Multi-Factor Authentication**

- Follow the prompts to enable and configure

2. Set Up Role-Based Access Control (RBAC)

Avoid using your main account for all tasks. Create roles and assign them only the permissions needed for specific duties.

Example: Assigning a contributor role to another user

```
az role assignment create \
  --assignee user@example.com \
  --role Contributor \
  --scope /subscriptions/<subscription-id>
```

3. Use Resource Locks and Policies

To prevent accidental deletion of critical resources, apply **resource locks** and **Azure Policies**.

Exploring the Azure Portal

Once your account is set up, head to https://portal.azure.com. This is the web-based UI for managing Azure services.

Key features of the portal include:

- **Dashboard**: Customizable widgets to monitor your environment

- **Resource Management**: View and configure all your resources

- **Marketplace**: Discover and deploy pre-configured apps and services

- **Search Bar**: Quickly find services, tools, and documentation

- **Cloud Shell**: Built-in terminal with CLI and PowerShell access

You can personalize the portal to suit your workflow by pinning frequently used services or creating custom dashboards.

Using Azure Cloud Shell

Azure Cloud Shell is a browser-accessible command-line interface embedded in the portal. It supports both **Bash** and **PowerShell** and comes pre-installed with tools like:

- Azure CLI

- Git

- Terraform

- Kubectl

To launch it:

- Click the **Cloud Shell icon** at the top of the Azure Portal

- Choose your shell type (Bash or PowerShell)

- Create a storage account if prompted (used to persist shell files)

Example: Listing all resource groups in Bash

```
az group list --output table
```

Cloud Shell allows you to script tasks, automate deployments, and manage infrastructure directly from your browser.

CLI Authentication Options

If you're using Azure CLI locally, authentication is required:

Option 1: Interactive Login

```
az login
```

This opens a browser window for login. Once authenticated, your CLI session is active.

Option 2: Service Principal (for automation)

```
az ad sp create-for-rbac --name "myApp" --role contributor --scopes
/subscriptions/<subscription-id>
```

This is ideal for CI/CD pipelines or automated scripts.

Setting Up Billing Alerts

To avoid surprises in your monthly Azure bill, set up **cost alerts**:

1. Go to **Cost Management + Billing**

2. Click **Budgets > Add**

3. Define a name, threshold, and email recipients

4. Set frequency (e.g., monthly) and recurrence

5. Save the alert

You can also tag resources to associate them with teams, departments, or projects for more granular cost tracking.

Example:

```
az tag create --name "department" --value "marketing"
az tag associate --resource-id /subscriptions/<subscription-
id>/resourceGroups/mygroup --tags department=marketing
```

Common Issues and Troubleshooting

Problem: Card declined during signup
 Solution: Use a valid international debit/credit card. Prepaid cards and virtual cards may not work.

Problem: Cloud Shell won't start
 Solution: Ensure a storage account is linked. Cloud Shell needs a mounted Azure File share.

Problem: Can't access subscription
 Solution: Check if the Microsoft account is linked properly or if you're logged into the correct tenant.

Summary

Creating and configuring your Azure account is the first step in your journey to mastering the cloud. From setting up secure authentication to choosing a subscription and exploring the portal, everything you do from this point on builds on these foundations.

Here's a quick checklist:

- ✓ Create your free Azure account

- ✓ Secure your identity with MFA

- ✓ Choose or upgrade your subscription

- ✓ Understand account hierarchy (Subscriptions → Resource Groups → Resources)

- ✓ Explore the Azure Portal and Cloud Shell

- ✓ Configure billing alerts and tags

- ✓ Begin deploying your first services

With your environment ready, you're now equipped to start working with real Azure services. In the next section, we'll take a deep dive into the Azure Portal, helping you navigate, customize, and operate it like a pro.

Navigating the Azure Portal

The Azure Portal is your primary web-based interface for managing and monitoring Azure resources. It offers a rich graphical environment that caters to users of all experience levels—from beginners deploying their first app to advanced administrators configuring complex enterprise environments. Mastering the Azure Portal not only makes you more efficient but also enables you to explore and experiment with Azure services confidently.

In this section, we'll explore the layout, key features, customization options, and advanced capabilities of the Azure Portal. We'll also cover time-saving tips, navigation techniques, troubleshooting methods, and how to integrate the portal with other tools.

What is the Azure Portal?

The Azure Portal is a unified web interface for managing Azure resources. Accessible at https://portal.azure.com, it allows you to:

- Deploy and configure services

- Monitor metrics and logs

- Set access controls and security

- Manage billing and usage

- Execute scripts using Cloud Shell

- Browse the Azure Marketplace

Every action in the portal corresponds to underlying API calls, meaning you can perform nearly all operations available via CLI or SDKs.

Logging In and First-Time Experience

After creating an Azure account, visit the portal URL and sign in using your Microsoft credentials. On your first login, you may be prompted to configure some basic settings and create your first resource.

You'll land on the **default dashboard**, a visual workspace where you can pin services, charts, shortcuts, and more. This dashboard is fully customizable and is often the first point of interaction for daily Azure operations.

Key Interface Areas

The portal is divided into several functional regions. Understanding how to use each will speed up your workflow significantly.

1. Global Search Bar

Located at the top, this bar lets you search for:

- Azure services (e.g., "Virtual Machines")

- Specific resources (e.g., "myVM")

- Documentation and tutorials

- Marketplace offers

You can type partial names, and suggestions will auto-complete in real-time.

2. Navigation Menu

On the left-hand side, you'll find:

- **Home**: Takes you to the main overview screen

- **Dashboard**: Access your customized dashboards

- **All Services**: Browse or search all available Azure services

- **Resource Groups**: View resources grouped by logical categories

- **Subscriptions**: Manage billing, quotas, and access

- **Cost Management + Billing**: View your usage and spending

You can pin any frequently used services to the menu for faster access.

3. Service Blades

When you click a service, a new "blade" opens. These are tab-like panels that cascade from right to left as you drill deeper into configurations. You can open multiple blades simultaneously, and each blade can be closed individually.

4. Top Bar Tools

- **Notifications (Bell Icon)**: Shows system alerts, deployment statuses, and errors

- **Settings (Gear Icon)**: Portal theme, language, and layout options

- **Feedback**: Report bugs or request features

- **Directory + Subscription Switcher**: Switch between tenants and subscriptions

Customizing Your Dashboard

The portal allows you to create multiple dashboards tailored to different projects, teams, or purposes.

Creating a Dashboard

1. Go to **Dashboard**

2. Click **New Dashboard**

3. Use the **Tile Gallery** to drag and drop widgets such as:

   ○ Service overviews (VM, SQL Database, etc.)

   ○ Charts and graphs

o   Markdown notes

o   Shortcuts to resources

Example: Pinning a VM to Your Dashboard

1. Navigate to your VM (e.g., "myVM")

2. Click the pin icon (📌) at the top

3. Select the dashboard you want to pin it to

You can rearrange, resize, and rename tiles for a fully customized view.

Managing Resources via the Portal

The portal offers intuitive, form-driven wizards for provisioning resources. Let's look at a few common workflows.

Creating a Virtual Machine

1. Click **Create a resource**

2. Choose **Virtual Machine**

3. Fill in required fields:

    o   Subscription

    o   Resource group

    o   Region

    o   OS image (e.g., Ubuntu, Windows)

    o   Size (e.g., B2s)

    o   Admin credentials

4. Click **Review + Create**, then **Create**

You'll see deployment progress in the **Notifications** area.

Accessing a Storage Account

1. Navigate to **Storage accounts**

2. Select a storage account (e.g., `mystorageacct`)

3. Manage:

   - Blob containers

   - File shares

   - Access keys

   - Networking rules

You can upload files directly via the UI or use a SAS (Shared Access Signature) token for temporary secure access.

Using Azure Marketplace

The Azure Marketplace is integrated into the portal and offers:

- Pre-configured virtual machine images (e.g., WordPress, Jenkins, SQL Server)

- SaaS solutions

- DevOps integrations

- Machine learning models

Example: Launching WordPress on Ubuntu

1. Go to **Marketplace**

2. Search for **WordPress**

3. Select **WordPress on Ubuntu**

4. Click **Create**

5. Complete the resource creation steps

Marketplace resources are billed according to their publisher's pricing, in addition to Azure infrastructure costs.

Monitoring and Alerts

Every Azure service includes built-in monitoring capabilities. Through the portal, you can:

- View usage and performance graphs

- Set thresholds for automatic alerts

- Trigger automated actions

Example: Creating a CPU Alert for a VM

1. Navigate to the VM

2. Click **Alerts > + New alert rule**

3. Select signal (e.g., "Percentage CPU > 80%")

4. Add an action group (e.g., email, webhook)

5. Name the rule and enable it

This ensures you're notified before critical thresholds are breached.

Portal Shortcuts and Productivity Tips

- Press **G + /** to focus the global search bar

- Press **G + D** to return to the dashboard

- Use **F1** to bring up a list of keyboard shortcuts

- Right-click any resource and choose **Open in new tab** to multitask efficiently

- Use tags (e.g., `Environment: Production`, `Team: DevOps`) for filtering and billing

Integrating Azure CLI and Cloud Shell

For power users, the portal includes **Cloud Shell**, a browser-accessible CLI environment.

Launch Cloud Shell

- Click the **Cloud Shell icon** (top menu)

- Choose **Bash** or **PowerShell**

- Start managing resources via commands

Example: Listing all VMs

```
az vm list --output table
```

Cloud Shell also supports `kubectl`, `terraform`, `git`, `npm`, and many other tools, making it perfect for DevOps tasks.

Troubleshooting Common Issues

Problem: Portal not loading or slow performance
 Solution: Try clearing your browser cache or switching browsers. Use Edge or Chrome for optimal experience.

Problem: Resource blade shows errors
 Solution: Check permissions. You may not have access under your current subscription or directory.

Problem: Can't find a service
 Solution: Use the **"All Services"** menu and use filters like category (e.g., compute, storage).

Problem: Can't launch Cloud Shell
 Solution: Ensure you've provisioned a storage account. It's required to store session files.

Summary

The Azure Portal is more than just a UI—it's a comprehensive control center for managing, deploying, and monitoring your cloud environment. Whether you're configuring a VM, setting access controls, tracking performance, or launching machine learning models, the portal simplifies every aspect of your interaction with Azure.

Here's what you should now be able to do:

- ✅ Navigate the Azure Portal confidently

- ✅ Use search, menus, and dashboards efficiently

- ✅ Deploy and manage common resources

- ✅ Customize dashboards to suit your workflow

- ✅ Monitor services and configure alerts

- ✅ Use Cloud Shell for script-based management

In the next section, we'll look deeper into how Azure organizes resources using **subscriptions and resource groups**—a fundamental concept that underpins billing, security, and operational strategy.

Understanding Azure Subscriptions and Resource Groups

A successful Azure environment begins with a solid understanding of its organizational structure. At the heart of this structure are **subscriptions** and **resource groups**, which define how resources are deployed, managed, billed, and secured. Without properly understanding and configuring these elements, you risk confusion, inefficiencies, and unnecessary costs.

This section will explore Azure subscriptions and resource groups in depth. We'll cover what they are, how they work together, how to structure them efficiently, and how to manage them using the Azure Portal, CLI, and PowerShell.

What is an Azure Subscription?

An **Azure subscription** is a logical container used to provision resources in Azure. It holds the details of all your resources—like virtual machines, databases, web apps, and storage—and governs how those resources are billed, secured, and accessed.

Each subscription is associated with:

- A **billing account** (payment method, invoice, credits)

- A **directory/tenant** (identity and access control)

- A set of **quotas** (e.g., how many VMs you can deploy)

- One or more **resource groups**

- A unique **subscription ID**

You can create multiple subscriptions under a single Azure account, which allows for logical and financial separation between environments or business units.

Why Use Multiple Subscriptions?

While you can run everything under a single subscription, using **multiple subscriptions** offers several benefits:

1. **Isolation** – Separate environments like development, staging, and production

2. **Security** – Apply distinct policies and access controls

3. **Cost Tracking** – Attribute costs to different departments or projects

4. **Quota Management** – Avoid hitting resource limits in large organizations

5. **Compliance** – Align subscriptions with legal or regulatory boundaries

Example Use Case

Subscription Name	Purpose
Dev-Test Subscription	Isolated environment for testing
Production Subscription	High-availability workloads
Marketing Subscription	Campaign-specific deployments
Research & AI Subscription	Experimental services, ML workloads

Creating and Managing Subscriptions

You can create new subscriptions through the **Azure Portal** or by contacting your Microsoft account manager (for enterprise agreements).

To view your subscriptions:

Azure Portal:

- Go to **Subscriptions**

- View your list of subscriptions with details like ID, name, billing status, and policies

Azure CLI:

```
az account list --output table
```

To switch between subscriptions in CLI:

```
az account set --subscription "<Subscription ID or Name>"
```

To rename a subscription (friendly name):

```
az account subscription rename --name "New Name"
```

Role-Based Access Control (RBAC) at Subscription Level

You can assign users or service principals access at the **subscription level** to manage all resources within it.

Example: Assign a user the Contributor role on a subscription

```
az role assignment create \
  --assignee user@example.com \
  --role Contributor \
  --scope /subscriptions/<subscription-id>
```

RBAC can also be scoped at **resource group** or **individual resource** levels for more granular control.

What is a Resource Group?

A **resource group** is a container that holds related Azure resources. Every resource (VM, storage account, web app, etc.) must be associated with one—and only one—resource group.

Resource groups:

- Are used for **logical organization**

- Share **lifecycle and deployment scope**

- Can be managed as a unit (start, stop, delete, tag)

- Are **regionless**, though the resources inside may have region-specific deployments

- Allow **role-based access control** at group level

Best Practices for Structuring Resource Groups

1. **Group by Lifecycle** – Put resources that share the same deployment and retirement cycle together.

2. **Group by Application** – Keep all components of an app (frontend, backend, database, storage) in one group.

3. **Avoid Cross-App Groups** – Don't mix unrelated services in a single group.

4. **Use Naming Conventions** – Establish clear, descriptive names (e.g., `rg-webapp-prod`, `rg-data-dev`).

5. **Apply Tags** – Assign metadata to resource groups to track ownership, cost, or environment.

Creating a Resource Group

Azure Portal:

1. Go to **Resource Groups**

2. Click **+ Create**

3. Provide:

   - Subscription

   - Resource group name

   - Region (for metadata storage)

4. Click **Review + Create**

Azure CLI:

```
az group create \
  --name myResourceGroup \
  --location eastus
```

Moving Resources Between Groups

Azure allows resources to be moved between groups or subscriptions with some caveats:

- Both source and target must be in the same region (for some services)

- Downtime may occur for specific resources (e.g., public IPs)

Azure CLI:

```
az resource move \
  --destination-group NewResourceGroup \
  --destination-subscription-id <target-subscription-id> \
  --ids <resource-id-1> <resource-id-2>
```

Always validate dependencies before moving resources.

Deleting a Resource Group

Deleting a resource group will **delete all resources within it**. This is powerful but dangerous.

Azure Portal:

- Go to the resource group

- Click **Delete resource group**

- Type the name to confirm

Azure CLI:

```
az group delete --name myResourceGroup --yes --no-wait
```

Use this with caution, especially in production environments.

Tagging Resource Groups

Tags help manage resources at scale. They are key-value pairs used for:

- Cost management

- Ownership tracking

- Environment labeling

- Automation (e.g., delete unused dev groups nightly)

Azure CLI:

```
az group update \
  --name myResourceGroup \
  --set tags.Environment=Development tags.Team=WebDev
```

To retrieve tagged groups:

```
az group list --tag Environment=Production --output table
```

Policies and Locks

You can apply **Azure Policies** and **resource locks** to resource groups for governance and protection.

Example: Prevent deletion of a group

Azure CLI:

```
az lock create \
  --name "LockRG" \
  --lock-type CanNotDelete \
  --resource-group myResourceGroup
```

Example: Apply a policy to enforce tags

Azure Policy Portal:

1. Go to **Policy**

2. Assign policy: **Require a tag on resource groups**

3. Set the enforcement mode to audit or deny

Viewing and Auditing Activity

Azure provides rich auditing features through **Activity Logs**. You can view:

- Who created or modified a resource

- When a resource was moved or deleted

- Changes in access control

Azure Portal:

- Navigate to a resource group

- Click **Activity log**

Azure CLI:

```
az monitor activity-log list \
  --resource-group myResourceGroup \
  --output table
```

Summary

Understanding and effectively managing Azure subscriptions and resource groups is foundational for building secure, scalable, and organized cloud environments.

Key takeaways:

- ✓ Subscriptions define billing and access boundaries

- ✓ Resource groups organize resources logically and manage them collectively

- ✅ Use multiple subscriptions to isolate environments or teams

- ✅ Apply RBAC, tags, policies, and locks for control and governance

- ✅ Manage all entities through Portal, CLI, or automation

With a strong grasp of these concepts, you're well-positioned to start provisioning Azure resources in a secure, structured, and maintainable way. In the next section, we'll dive into essential tools like Azure CLI, PowerShell, and Cloud Shell to automate and streamline your development and operations workflow.

Essential Tools: Azure CLI, PowerShell, and Cloud Shell

To fully harness the power and flexibility of Microsoft Azure, you need the right tools. While the Azure Portal provides a rich graphical user interface, many developers and IT professionals prefer command-line tools for their speed, automation capabilities, and support for scripting repeatable tasks. The three primary tools for interacting with Azure programmatically are **Azure CLI**, **Azure PowerShell**, and **Azure Cloud Shell**.

This section provides an in-depth exploration of each tool, highlighting their differences, strengths, use cases, and best practices. We'll walk through real-world examples, scripting workflows, and how to integrate these tools into your development and operational environments.

Overview of Azure Command-Line Tools

Tool	Platform Support	Syntax Style	Ideal For
Azure CLI	Cross-platform (Linux, macOS, Windows)	Unix-style (bash, zsh)	Developers, DevOps, quick tasks
Azure PowerShell	Windows, Linux, macOS	PowerShell cmdlets	Admins, infrastructure scripting
Azure Cloud Shell	Browser-based (in Portal)	CLI or PowerShell	On-the-go management, no install

Each of these tools provides access to the full range of Azure services and APIs. Depending on your background—whether you're coming from a DevOps, admin, or software engineering perspective—one may feel more natural than another.

Azure CLI

Azure CLI (`az`) is a cross-platform command-line tool built with Python that uses simple, consistent syntax for managing Azure resources. It works well on any OS and integrates seamlessly with automation tools and DevOps pipelines.

Installing Azure CLI

- **Windows**:
  Use the MSI installer from Microsoft:
  https://aka.ms/installazurecliwindows

macOS:

```
brew update && brew install azure-cli
```

-

Linux (Ubuntu/Debian):

```
curl -sL https://aka.ms/InstallAzureCLIDeb | sudo bash
```

-

To confirm installation:

```
az --version
```

Logging In

Interactive login:

```
az login
```

This opens a browser window for authentication.

Service principal login (for automation):

```
az login --service-principal \
  --username <app-id> \
  --password <password-or-cert> \
  --tenant <tenant-id>
```

Common CLI Operations

Create a Resource Group:

```
az group create \
  --name myResourceGroup \
  --location eastus
```

Create a Virtual Machine:

```
az vm create \
  --resource-group myResourceGroup \
  --name myVM \
  --image UbuntuLTS \
  --admin-username azureuser \
  --generate-ssh-keys
```

Deploy a Web App:

```
az webapp up \
  --name mywebapp123 \
  --resource-group myResourceGroup \
  --runtime "NODE|14-lts"
```

List Resources:

```
az resource list --output table
```

Azure CLI is especially powerful when combined with automation tools like GitHub Actions, Azure DevOps, or CI/CD pipelines.

Azure PowerShell

Azure PowerShell is a set of modules that let you manage Azure using PowerShell scripts. It's ideal for administrators who are familiar with PowerShell syntax and need fine-grained control over resource states and configurations.

Installing Azure PowerShell

- **Windows (PowerShell 5.1+)**:

```
Install-Module -Name Az -AllowClobber -Scope CurrentUser
```

- **macOS/Linux (PowerShell Core)**:

```
pwsh
Install-Module -Name Az -AllowClobber -Scope CurrentUser
```

Check module installation:

```
Get-Module -Name Az -ListAvailable
```

Logging In

```
Connect-AzAccount
```

You'll be prompted to log in through a browser.

Common PowerShell Cmdlets

Create a Resource Group:

```
New-AzResourceGroup -Name "myResourceGroup" -Location "EastUS"
```

Create a VM:

```
New-AzVM -ResourceGroupName "myResourceGroup" -Name "myVM" -Location "EastUS"
```

List All Resource Groups:

```
Get-AzResourceGroup
```

Delete a Resource:

```
Remove-AzResourceGroup -Name "myResourceGroup" -Force
```

PowerShell's strength lies in its ability to automate complex scenarios and configurations across multiple Azure services using a consistent scripting language.

Azure Cloud Shell

Azure Cloud Shell is a browser-based terminal built directly into the Azure Portal. It supports both **Bash (Azure CLI)** and **PowerShell** environments and is perfect for quick tasks, learning, or when you don't have access to your development machine.

Launching Cloud Shell

1. Go to https://portal.azure.com

2. Click the **Cloud Shell icon** in the top menu

3. Choose **Bash** or **PowerShell**

4. The shell will provision a storage account on first use

Cloud Shell automatically authenticates using your portal session, meaning no need to run `az login`.

Advantages of Cloud Shell

- No local installation required

- Comes pre-loaded with Azure CLI, PowerShell, Terraform, Kubectl, Git, and more

- Persistent home directory backed by Azure Files

- Access to saved scripts, aliases, and profile configurations

Example: Create a Storage Account

```
az storage account create \
  --name mystorageacct \
  --resource-group myResourceGroup \
  --location eastus \
  --sku Standard_LRS
```

Uploading/Editing Files

You can upload and download files in Cloud Shell using the built-in file browser or command-line tools like `curl` and `wget`.

To edit files:

```
code myscript.sh
```

This opens a lightweight, browser-based editor inside Cloud Shell.

Choosing the Right Tool

Scenario	Recommended Tool
Cross-platform scripting	Azure CLI
Admin automation and compliance	Azure PowerShell
On-the-go management	Cloud Shell
DevOps pipeline integration	Azure CLI
Deep PowerShell ecosystem usage	Azure PowerShell
Education, demos, or training	Cloud Shell

There's no strict rule—you can mix and match tools depending on your context. For example, a DevOps engineer might write deployment scripts in Azure CLI but use Cloud Shell for monitoring live systems, while a sysadmin may prefer Azure PowerShell for auditing and policy enforcement tasks.

Integrating Tools with DevOps Workflows

You can embed these tools into CI/CD pipelines, scheduled automation tasks, and provisioning scripts. Examples include:

- **Azure DevOps Pipelines** with CLI or PowerShell tasks

- **GitHub Actions** that use Azure CLI or `az login` via a service principal

- **Terraform** scripts called from Cloud Shell

- **ARM/Bicep templates** deployed with CLI automation

Example: Use CLI in GitHub Action

```
jobs:
  deploy:
```

```
runs-on: ubuntu-latest
steps:
  - name: Azure Login
    uses: azure/login@v1
    with:
      creds: ${{ secrets.AZURE_CREDENTIALS }}
  - name: Deploy Web App
    run: |
      az webapp up --name mywebapp123 --resource-group myRG
```

Troubleshooting Common Issues

Problem: CLI or PowerShell commands failing with "permission denied"
Solution: Ensure the signed-in user or service principal has correct RBAC roles.

Problem: CLI version outdated
Solution: Run `az upgrade` or reinstall using the latest installer.

Problem: Module conflicts in PowerShell
Solution: Use `-AllowClobber` during install or uninstall older AzureRM modules.

Problem: Cloud Shell not starting
Solution: Create a new storage account manually or clear cached configurations.

Summary

Azure CLI, PowerShell, and Cloud Shell are indispensable tools for any Azure professional. They offer flexibility, speed, and automation capabilities that far surpass manual management via the portal.

Key takeaways:

- ✓ Use **Azure CLI** for cross-platform scripting and DevOps

- ✓ Use **Azure PowerShell** for infrastructure automation and administration

- ✓ Use **Azure Cloud Shell** for browser-based, on-the-fly management

- ✓ Learn both CLI and PowerShell to adapt to team and project needs

- ✓ Integrate these tools into CI/CD and automation pipelines

With these tools at your disposal, you're well-equipped to build, deploy, and manage anything in Azure efficiently. In the next chapter, we'll dive into Azure's core services—compute, storage, networking, and databases—to start building real solutions.

Chapter 3: Core Azure Services Explained

Compute Services (VMs, App Services, Functions)

Microsoft Azure offers a rich set of compute services designed to support a wide array of application types, deployment styles, and scalability requirements. Compute services are the backbone of any cloud solution—they provide the processing power and runtime environment for your applications, ranging from simple scripts to global-scale web applications.

In this section, we'll break down the core compute services on Azure:

- Virtual Machines (VMs)

- Azure App Services

- Azure Functions

We'll also explore when to use each, how to set them up, and key considerations for scaling and cost management.

Virtual Machines (VMs)

Azure Virtual Machines allow you to run Windows or Linux-based workloads in a highly customizable environment. This infrastructure-as-a-service (IaaS) offering gives full control over the operating system, installed software, and the VM's networking.

Key Features

- **Full OS-level control**: Install and configure any software or runtime.

- **Wide OS selection**: Windows, Ubuntu, Red Hat, CentOS, and more.

- **Scalability**: VMs can be scaled manually or automatically.

- **Availability Sets & Zones**: Improve uptime and fault tolerance.

Creating a Virtual Machine

You can create a VM using the Azure Portal, Azure CLI, or PowerShell.

Azure CLI Example:

```
az vm create \
  --name myVM \
  --resource-group myResourceGroup \
  --image UbuntuLTS \
  --admin-username azureuser \
  --generate-ssh-keys
```

This command creates a basic Ubuntu VM with SSH keys. You can customize the VM size, disk, and network settings further.

Use Cases

- Hosting legacy applications that require full OS access.

- Running custom server software.

- Development and test environments.

- Running container orchestration tools like Docker Swarm or Kubernetes.

Considerations

- VMs require manual patching and maintenance unless configured with Azure Automation or Update Management.

- Pricing is based on VM size, region, and usage hours.

- High availability requires additional setup, such as Load Balancers or Availability Zones.

Azure App Services

Azure App Services is a platform-as-a-service (PaaS) offering that simplifies the deployment of web apps, REST APIs, and mobile backends. It abstracts away infrastructure management, letting you focus on writing code.

Key Features

- **Managed hosting**: No need to manage OS updates or hardware.

- **Language support**: .NET, Node.js, Python, PHP, Java, and more.

- **Deployment slots**: Swap staging and production environments with zero downtime.

- **Built-in scaling**: Autoscale based on CPU, memory, or schedule.

- **CI/CD integration**: Seamless deployment from GitHub, Azure Repos, or Bitbucket.

Creating an App Service

You can create and deploy using the Azure Portal or CLI.

Azure CLI Example:

```
az webapp up \
  --name myAppService \
  --resource-group myResourceGroup \
  --location eastus \
  --runtime "NODE|18-lts"
```

This command uploads your local app and hosts it using the specified runtime.

Use Cases

- Hosting public-facing websites or APIs.

- Backend services for mobile apps.

- Multi-language enterprise-grade web apps.

- Applications that require high availability and easy scaling.

Considerations

- Limited control over the underlying infrastructure.

- May not be suitable for apps with low-level OS dependencies.

- Pricing is based on service plan tiers and instance count.

Azure Functions

Azure Functions is a serverless compute option that runs event-driven code without managing infrastructure. It's perfect for building lightweight services, background tasks, or processing data in real time.

Key Features

- **Event-driven**: Triggered by HTTP requests, timers, queues, blobs, and more.

- **Auto-scaling**: Instantly scales based on load.

- **Micro-billing**: Pay only for the execution time and number of executions.

- **Flexible language support**: Write functions in C#, JavaScript, Python, Java, and PowerShell.

Creating an Azure Function

You can create a Function App in the portal or use the Azure Functions Core Tools locally.

Azure CLI Example:

```
az functionapp create \
  --resource-group myResourceGroup \
  --consumption-plan-location westus \
  --runtime python \
  --functions-version 4 \
  --name myFunctionApp \
  --storage-account mystorageaccount
```

Sample Python Function (HTTP Trigger):

```python
import logging
import azure.functions as func

def main(req: func.HttpRequest) -> func.HttpResponse:
    name = req.params.get('name')
    if not name:
        return func.HttpResponse(
            "Please pass a name on the query string.",
            status_code=400
        )
    return func.HttpResponse(f"Hello, {name}!")
```

Use Cases

- Real-time data processing (e.g., image resizing, log parsing).

- Webhooks and event triggers (e.g., when a new blob is added).

- Lightweight backend APIs.

- Automated workflows or scheduled tasks.

Considerations

- Cold starts may introduce latency for infrequently used functions.

- Execution timeout limits (configurable, but limited in consumption plan).

- Best suited for stateless, short-lived functions.

Choosing the Right Compute Service

Requirement	Best Option
Full OS control	Azure Virtual Machines
Rapid web app/API development	Azure App Services
Event-driven workflows	Azure Functions
High scalability with containers	Azure Kubernetes Service (discussed in Chapter 8)

Consider the following when making your decision:

- **Deployment speed**: App Services and Functions are quicker to deploy.

- **Maintenance effort**: Serverless and PaaS options reduce maintenance.

- **Scalability needs**: Azure Functions scales automatically; VMs need configuration.

- **Budget**: Serverless options can reduce costs significantly for low-traffic workloads.

Summary

Azure's compute offerings provide solutions for virtually every scenario—whether you need full control with Virtual Machines, a managed platform with App Services, or a highly scalable and cost-effective serverless model with Azure Functions.

As you become familiar with these services, you'll learn to choose the right one for the task at hand. In practice, many applications use a combination—for example, using App Services for the main application, Azure Functions for background jobs, and VMs for special-purpose tasks.

In the next section, we'll cover Azure's versatile storage solutions that work hand-in-hand with compute services to power robust cloud applications.

Storage Solutions (Blob, Table, File, Queue)

Azure provides a highly scalable and secure storage platform with services designed for a wide variety of use cases, from serving media to managing application state and enabling distributed processing. This section explores the four core types of storage offered by Azure Storage: Blob, Table, File, and Queue. We will cover their core features, use cases, and integration tips for real-world applications.

Azure Storage Overview

Azure Storage is a cloud-based storage solution that provides redundancy, high availability, and integration with virtually all Azure services. All data in Azure Storage is encrypted at rest and can be replicated across regions for disaster recovery.

The four main storage types include:

- **Blob Storage**: Object storage for unstructured data like documents, images, and backups.

- **Table Storage**: NoSQL key-value store for structured data.

- **File Storage**: Fully managed file shares for legacy applications and shared access.

- **Queue Storage**: Message storage for asynchronous communication between components.

Each type is part of an Azure Storage Account, which is the foundational resource needed to use any of the above.

Creating a Storage Account (Azure CLI):

```
az storage account create \
  --name mystorageaccount \
  --resource-group myResourceGroup \
  --location eastus \
  --sku Standard_LRS
```

Blob Storage

Azure Blob Storage is optimized for storing massive amounts of unstructured data. It supports three blob types: block blobs, append blobs, and page blobs.

Key Features

- Highly scalable and accessible.

- Supports hot, cool, and archive tiers.

- Secure with shared access signatures (SAS) and Azure AD.

- Supports lifecycle management rules.

Use Cases

- Media content storage (images, videos, PDFs).

- Static website hosting.

- Data backup and recovery.

- Logging and telemetry data.

Uploading a Blob (Azure CLI):

```
az storage blob upload \
  --account-name mystorageaccount \
  --container-name mycontainer \
  --name example.txt \
  --file ./example.txt \
  --auth-mode login
```

Downloading a Blob:

```
az storage blob download \
  --container-name mycontainer \
  --name example.txt \
  --file ./downloaded-example.txt \
  --account-name mystorageaccount
```

Lifecycle Rule Example (JSON):

```
{
```

```
"rules": [
  {
    "enabled": true,
    "name": "move-to-cool",
    "type": "Lifecycle",
    "definition": {
      "filters": {
        "blobTypes": ["blockBlob"],
        "prefixMatch": ["logs/"]
      },
      "actions": {
        "baseBlob": {
          "tierToCool": {
            "daysAfterModificationGreaterThan": 30
          }
        }
      }
    }
  }
]
}
```

Table Storage

Table Storage is a key-value NoSQL store that offers schema-less storage of structured data. It's ideal for datasets that need to grow quickly and require fast read/write operations.

Key Features

- Schemaless storage.

- Supports partitions for scalability.

- Accessible via REST API or SDKs.

- Low-cost and fast access for structured data.

Use Cases

- Storing metadata or configuration.

- IoT device data.

- User profile data.

- Logging information.

Insert Data Using Azure SDK (Node.js Example):

```
const { TableClient, AzureNamedKeyCredential } =
require("@azure/data-tables");

const account = "<account-name>";
const accountKey = "<account-key>";
const tableName = "MyTable";

const client = new TableClient(
  `https://${account}.table.core.windows.net`,
  tableName,
  new AzureNamedKeyCredential(account, accountKey)
);

await client.createTable();

await client.createEntity({
  partitionKey: "user001",
  rowKey: "profile",
  email: "test@example.com",
  age: 32
});
```

Considerations

- Table Storage supports only basic querying—no joins or foreign keys.

- For complex queries, consider using Cosmos DB Table API.

- Data is partitioned to optimize performance, so choose keys wisely.

File Storage

Azure File Storage provides fully managed SMB file shares that can be mounted on Windows, macOS, and Linux systems. It is especially useful for migrating legacy apps to the cloud that expect a file system.

Key Features

- SMB protocol support (v3.x).

- NFS support (premium tier).

- Snapshot support for backups.

- Integration with Azure File Sync for hybrid scenarios.

Use Cases

- File shares between VMs or applications.

- Lift-and-shift legacy applications.

- Shared application state or media assets.

- On-premise file system extension with Azure File Sync.

Mounting on Windows:

```
net use Z: \\<storage-account-name>.file.core.windows.net\myshare
/user:Azure\<storage-account-name> <storage-key>
```

Mounting on Linux:

```
sudo mount -t cifs //<storage-account-
name>.file.core.windows.net/myshare /mnt/azurefiles -o
vers=3.0,username=<storage-account-name>,password=<storage-
key>,dir_mode=0777,file_mode=0777
```

File Share Limits

- Max size per file share: Up to 100 TB.

- Max file size: 1 TB (standard), 4 TB (premium).

- Quotas can be configured to restrict usage.

Queue Storage

Azure Queue Storage offers a simple message queueing mechanism for building scalable and decoupled systems. It's particularly effective for distributed applications where components need to communicate asynchronously.

Key Features

- Message sizes up to 64 KB.

- Up to 200 TB total queue size per storage account.

- Time-to-live (TTL) support for messages.

- Poison message handling for failed processing.

Use Cases

- Decoupling microservices.

- Implementing retry logic for background jobs.

- Event-driven application designs.

- Workflow management systems.

Creating and Adding a Message (Azure CLI):

```
az storage queue create \
  --name myqueue \
  --account-name mystorageaccount

az storage message put \
  --queue-name myqueue \
  --content "Process this task" \
  --account-name mystorageaccount
```

Retrieving and Deleting a Message:

```
az storage message get \
  --queue-name myqueue \
  --account-name mystorageaccount
```

```
az storage message delete \
  --queue-name myqueue \
  --id <message-id> \
  --pop-receipt <receipt>
```

Security and Access

Azure Storage supports multiple layers of security:

- **Azure RBAC**: Assign users or services access roles.

- **Shared Access Signatures (SAS)**: Fine-grained, time-limited access.

- **Storage Account Keys**: Primary and secondary keys for full access.

- **Private Endpoints**: Secure traffic over Azure backbone.

- **Firewall Rules**: IP whitelisting and VNet integration.

Generating a SAS Token:

```
az storage container generate-sas \
  --account-name mystorageaccount \
  --name mycontainer \
  --permissions r \
  --expiry 2025-12-31T23:59:00Z \
  --output tsv
```

Monitoring and Management

Use Azure Monitor, Metrics, and Alerts to track storage usage and performance.

Enable Diagnostic Logs:

```
az monitor diagnostic-settings create \
  --resource <storage-resource-id> \
  --name "diag-settings" \
  --logs '[{"category": "StorageRead", "enabled": true}]' \
  --workspace <log-analytics-workspace-id>
```

You can also use the **Azure Storage Explorer** desktop application to interact with your storage accounts visually—uploading, downloading, editing, and organizing data across all types.

Summary

Azure Storage solutions provide a comprehensive toolkit for managing data in the cloud. Whether you're serving high-resolution media, storing logs from millions of IoT devices, sharing files across regions, or coordinating microservices, there's an Azure storage option tailored to your needs.

Choosing the right storage type depends on your application's data structure, access pattern, and integration model:

Need	Best Storage Type
Unstructured files & media	Blob Storage
NoSQL structured data	Table Storage
Legacy app file sharing	File Storage
Asynchronous messaging	Queue Storage

By understanding and leveraging each of these options, you'll be able to architect resilient, scalable, and efficient cloud-native applications on Azure.

Networking Basics (VNets, Load Balancers, DNS)

Networking in Microsoft Azure is foundational to building secure, scalable, and highly available cloud solutions. Azure provides a range of networking services to help you connect, secure, and manage your resources efficiently. This section dives deep into the core networking components—Virtual Networks (VNets), Load Balancers, and Domain Name System (DNS)—exploring their purposes, architecture, and practical implementation patterns.

Azure Virtual Networks (VNets)

A Virtual Network (VNet) in Azure is akin to a traditional on-premises network, providing isolated and secure environments for deploying and managing your resources. VNets form the basis for many Azure services to communicate privately.

Key Features

- **Isolation and segmentation**: Each VNet is logically isolated from others.

- **Subnets**: Divide VNets into smaller segments for organizing and securing resources.

- **IP address management**: Assign static or dynamic private IPs.

- **Peering**: Connect VNets for inter-region or inter-subscription communication.

- **Hybrid Connectivity**: VPN and ExpressRoute support for on-premises integration.

Creating a VNet

Azure CLI Example:

```
az network vnet create \
  --name myVNet \
  --resource-group myResourceGroup \
  --address-prefix 10.0.0.0/16 \
  --subnet-name mySubnet \
  --subnet-prefix 10.0.1.0/24
```

This command creates a VNet with an address space and a subnet.

Subnets and IP Planning

Organize resources using subnets for logical segmentation:

- **WebSubnet** for public-facing services.

- **AppSubnet** for internal services.

- **DBSubnet** for database services.

Each subnet should have appropriate **Network Security Groups (NSGs)** applied to control traffic flow.

VNet Peering

Allows communication between VNets without a VPN or public internet exposure.

Azure CLI:

```
az network vnet peering create \
  --name LinkVNet1ToVNet2 \
  --resource-group myResourceGroup \
```

```
--vnet-name VNet1 \
--remote-vnet VNet2 \
--allow-vnet-access
```

Network Security Groups (NSGs)

NSGs act like firewalls that control inbound and outbound traffic at both the subnet and NIC levels. Each rule includes properties like priority, source/destination, port, and protocol.

Example NSG Rule (Allow SSH):

```
az network nsg rule create \
  --resource-group myResourceGroup \
  --nsg-name myNSG \
  --name AllowSSH \
  --protocol Tcp \
  --direction Inbound \
  --priority 1000 \
  --source-address-prefix '*' \
  --source-port-range '*' \
  --destination-address-prefix '*' \
  --destination-port-range 22 \
  --access Allow
```

Always apply least privilege—only open ports and protocols that are necessary.

Azure Load Balancer

Azure Load Balancer distributes incoming network traffic across multiple resources to increase availability and reliability.

Types of Load Balancers

- **Public Load Balancer**: Exposes apps to the internet.

- **Internal Load Balancer**: Distributes traffic inside a private VNet.

Key Features

- Layer 4 (TCP/UDP) traffic distribution.

- Health probes for endpoint availability.

- NAT rules for VM access.

- Supports inbound/outbound scenarios.

Creating a Load Balancer (Public)

```
az network public-ip create \
  --name myPublicIP \
  --resource-group myResourceGroup \
  --allocation-method Static \
  --sku Standard

az network lb create \
  --resource-group myResourceGroup \
  --name myLoadBalancer \
  --frontend-ip-name myFrontEnd \
  --backend-pool-name myBackEndPool \
  --public-ip-address myPublicIP \
  --sku Standard
```

Adding a Rule

```
az network lb rule create \
  --resource-group myResourceGroup \
  --lb-name myLoadBalancer \
  --name myHTTPRule \
  --protocol tcp \
  --frontend-port 80 \
  --backend-port 80 \
  --frontend-ip-name myFrontEnd \
  --backend-pool-name myBackEndPool \
  --probe-name myHealthProbe
```

Health Probes

Health probes determine if backend resources are available.

Example Probe:

```
az network lb probe create \
  --resource-group myResourceGroup \
  --lb-name myLoadBalancer \
```

```
--name myHealthProbe \
--protocol tcp \
--port 80
```

Azure DNS

Azure DNS allows you to host your DNS domain in Azure, managing your records using the same credentials and billing as other Azure services.

Key Features

- Fast and reliable global DNS service.

- Custom domain hosting (e.g., mysite.com).

- Supports all common DNS record types.

- Integration with Azure services and automation.

Creating a DNS Zone

```
az network dns zone create \
  --resource-group myResourceGroup \
  --name mysite.com
```

Adding DNS Records

A Record:

```
az network dns record-set a add-record \
  --resource-group myResourceGroup \
  --zone-name mysite.com \
  --record-set-name www \
  --ipv4-address 10.0.0.4
```

CNAME Record:

```
az network dns record-set cname set-record \
  --resource-group myResourceGroup \
  --zone-name mysite.com \
  --record-set-name blog \
  --cname www.example.com
```

Custom Domain Integration with App Services

You can map a custom domain hosted in Azure DNS to an Azure App Service by validating ownership via TXT or A records.

Application Gateway

For layer 7 (HTTP/HTTPS) load balancing, Azure provides **Application Gateway**, which includes:

- SSL termination.

- URL-based routing.

- Web Application Firewall (WAF).

- Session affinity.

Use Cases

- Hosting multiple sites on the same IP.

- Advanced path-based routing.

- Protecting against common web vulnerabilities.

Example Scenario:

You can direct traffic based on URL:

- `/api` → API backend pool

- `/images` → Blob static content

- `/` → Frontend web app

Private Endpoints and Service Endpoints

For secure access to Azure PaaS services from your VNet, Azure offers:

- **Service Endpoints**: Extend your VNet to Azure services over Microsoft's backbone.

- **Private Endpoints**: Assign a private IP to Azure resources for isolated access.

Private Endpoint Example (Azure CLI):

```
az network private-endpoint create \
  --name myPrivateEndpoint \
  --resource-group myResourceGroup \
  --vnet-name myVNet \
  --subnet mySubnet \
  --private-connection-resource-id <resource-id> \
  --group-ids blob \
  --connection-name myConnection
```

Traffic Manager and Front Door

- **Azure Traffic Manager**: DNS-based global traffic routing across regions.

- **Azure Front Door**: Global HTTP/HTTPS load balancing with caching and acceleration.

Traffic Manager Use Cases:

- Route traffic to the closest regional endpoint.

- Distribute load across deployments in multiple geographies.

- Provide geo-failover for disaster recovery.

Front Door Use Cases:

- Faster content delivery with edge POPs.

- Central entry point with intelligent routing.

- WAF for protection against attacks.

Best Practices for Azure Networking

1. **Use NSGs strategically**: Apply at both subnet and NIC levels for layered protection.

2. **Segment networks with subnets**: Apply principles of Zero Trust.

3. **Use Private Endpoints for sensitive services**: Avoid exposing resources to the public internet.

4. **Monitor network flows**: Enable NSG flow logs and use Network Watcher.

5. **Plan IP ranges carefully**: Ensure non-overlapping address spaces for peering and hybrid scenarios.

6. **Enable DDoS Protection**: Use Azure's built-in and standard DDoS protection plans.

7. **Use BGP with ExpressRoute**: For dynamic route advertisement and failover.

8. **Implement WAF and SSL**: Protect apps behind Application Gateway or Front Door.

Summary

Networking in Azure is powerful, flexible, and essential to every cloud architecture. From creating virtual networks to enabling global failover, Azure provides enterprise-grade tools for every scenario.

Networking Component	Purpose
VNet	Private IP-based isolation and control
NSG	Firewall rules at NIC/subnet levels
Load Balancer	Distribute traffic at Layer 4
Application Gateway	Layer 7 routing with WAF
DNS	Domain management and resolution
Private Endpoints	Secure access to PaaS
Traffic Manager	Global DNS-based routing

Front Door	HTTP/HTTPS acceleration and security

Understanding and implementing these services allows you to design secure, scalable, and highly performant cloud applications that align with modern best practices.

Databases on Azure (SQL Database, Cosmos DB, MySQL)

Databases are the backbone of almost every modern application, and Azure provides a robust suite of database solutions to meet a wide variety of use cases—from traditional relational models to globally distributed NoSQL options. In this section, we'll explore the major database services available on Microsoft Azure, focusing on SQL Database, Cosmos DB, and MySQL. We'll look at their features, when to use them, and how to deploy and manage them effectively.

Azure SQL Database

Azure SQL Database is a fully managed relational database-as-a-service (DBaaS) built on SQL Server. It's ideal for applications that require strong consistency, structured data, and complex querying capabilities.

Key Features

- Fully managed by Microsoft (patching, backups, replication).

- High availability with zone redundancy and failover.

- Built-in threat detection and advanced security.

- Elastic pools to share resources between databases.

- Autoscaling compute and storage.

Deployment Models

1. **Single Database**: Isolated, single-instance database.

2. **Elastic Pool**: Multiple databases sharing a set of resources.

3. **Managed Instance**: Full SQL Server compatibility in a PaaS environment.

Creating an Azure SQL Database (CLI Example)

```
az sql server create \
  --name my-sql-server \
  --resource-group myResourceGroup \
  --location eastus \
  --admin-user myadmin \
  --admin-password mypassword123!

az sql db create \
  --resource-group myResourceGroup \
  --server my-sql-server \
  --name myDatabase \
  --service-objective S1
```

Connecting to Azure SQL

You can connect using tools like **Azure Data Studio**, **SQL Server Management Studio (SSMS)**, or programmatically via JDBC/ODBC/.NET providers.

Connection string (.NET):

```
Server=tcp:my-sql-server.database.windows.net,1433;
Initial Catalog=myDatabase;
Persist Security Info=False;
User ID=myadmin;
Password=mypassword123!;
MultipleActiveResultSets=False;
Encrypt=True;
TrustServerCertificate=False;
Connection Timeout=30;
```

Use Cases

- Enterprise-grade OLTP systems.

- Applications with strong relational data dependencies.

- Reporting and business intelligence solutions.

- Systems needing compliance and high security.

Azure Cosmos DB

Cosmos DB is Microsoft's globally distributed, multi-model NoSQL database designed for modern app development at scale. It supports document, key-value, column-family, and graph data models with APIs for MongoDB, Cassandra, Gremlin, and SQL (Core).

Key Features

- Multi-model: Document, key-value, graph, table, column-family.

- Multi-API: SQL, MongoDB, Cassandra, Table, Gremlin.

- Global distribution with multi-master replication.

- Tunable consistency levels (Strong, Bounded Staleness, Session, Consistent Prefix, Eventual).

- Instant elasticity with autoscale throughput.

Provisioning Cosmos DB (CLI Example)

```
az cosmosdb create \
  --name mycosmosdb \
  --resource-group myResourceGroup \
  --locations regionName=eastus failoverPriority=0
isZoneRedundant=False \
  --default-consistency-level Session \
  --kind MongoDB
```

Creating a Database and Container

```
az cosmosdb mongodb database create \
  --account-name mycosmosdb \
  --name myDatabase \
  --resource-group myResourceGroup

az cosmosdb mongodb collection create \
  --account-name mycosmosdb \
  --database-name myDatabase \
  --name myCollection \
  --resource-group myResourceGroup \
  --throughput 400
```

Use Cases

- Applications with dynamic schema or high ingestion rates.

- Real-time personalization and recommendation engines.

- IoT telemetry and time-series data.

- Social apps and e-commerce platforms.

- Global apps requiring low latency and high availability.

Example Document (JSON)

```json
{
  "id": "product123",
  "name": "Azure T-Shirt",
  "price": 24.99,
  "tags": ["clothing", "azure", "tshirt"],
  "inventory": {
    "warehouse": 50,
    "store": 15
  }
}
```

Azure Database for MySQL

Azure Database for MySQL is a managed database service that supports community MySQL with high availability, backup, monitoring, and scaling built-in.

Key Features

- Fully managed MySQL database.

- Versions 5.7 and 8.0 supported.

- Built-in high availability and backup.

- Autoscaling storage and compute (in flexible server model).

- SSL/TLS encryption.

Deployment Models

1. **Single Server**: Basic deployment with automatic backups.

2. **Flexible Server**: Custom maintenance window, zone redundancy, and stop/start capabilities.

Creating MySQL Flexible Server (CLI)

```
az mysql flexible-server create \
  --name mymysqlserver \
  --resource-group myResourceGroup \
  --location eastus \
  --admin-user myadmin \
  --admin-password mypassword123! \
  --sku-name Standard_B1ms \
  --version 8.0
```

Connecting via MySQL CLI

```
mysql -h mymysqlserver.mysql.database.azure.com \
  -u myadmin@mymysqlserver \
  -p
```

Use Cases

- Web applications built on LAMP/LEMP stacks.

- CMS platforms like WordPress and Drupal.

- eCommerce applications like Magento.

- Any open-source application requiring MySQL.

Security and Compliance

All Azure database services offer enterprise-grade security out-of-the-box:

- **Encryption**: Data is encrypted at rest using Transparent Data Encryption (TDE) and in transit using TLS/SSL.

- **Network Isolation**: VNet integration and private endpoints.

- **Firewall Rules**: Define access by IP range.

- **Azure AD Integration**: Centralized identity and access management.

- **Advanced Threat Protection**: Detects vulnerabilities and anomalous activities.

Add Firewall Rule Example (Azure SQL):

```
az sql server firewall-rule create \
  --resource-group myResourceGroup \
  --server my-sql-server \
  --name AllowMyIP \
  --start-ip-address 203.0.113.1 \
  --end-ip-address 203.0.113.1
```

Backup and Disaster Recovery

Each Azure DB service includes robust backup features:

- **Point-in-time restore**: Up to 35 days for SQL/MySQL/PostgreSQL.

- **Geo-redundant backups**: Optional for cross-region restoration.

- **Automatic failover**: In case of zone failures (Premium tiers or geo-replication setups).

Geo-Replication Example (Azure SQL):

```
az sql db replica create \
  --name myDatabase \
  --partner-server mySecondaryServer \
  --resource-group myResourceGroup \
  --server my-sql-server
```

Monitoring and Performance Tuning

Azure provides built-in tools to monitor and tune your databases:

- **Query Performance Insight** (SQL Database)

- **Metrics Explorer** (Cosmos DB throughput, latency)

- **Slow Query Logs** (MySQL Flexible Server)

- **Azure Monitor Integration**: Alerts, dashboards, diagnostics.

Enable Diagnostics (SQL Database):

```
az monitor diagnostic-settings create \
  --resource <sql-database-id> \
  --workspace <log-analytics-workspace-id> \
  --name "SQLDiagnostics" \
  --logs '[{"category": "SQLSecurityAuditEvents", "enabled": true}]'
```

Cost Optimization Tips

1. **Use serverless SQL for infrequent use cases**.

2. **Autoscale Cosmos DB throughput** to avoid over-provisioning.

3. **Flexible Server MySQL** allows for pause/resume to save cost during idle times.

4. **Elastic pools** in SQL reduce cost for multi-tenant SaaS models.

5. **Monitor usage patterns** to right-size compute and storage resources.

Choosing the Right Azure Database

Requirement	Recommended Service
Structured, relational data	Azure SQL Database
Globally distributed NoSQL with low latency	Azure Cosmos DB
Open-source app with MySQL backend	Azure Database for MySQL
Dynamic schema with high availability	Cosmos DB (SQL or Mongo)
WordPress, Magento, Drupal	Azure MySQL
Complex joins and stored procedures	SQL Database or Managed Instance

Summary

Azure offers a powerful suite of database solutions that cater to nearly every workload scenario—from traditional relational models to flexible, distributed NoSQL data stores. Whether you're building a data-driven web app, a globally available mobile backend, or a scalable e-commerce system, Azure provides the tools and services to store, secure, and manage your data effectively.

Understanding the strengths and trade-offs of SQL Database, Cosmos DB, and MySQL on Azure enables you to make architecture decisions that support performance, scalability, security, and cost efficiency. As your application evolves, Azure's flexible database offerings ensure that your data strategy can evolve right along with it.

Chapter 4: Building and Deploying Your First Azure App

Choosing the Right Azure Services

Building an application on Azure begins with a crucial first step: selecting the appropriate Azure services for your needs. With the vast range of offerings available, it's important to make decisions based on the application's architecture, scalability requirements, target audience, compliance standards, and development workflow.

This section will guide you through evaluating requirements, understanding common architectural patterns, comparing similar services, and ultimately choosing the best Azure components to bring your application to life. We'll explore real-world decision-making criteria, service recommendations for different scenarios, and tips to avoid common pitfalls.

Understanding Your Application Requirements

Before selecting services, it's vital to have a clear understanding of what your application needs. Begin by answering these core questions:

- **Is this a web, mobile, desktop, or hybrid application?**

- **Does it need to scale globally or regionally?**

- **Will the app process real-time data or batch jobs?**

- **What types of data will it store? Structured, unstructured, or both?**

- **What are the security and compliance considerations?**

- **Do you need high availability or disaster recovery?**

- **Will you be working in a CI/CD workflow?**

These answers will guide your architectural choices. Let's walk through different service categories and how to match them to your application's needs.

Selecting the Compute Service

Compute is the engine of your app. Azure offers multiple ways to run your application code:

Azure App Service

- Best for web applications and REST APIs.

- Supports multiple languages (Node.js, Python, .NET, Java).

- Managed platform: handles OS, patching, scaling.

- Supports deployment slots, CI/CD, and autoscaling.

Azure Functions

- Ideal for event-driven, serverless architectures.

- Billed only for execution time.

- Great for background tasks, webhook handlers, and lightweight APIs.

Azure Kubernetes Service (AKS)

- For containerized microservices with complex orchestration needs.

- Managed Kubernetes with full control over container behavior.

- Ideal for scalable, modular systems with DevOps pipelines.

Azure Virtual Machines

- Full control over the OS and installed software.

- Required for legacy workloads or special configurations.

- Heavier management overhead.

Recommendation Matrix:

Use Case	Recommended Service
Simple web app	Azure App Service
Background tasks	Azure Functions

Microservices with containers	AKS
Full control environment	Virtual Machines
APIs with autoscaling	App Service or Functions

Choosing the Right Database

Database selection should be guided by your data structure, query patterns, and consistency needs.

Azure SQL Database

- Fully managed relational database.

- Ideal for OLTP apps with structured data and strong consistency.

Azure Cosmos DB

- Globally distributed, multi-model NoSQL.

- Suitable for fast, scalable apps with dynamic schemas.

Azure Database for MySQL/PostgreSQL

- Community edition support.

- Best for open-source app stacks like WordPress, Drupal, Magento.

Azure Table Storage

- NoSQL key-value store.

- Best for simple, large-scale datasets without complex queries.

Decision Guide:

Requirement	Service
Relational structure	Azure SQL, MySQL, PostgreSQL

Flexible schema	Azure Cosmos DB
High global availability	Cosmos DB with geo-replication
Simple key/value store	Azure Table Storage

Storing Application Files and Assets

Your app may need to store media files, documents, logs, or other unstructured data.

Azure Blob Storage

- Best for storing any binary or text-based unstructured data.

- Scalable and cost-efficient.

- Integration with Content Delivery Network (CDN) for global distribution.

Azure File Storage

- Offers SMB/NFS file share access.

- Suitable for legacy apps or shared access between services.

Example CLI for Blob Storage:

```
az storage account create \
  --name mystorageacct \
  --resource-group myResourceGroup \
  --location westus \
  --sku Standard_LRS

az storage container create \
  --account-name mystorageacct \
  --name mycontainer \
  --public-access off
```

Networking and Access Control

Controlling access and enabling secure communications is critical for any application.

Azure Virtual Network (VNet)

- Needed if you're connecting multiple resources securely.

- Supports network security groups, private endpoints.

Azure Front Door

- Global entry point for web applications.

- Supports HTTPS termination, routing, and Web Application Firewall.

Azure API Management (APIM)

- Full lifecycle API management: gateway, rate limiting, authentication.

- Perfect for public and partner-facing APIs.

Azure Active Directory (Azure AD)

- Identity management and single sign-on for users and apps.

- Integrates with RBAC for access control.

CI/CD and DevOps Integration

To deploy and maintain your app efficiently, DevOps is essential. Azure provides several tools:

Azure DevOps

- Provides Boards, Pipelines, Repos, and Artifacts.

- Excellent for full project management and deployment automation.

GitHub Actions for Azure

- Seamlessly integrates with GitHub repos.

- Supports deployment to App Services, Functions, AKS, and more.

Azure Container Registry (ACR)

- Stores and manages container images for AKS and App Services.

- Easily integrates into pipelines.

Example GitHub Workflow (Deploy to Azure App Service):

```
name: Deploy to Azure App Service
on:
  push:
    branches:
      - main
jobs:
  build-and-deploy:
    runs-on: ubuntu-latest
    steps:
      - name: Checkout code
        uses: actions/checkout@v2

      - name: Login to Azure
        uses: azure/login@v1
        with:
          creds: ${{ secrets.AZURE_CREDENTIALS }}

      - name: Deploy to Web App
        uses: azure/webapps-deploy@v2
        with:
          app-name: my-webapp
          slot-name: production
          package: .
```

Logging, Monitoring, and Alerting

Observability ensures you can debug and optimize your application effectively.

Azure Monitor

- Aggregates metrics and logs from all Azure services.

Application Insights

- Performance monitoring and usage analytics.

- Works with App Services, Functions, containers.

Log Analytics

- Query logs using Kusto Query Language (KQL).

- Build dashboards and trigger alerts.

Enable Application Insights (App Service):

```
az monitor app-insights component create \
  --app myAppInsights \
  --location eastus \
  --resource-group myResourceGroup \
  --application-type web
```

Security Considerations

Always bake in security from the beginning:

- Use **Azure Key Vault** to store secrets, connection strings, and certificates.

- Apply **Role-Based Access Control (RBAC)** to limit developer access to sensitive resources.

- Enable **DDoS Protection** for public apps.

- Secure APIs with **OAuth2 and OpenID Connect** via Azure AD.

Sample Architecture Scenarios

1. Serverless E-Commerce App

- Azure Functions for backend

- Cosmos DB for product and order data

- Blob Storage for product images

- Azure Front Door + CDN for global delivery

- Azure AD B2C for user auth

2. SaaS Web App

- Azure App Service for frontend

- Azure SQL Database for relational data

- Azure Redis for session caching

- Azure API Management for public API layer

- Azure DevOps for CI/CD

3. Enterprise Microservices Platform

- AKS for containers

- ACR for image storage

- Azure PostgreSQL Flexible Server for DB

- Azure Key Vault for secrets

- Azure Monitor + Log Analytics

Summary

Choosing the right Azure services sets the stage for your application's success. Instead of jumping into development with a one-size-fits-all mindset, take time to assess requirements, compare options, and consider trade-offs.

Start small, validate with prototypes, and scale with confidence using Azure's broad ecosystem. By combining the appropriate compute, database, storage, networking, and DevOps services, you can build resilient, high-performing, and future-proof applications on the Microsoft Azure cloud platform.

Setting Up a Development Environment

Building applications on Microsoft Azure efficiently requires a well-prepared development environment. This environment must support rapid development, debugging, testing, and deployment across various services and stacks. Whether you are building a simple web application, a serverless function, or a microservices-based architecture, your tooling, SDKs, CLI, IDEs, and extensions play a critical role.

In this section, we'll walk through the key components of setting up your development environment for Azure, including:

- Configuring your local machine

- Installing essential tools (CLI, SDKs, IDEs)

- Setting up code repositories and version control

- Establishing CI/CD pipelines

- Testing and debugging with Azure integrations

Choosing Your Development Machine Setup

Azure supports development on **Windows**, **macOS**, and **Linux**, giving flexibility depending on your preference or the tech stack of your app.

Recommended Minimum Specifications:

- 8 GB RAM (16 GB for container-based development)

- SSD storage for quick I/O

- VS Code or Visual Studio 2022

- Docker installed (for container work)

- Node.js, Python, Java, or .NET SDKs depending on your stack

For consistent tooling, using **WSL 2** on Windows provides a Linux-like experience that matches Azure runtime environments closely.

Installing Azure CLI and PowerShell

The **Azure CLI** is the primary command-line tool for interacting with Azure resources. It allows you to script common tasks, deploy services, and manage infrastructure.

Azure CLI Installation:

On Windows:

```
Invoke-WebRequest -Uri https://aka.ms/installazurecliwindows -
OutFile .\AzureCLI.msi; Start-Process msiexec.exe -Wait -
ArgumentList '/I AzureCLI.msi /quiet'
```

On macOS:

```
brew install azure-cli
```

On Linux (Debian/Ubuntu):

```
curl -sL https://aka.ms/InstallAzureCLIDeb | sudo bash
```

After installation:

```
az login
```

This opens a browser window to authenticate using your Azure account.

Azure PowerShell Installation:

If you prefer PowerShell, install the Azure module:

```
Install-Module -Name Az -Scope CurrentUser -Repository PSGallery -
Force
```

Check installed modules:

```
Get-Module -ListAvailable Az
```

Setting Up Visual Studio Code (VS Code)

VS Code is a lightweight, cross-platform editor widely used in Azure development.

Recommended Extensions:

- **Azure Account**: For signing in and managing subscriptions.
- **Azure App Service**: Deploy apps to App Services.

- **Azure Functions**: Create, debug, and deploy Functions locally.

- **Docker**: Build and manage containers.

- **Remote - WSL/SSH**: Develop in Linux environments directly from Windows.

- **Bicep** or **ARM Tools**: Write infrastructure as code.

- **Terraform**: Manage infrastructure using HCL.

- **Azure CLI Tools**: IntelliSense for CLI commands.

VS Code also includes integrated Git support, terminal, and debugging tools, making it an all-in-one IDE for cloud-native development.

Configuring SDKs and Runtime Environments

Depending on your app's stack, you'll need to install the appropriate SDKs and runtimes:

.NET (Windows/macOS/Linux)

```
https://dotnet.microsoft.com/en-us/download
```

Node.js (macOS/Linux/Windows)

```
https://nodejs.org/
```

Verify installation:

```
node -v
npm -v
```

Python

```
sudo apt install python3-pip
pip3 install virtualenv
```

Java (OpenJDK 11+)

```
sudo apt install openjdk-17-jdk
```

Ensure environment variables like JAVA_HOME are configured for your IDE or build tool.

Setting Up Docker and Kubernetes

For container-based development, install Docker Desktop and Kubernetes locally.

Docker Installation:

- Windows/macOS: Download from https://www.docker.com/products/docker-desktop

- Linux:

```
sudo apt install docker.io
sudo systemctl start docker
sudo usermod -aG docker $USER
```

Verify Docker:

```
docker --version
```

Enable Kubernetes from Docker Desktop to create local clusters.

Install **kubectl** (Kubernetes CLI):

```
az aks install-cli
```

Using Azure Dev CLI (azd)

Azure Developer CLI (`azd`) is a newer tool for scaffolding, provisioning, and deploying apps using templates.

Install:

```
curl -fsSL https://aka.ms/install-azd.sh | bash
```

Login:

```
azd auth login
```

Initialize a template:

```
azd init --template todo-nodejs-mongo
azd up
```

This will:

- Set up your infrastructure

- Deploy your app

- Configure environment variables

Version Control and GitHub Integration

Git is essential for source control and CI/CD automation. If you haven't already:

```
git config --global user.name "Your Name"
git config --global user.email "your@example.com"
```

Create a new repository:

```
git init
git remote add origin https://github.com/youruser/yourrepo.git
```

Push code:

```
git add .
git commit -m "initial commit"
git push -u origin main
```

GitHub Integration with Azure:

- Use **GitHub Actions** to deploy apps automatically.

- Configure secrets like AZURE_CREDENTIALS securely.

- Link your Azure subscription to GitHub through the Azure Portal or GitHub Marketplace.

Emulators and Local Services

Azure provides several local emulators for offline development and testing:

Azurite: Emulator for Blob, Queue, and Table Storage.

```
npm install -g azurite
azurite
```

•

Azure Functions Core Tools: Run and debug functions locally.

```
npm install -g azure-functions-core-tools@4 --unsafe-perm true
func start
```

•
• **Cosmos DB Emulator**: Windows-only tool for developing Cosmos DB apps locally.

Use these emulators to build and test without consuming cloud resources.

Environment Variables and Configuration

Use .env files or environment variables to manage sensitive configuration locally.

Example .env:

```
DB_HOST=localhost
DB_USER=admin
DB_PASS=password123
```

In Node.js:

```
require('dotenv').config();
console.log(process.env.DB_HOST);
```

Use Azure App Configuration or Key Vault to store these securely in production.

Setting Up CI/CD with Azure DevOps or GitHub Actions

Azure DevOps Setup:

1. Create a project at dev.azure.com.

2. Set up a repo and push code.

3. Define pipelines in `azure-pipelines.yml`.

Example pipeline:

```
trigger:
- main

pool:
  vmImage: ubuntu-latest

steps:
- task: NodeTool@0
  inputs:
    versionSpec: '18.x'
  displayName: 'Install Node.js'

- script: |
    npm install
    npm run build
  displayName: 'Install and Build'
```

GitHub Actions:

Already covered earlier, integrates easily with your repo and secrets.

Debugging and Live Testing

Use **Visual Studio Code Debugger** with breakpoints and watches. For Azure resources:

- Attach debugger to App Services.

- Use **Live Share** to collaborate remotely.

- View logs in **Application Insights** or **Log Stream**.

For Azure Functions:

```
func start --verbose
```

Monitor HTTP triggers, output logs, and return values instantly.

Summary

Setting up a professional-grade development environment for Azure isn't just about installing a few tools—it's about creating a reliable, automated, and productive workflow. With the right IDEs, SDKs, version control, emulators, and automation pipelines, you empower yourself and your team to develop, test, and deploy high-quality applications efficiently.

Whether you're coding from a Windows laptop, macOS workstation, or Linux terminal, Azure's flexible ecosystem supports your journey from idea to production with minimal friction and maximum speed.

Deploying via Azure App Services

Azure App Services provides a powerful, fully managed platform-as-a-service (PaaS) solution for hosting web applications, REST APIs, and mobile backends. It abstracts the underlying infrastructure, allowing developers to focus on writing and deploying code rather than managing servers or worrying about patching, scaling, or security maintenance.

In this section, we'll walk through everything you need to know to successfully deploy an application using Azure App Services—from understanding the service tiers to setting up deployment slots, configuring environment variables, deploying from source control, and troubleshooting live applications.

Why Use Azure App Services?

Azure App Services simplifies deployment with features such as:

- **Built-in CI/CD integration** with GitHub, Azure DevOps, Bitbucket.

- **Support for multiple languages** (.NET, Java, Node.js, Python, PHP, Ruby).

- **Custom domains and SSL certificates**.

- **Auto-scaling and load balancing**.

- **Staging environments with deployment slots**.

- **Integration with Virtual Networks** for secure backend connectivity.

- **Managed platform updates** and patching.

Creating an App Service Plan

Before deploying an app, you must create an App Service Plan, which determines the compute resources allocated to your app.

Azure CLI Example:

```
az appservice plan create \
  --name myAppPlan \
  --resource-group myResourceGroup \
  --sku B1 \
  --is-linux
```

This creates a Basic tier Linux-based hosting plan. For production apps, consider higher SKUs like P1v3 (Premium) or S1 (Standard) for features like scaling and custom domains.

Creating the Web App

Once you have a plan, create the web app that will host your application.

```
az webapp create \
  --resource-group myResourceGroup \
  --plan myAppPlan \
  --name myUniqueAppName \
  --runtime "NODE|18-lts"
```

Replace NODE|18-lts with your desired runtime. Other examples:

- .NET|6

- PYTHON|3.11

- JAVA|11-java11

After creation, your app is accessible at https://myUniqueAppName.azurewebsites.net.

Deploying Code

There are several ways to deploy your code to an App Service:

1. Via Zip Deployment

```
az webapp deployment source config-zip \
  --resource-group myResourceGroup \
  --name myUniqueAppName \
  --src path/to/deployment.zip
```

2. From Local Git Repository

```
az webapp deployment source config-local-git \
  --name myUniqueAppName \
  --resource-group myResourceGroup
```

This returns a Git endpoint. Push code:

```
git remote add azure https://<git-endpoint>
git push azure main
```

3. GitHub Integration

```
az webapp deployment source config \
  --name myUniqueAppName \
  --resource-group myResourceGroup \
  --repo-url https://github.com/myuser/myrepo \
  --branch main \
  --manual-integration
```

Setting Environment Variables

Environment variables (Application Settings) are critical for configuration without code changes.

CLI Example:

```
az webapp config appsettings set \
  --name myUniqueAppName \
  --resource-group myResourceGroup \
  --settings "ENV=production" "API_KEY=abcdef123456"
```

These can be accessed in your code via:

- Node.js: `process.env.ENV`

- Python: `os.environ['ENV']`

- .NET: `Environment.GetEnvironmentVariable("ENV")`

Using Deployment Slots

Deployment slots allow you to deploy and test your app in a production-like environment without affecting live traffic. You can later swap the staging slot into production.

Create a Slot:
```
az webapp deployment slot create \
  --name myUniqueAppName \
  --resource-group myResourceGroup \
  --slot staging
```

Deploy your app to the `staging` slot using any method above, then test it live at:

```
https://myUniqueAppName-staging.azurewebsites.net
```

Swap Slots:
```
az webapp deployment slot swap \
  --name myUniqueAppName \
  --resource-group myResourceGroup \
  --slot staging \
  --target-slot production
```

Managing Application Configuration

Configure Startup Command (Linux Apps):
```
az webapp config set \
  --resource-group myResourceGroup \
  --name myUniqueAppName \
  --startup-file "npm start"
```

Configure Custom Domain:
```
az webapp config hostname add \
```

```
  --webapp-name myUniqueAppName \
  --resource-group myResourceGroup \
  --hostname www.mycustomdomain.com
```

Add SSL Certificate:
```
az webapp config ssl upload \
  --name myUniqueAppName \
  --resource-group myResourceGroup \
  --certificate-file /path/to/cert.pfx \
  --certificate-password mypassword
```

Monitoring and Logging

App Services integrates with Azure Monitor and Application Insights for full observability.

Enable Logging:
```
az webapp log config \
  --name myUniqueAppName \
  --resource-group myResourceGroup \
  --application-logging filesystem \
  --level information
```

View Logs:
```
az webapp log tail \
  --name myUniqueAppName \
  --resource-group myResourceGroup
```

This live log stream helps debug runtime issues immediately after deployment.

Enable Application Insights:
```
az monitor app-insights component create \
  --app myInsightsApp \
  --location eastus \
  --resource-group myResourceGroup \
  --application-type web
```

Then link it:

```
az webapp config appsettings set \
```

```
--resource-group myResourceGroup \
--name myUniqueAppName \
--settings APPINSIGHTS_INSTRUMENTATIONKEY=<key>
```

Scaling the App

App Services supports manual and automatic scaling based on metrics like CPU usage or request count.

Manual Scaling:

```
az appservice plan update \
  --name myAppPlan \
  --resource-group myResourceGroup \
  --number-of-workers 3
```

Autoscaling (Portal or CLI via Rules):

Use Azure Monitor's autoscale settings to scale based on load conditions.

Secure Your App

- Use **Azure Key Vault** to store secrets securely.

- Enable **HTTPS only**:

```
az webapp update \
  --name myUniqueAppName \
  --resource-group myResourceGroup \
  --https-only true
```

- Set up **Authentication / Authorization** with Azure Active Directory or social providers via the portal.

Common Deployment Scenarios

Node.js Express App

1. Install dependencies

2. Define `startup command`: `npm start`

3. Deploy via ZIP or GitHub

4. Set environment variables

Python Flask App

1. Create `requirements.txt`

2. Add `startup command`: `gunicorn --bind=0.0.0.0 app:app`

3. Deploy via GitHub Actions

4. Monitor logs and performance

.NET Core Web API

1. Publish project: `dotnet publish -c Release`

2. Zip the `publish` folder

3. Deploy with `az webapp deployment source config-zip`

Troubleshooting Deployments

1. **App not starting**:

   - Check startup command.

   - View logs via `az webapp log tail`.

2. **Environment variables not loading**:

   - Ensure variables are set at App Service level, not in deployment slot.

3. **Deployment failed**:

   - Check GitHub Actions or zip logs.

- ○ Try a local deployment to isolate issue.

4. **App unreachable**:

   - ○ Check networking rules, custom domain DNS, and SSL bindings.

Summary

Deploying applications using Azure App Services is a streamlined, scalable, and powerful way to bring cloud-native apps to life. With support for multiple runtimes, deployment options, autoscaling, slot-based releases, integrated monitoring, and tight DevOps integration, App Services serves as a go-to choice for modern application hosting on Azure.

By mastering deployment through CLI, GitHub, or CI/CD pipelines—and integrating services like Application Insights, Key Vault, and Azure Monitor—you can deliver robust, secure, and reliable applications without managing underlying infrastructure.

Continuous Integration and Delivery with Azure DevOps

Continuous Integration (CI) and Continuous Delivery (CD) are critical practices in modern software development that enable faster, more reliable deployments by automating the process of building, testing, and releasing code. Azure DevOps provides an end-to-end suite of tools that allow development teams to implement CI/CD pipelines efficiently.

In this section, you'll learn how to use Azure DevOps to build and release your applications automatically, from committing code in a Git repository to deploying it to Azure services like App Services, Azure Functions, and Kubernetes clusters. We'll also cover YAML pipelines, environment promotion, test automation, secrets management, and best practices for managing CI/CD workflows in real-world scenarios.

Overview of Azure DevOps Services

Azure DevOps offers a suite of services that integrate seamlessly:

- **Azure Repos** – Source code hosting with Git or Team Foundation Version Control (TFVC)

- **Azure Pipelines** – CI/CD automation with support for YAML and classic editors

- **Azure Boards** – Work tracking, Kanban, and Scrum planning

- **Azure Test Plans** – Manual and exploratory testing

- **Azure Artifacts** – Package hosting (NuGet, npm, Maven)

For CI/CD workflows, the core focus is on **Azure Repos** and **Azure Pipelines**.

Setting Up a CI/CD Pipeline

Start by creating a project in Azure DevOps:

1. Navigate to https://dev.azure.com

2. Create a new organization and project

3. Initialize a Git repo under **Repos**

Push your local code:

```
git remote add origin
https://dev.azure.com/<org>/<project>/_git/<repo>
git push -u origin main
```

4.

Configuring a Build Pipeline (CI)

A build pipeline compiles your code, runs tests, and produces artifacts. The most efficient way to define this pipeline is via a YAML file.

Example: Node.js CI Pipeline (`azure-pipelines.yml`)

```
trigger:
  branches:
    include:
      - main

pool:
  vmImage: 'ubuntu-latest'

steps:
  - task: NodeTool@0
    inputs:
```

```
      versionSpec: '18.x'
    displayName: 'Install Node.js'

  - script: npm install
    displayName: 'Install dependencies'

  - script: npm run test
    displayName: 'Run tests'

  - task: ArchiveFiles@2
    inputs:
      rootFolderOrFile: '$(Build.SourcesDirectory)'
      includeRootFolder: false
      archiveType: 'zip'
      archiveFile: '$(Build.ArtifactStagingDirectory)/app.zip'
      replaceExistingArchive: true

  - task: PublishBuildArtifacts@1
    inputs:
      PathtoPublish: '$(Build.ArtifactStagingDirectory)'
      ArtifactName: 'drop'
```

This pipeline is triggered on every push to main, installs Node.js, runs tests, archives the application, and publishes the result as a build artifact.

Setting Up a Release Pipeline (CD)

Release pipelines automate deployment to Azure environments. While Azure DevOps supports GUI-based pipelines, YAML is the preferred method for consistency and source control.

Example: Deployment to Azure App Service

Add the following step to a new pipeline or combine it into the same YAML file:

```
- task: AzureWebApp@1
  inputs:
    azureSubscription: 'AzureServiceConnection'
    appType: 'webApp'
    appName: 'myAppServiceName'
    package: '$(Build.ArtifactStagingDirectory)/app.zip'
```

To create a service connection (used by `azureSubscription`), navigate to Project Settings > Service Connections > New connection > Azure Resource Manager, then authorize it.

Environments and Approvals

Azure DevOps allows you to define **environments** (e.g., dev, staging, production) and assign **approvals** for each stage. This promotes safe deployment practices and manual oversight where necessary.

Define Environments in YAML

```yaml
stages:
  - stage: Deploy_Dev
    jobs:
      - deployment: DeployDev
        environment: 'dev'
        strategy:
          runOnce:
            deploy:
              steps:
                - script: echo "Deploying to dev"

  - stage: Deploy_Prod
    dependsOn: Deploy_Dev
    jobs:
      - deployment: DeployProd
        environment: 'production'
        strategy:
          runOnce:
            deploy:
              steps:
                - script: echo "Deploying to production"
```

Set manual approvals in the Azure DevOps portal under Environment settings.

Running Tests Automatically

Automated testing is essential for ensuring quality and confidence before releases.

Example: Adding Unit Tests (Jest)

```
- script: npm test
  displayName: 'Run Unit Tests'
```

Example: Adding Code Coverage

```
- script: |
    npm run test -- --coverage
  displayName: 'Run tests with coverage'

- task: PublishCodeCoverageResults@1
  inputs:
    codeCoverageTool: 'Cobertura'
    summaryFileLocation: 'coverage/cobertura-coverage.xml'
```

Azure DevOps will visualize test results and coverage in the build summary.

Managing Secrets with Azure Key Vault

Avoid storing credentials in the pipeline directly. Use Azure Key Vault and link it to the pipeline securely.

Steps:

1. Create a Key Vault

2. Add secrets: `DB_PASSWORD`, `API_KEY`

3. Grant pipeline service principal access

4. Reference in YAML:

```
- task: AzureKeyVault@2
  inputs:
    azureSubscription: 'AzureServiceConnection'
    KeyVaultName: 'myKeyVault'
    SecretsFilter: '*'
    RunAsPreJob: true
```

Secrets are exposed as environment variables in the format `$(DB_PASSWORD)`.

Parallel Jobs and Matrix Builds

CI pipelines can run tests across multiple platforms or configurations simultaneously using matrix builds.

Example: Matrix Strategy

```
strategy:
  matrix:
    linux_node14:
      OS: ubuntu-latest
      NodeVersion: 14.x
    linux_node18:
      OS: ubuntu-latest
      NodeVersion: 18.x
    windows_node18:
      OS: windows-latest
      NodeVersion: 18.x

pool:
  vmImage: $(OS)

steps:
  - task: NodeTool@0
    inputs:
      versionSpec: '$(NodeVersion)'
```

Notifications and Integration

You can configure notifications for pipeline status via:

- Email

- Microsoft Teams

- Slack (via Webhooks)

- Azure DevOps Extensions

Set up alerts in Project Settings > Notifications.

Deploying to Kubernetes (AKS)

CI/CD for microservices or containerized apps is commonly done with Azure Kubernetes Service.

Steps:
Build Docker image:

```
- task: Docker@2
  inputs:
    command: buildAndPush
    containerRegistry: 'MyACR'
    repository: 'myrepo/web'
    dockerfile: '**/Dockerfile'
    tags: '$(Build.BuildId)'
```

1.

Deploy using `kubectl`:

```
- task: Kubernetes@1
  inputs:
    connectionType: 'Azure Resource Manager'
    azureSubscription: 'AzureServiceConnection'
    azureResourceGroup: 'myResourceGroup'
    kubernetesCluster: 'myAKSCluster'
    namespace: 'default'
    command: 'apply'
    arguments: '-f k8s/deployment.yaml'
```

2.

Best Practices for CI/CD

- **Use separate pipelines for build and release**: Easier to manage and troubleshoot.

- **Version artifacts and use build numbers**: Avoid overwriting packages.

- **Fail fast**: Use small, frequent commits with fast tests.

- **Secure everything**: Never hard-code secrets.

- **Use pull request validations**: Ensure every PR triggers a CI build.

Summary

Implementing CI/CD with Azure DevOps automates the entire application lifecycle—from code commit to production deployment. It reduces human error, increases development speed, and ensures software quality through consistent testing and deployment practices.

By combining source control, YAML pipelines, automated tests, secrets management, and deployment environments, you can build a reliable and repeatable delivery process for your Azure-based applications. With these tools and best practices in place, teams can move confidently from development to delivery, deploying updates with speed and stability.

Chapter 5: Security and Identity Management in Azure

Introduction to Azure Active Directory

Security and identity management are foundational pillars of a robust cloud strategy. As organizations increasingly move their workloads to the cloud, the ability to manage who can access what—under what conditions and from where—has become more critical than ever. Microsoft Azure provides a powerful identity and access management (IAM) solution called **Azure Active Directory (Azure AD)** to meet these needs.

Azure AD is a cloud-based identity service that offers a broad range of capabilities including authentication, authorization, single sign-on (SSO), multi-factor authentication (MFA), conditional access policies, and integration with thousands of SaaS applications. It can serve as a primary directory for cloud-only organizations or work in a hybrid setup alongside an on-premises Active Directory.

This section will explore Azure AD in-depth, covering its core features, how it integrates with your Azure environment, and how you can leverage it to build a secure, scalable identity solution for your apps and users.

What is Azure Active Directory?

Azure Active Directory is Microsoft's multi-tenant, cloud-based directory and identity management service. It serves as the backbone for identity management in Azure and integrates with both Microsoft services (like Microsoft 365) and third-party applications.

Some core concepts to understand:

- **Tenant**: Each Azure AD directory is tied to a single tenant, which represents an organization.

- **Users**: Individual identities in Azure AD. Users can be internal employees or external partners/contractors.

- **Groups**: Collections of users for simplified permission management.

- **Roles**: Define what actions a user or group can perform in Azure.

- **Applications**: Services or APIs that can authenticate users via Azure AD.

Azure AD is used not just for Azure resources, but also for user sign-ins across Microsoft services and many third-party platforms.

Azure AD Editions

Azure AD is available in several tiers:

- **Free**: Basic identity features, limited to directory services and SSO to some apps.

- **Premium P1**: Adds conditional access, dynamic groups, and hybrid identity support.

- **Premium P2**: Includes identity protection, access reviews, and privileged identity management.

The right edition for your needs depends on your organization's size, security requirements, and whether you're operating in a hybrid environment.

Authentication and SSO

Azure AD supports various authentication protocols including:

- **OAuth 2.0**

- **OpenID Connect**

- **SAML 2.0**

- **WS-Federation**

With these protocols, Azure AD can provide **single sign-on (SSO)** capabilities to thousands of cloud (SaaS) applications like Salesforce, Google Workspace, and Dropbox. SSO ensures that users authenticate once and gain access to all assigned applications, improving both user experience and security.

To enable SSO for an app:

1. Navigate to **Azure Active Directory > Enterprise Applications**.

2. Add a new application from the gallery or register a custom app.

3. Configure the authentication settings, including protocol (SAML/OIDC).

4. Assign users or groups to the application.

```
# Example: List all assigned enterprise applications via Azure CLI
az ad app list --query "[].{AppName:displayName, AppId:appId}" --output table
```

Multi-Factor Authentication (MFA)

Multi-Factor Authentication adds an extra layer of protection by requiring users to verify their identity using more than just a password. Azure AD MFA can be enforced using:

- Microsoft Authenticator app

- SMS or voice call

- Hardware tokens (via FIDO2 or OATH)

You can enable MFA for users directly or use **Conditional Access** to enforce it based on specific conditions (like user location, device compliance, or app sensitivity).

Steps to enable MFA:

1. Go to **Azure AD > Users > Multi-Factor Authentication**.

2. Select users and enable MFA.

3. Configure user settings and registration requirements.

For Conditional Access MFA:

1. Go to **Azure AD > Security > Conditional Access**.

2. Create a new policy targeting specific users or apps.

3. Set conditions (e.g., sign-in risk, device platform).

4. Under **Access controls**, select **Grant > Require multi-factor authentication**.

```
# Check user MFA status using PowerShell
Get-MsolUser -All | Select
DisplayName,UserPrincipalName,StrongAuthenticationMethods
```

Conditional Access

Conditional Access policies allow fine-grained control over how users access your resources. A policy consists of **conditions** (e.g., user location, device state, sign-in risk) and **controls** (e.g., require MFA, block access).

Common use cases:

- Require MFA when signing in from outside the corporate network.

- Block access from countries with high risk.

- Allow only compliant devices to access sensitive apps.

Creating a Conditional Access Policy:

1. Go to **Azure AD > Security > Conditional Access**.

2. Click **New policy**.

3. Define **Assignments** (users, groups, apps).

4. Define **Conditions** (location, device state, etc.).

5. Define **Access controls**.

Azure AD B2B and B2C

Azure AD supports two models for external identities:

- **B2B (Business to Business)**: Share your apps and services with guest users from other organizations. Useful for collaborations and joint ventures.

- **B2C (Business to Consumer)**: A separate identity system to allow consumers to sign up and use your applications with social logins (e.g., Google, Facebook) or local accounts.

B2B Example Workflow:

1. Invite a guest user via Azure portal or CLI.

2. Assign them to groups or roles.

3. Control their access via Conditional Access policies.

```
# Invite a B2B user via CLI
az ad user create --display-name "John Guest" --user-principal-name
john.guest@externaldomain.com --invite-redirect-url
https://yourapp.com
```

B2C Use Case:

When building consumer-facing apps, Azure AD B2C offers:

- Customizable login and signup pages

- User flows (sign-up/sign-in, password reset)

- Social and local account federation

- Secure token issuance for authentication

Integration with On-Premises Active Directory

Hybrid environments often need to synchronize on-premises Active Directory with Azure AD. This is achieved using **Azure AD Connect**.

Azure AD Connect supports:

- Password hash synchronization

- Pass-through authentication

- Federation with ADFS

- Writeback for passwords and group memberships

Steps to configure Azure AD Connect:

1. Install Azure AD Connect on a Windows Server machine.

2. Choose the sync method.

3. Connect to both Azure AD and on-prem AD.

4. Configure filtering and sync options.

5. Start the synchronization process.

```
# Force a sync from PowerShell
Start-ADSyncSyncCycle -PolicyType Delta
```

Privileged Identity Management (PIM)

Azure AD Premium P2 introduces **Privileged Identity Management**, which allows for just-in-time access to privileged roles. This reduces the attack surface by ensuring users only have elevated permissions when absolutely necessary.

With PIM, you can:

- Require approval for role activation.

- Set time limits for elevated access.

- Enforce MFA before activation.

- Monitor and audit privileged role use.

PIM Setup:

1. Go to **Azure AD > Privileged Identity Management**.

2. Onboard your directory.

3. Assign eligible roles.

4. Configure activation settings and notifications.

Best Practices for Azure AD

- Use groups and roles to manage access, not individual user assignments.

- Require MFA for all users, especially admins.

- Regularly audit sign-in logs and access reviews.

- Enable Conditional Access to adapt security to context.

- Use PIM for managing administrative roles.

- Minimize guest user access and review it frequently.

- Secure legacy authentication protocols or block them entirely.

Conclusion

Azure Active Directory is far more than a simple user database—it's a comprehensive identity platform that underpins secure access to Azure, Microsoft 365, and countless other services. By understanding its features—from MFA to Conditional Access to B2C scenarios—you can build a secure, scalable, and flexible identity solution for your cloud infrastructure.

Security starts with identity. And Azure AD provides the tools to manage it effectively.

Managing Users, Groups, and Roles

Managing identities within an Azure environment is a critical responsibility for any administrator. Azure Active Directory (Azure AD) provides robust tools to manage users, organize them into groups, and assign roles to control access to resources across Azure and beyond. This section covers the essential tasks and best practices related to managing users, groups, and roles in Azure AD to establish a secure and well-governed identity structure.

User Management in Azure AD

Users in Azure AD can be internal (organizational) or external (guest). Each user is represented by a unique **User Principal Name (UPN)** and has associated attributes such as name, email, job title, department, etc. Azure AD supports cloud-only users and synchronized users from on-premises Active Directory.

Creating Users

There are several ways to create users:

1. **Azure Portal**:

   - Navigate to **Azure Active Directory > Users > New user**.

   - Choose **Create user** for a cloud-only user.

   - Fill in required fields such as Name, UPN, and initial password.

   - Assign roles or groups during creation if needed.

Azure CLI:

```
az ad user create \
  --display-name "Jane Doe" \
  --user-principal-name janedoe@yourtenant.onmicrosoft.com \
  --password 'P@ssword123!' \
  --force-change-password-next-login true
```

2.

PowerShell (MSOnline module):

```
New-MsolUser -UserPrincipalName janedoe@yourdomain.com `
            -DisplayName "Jane Doe" `
            -FirstName "Jane" `
            -LastName "Doe" `
            -Password "P@ssword123" `
            -ForceChangePassword $true
```

3.

User Attributes and Directory Schema

Azure AD supports an extended set of attributes for user objects, including:

- `givenName`, `surname`, `displayName`

- `jobTitle`, `department`

- `mail`, `userType`, `usageLocation`

You can manage custom attributes through **Directory Schema Extensions**, which allow you to store additional metadata on user profiles for your organization's needs.

Managing Groups

Groups are used to organize users and manage permissions collectively. Azure AD supports two types of groups:

- **Security Groups**: Used to grant access to resources.

- **Microsoft 365 Groups**: Include collaborative features like shared mailboxes, calendars, and Teams integration.

Creating Groups

1. **Azure Portal**:

   - Go to **Azure Active Directory > Groups > New group**.

   - Choose **Security** or **Microsoft 365**.

   - Provide a name and optional description.

   - Assign membership (static or dynamic).

Azure CLI:

```
az ad group create \
  --display-name "Developers" \
  --mail-nickname "devgroup"
```

2.

PowerShell:

```
New-AzureADGroup -DisplayName "Developers" `
                -MailEnabled $false `
                -MailNickname "devgroup" `
                -SecurityEnabled $true
```

   3.

Dynamic Membership

Dynamic groups automatically manage membership based on rules. For example, a group for all users in the "Engineering" department:

```
# Example rule syntax for dynamic membership
(user.department -eq "Engineering")
```

Dynamic membership rules are defined during group creation or updated later in the Azure Portal.

Assigning Users to Groups

You can assign users to groups manually (static) or via automation.

Portal:

- Go to **Azure AD > Groups > [Group Name] > Members > Add members**.

CLI:

```
az ad group member add \
  --group "Developers" \
  --member-id <userObjectId>
```

PowerShell:

```
Add-AzureADGroupMember -ObjectId <groupObjectId> -RefObjectId <userObjectId>
```

Role-Based Access Control (RBAC)

Role-Based Access Control (RBAC) allows you to assign **roles** to users, groups, or service principals to control access to Azure resources. RBAC is scoped at four levels:

- **Management Group**

- **Subscription**

- **Resource Group**

- **Resource**

Built-in Roles

Azure provides over 70 built-in roles, including:

- **Owner**: Full access, including the ability to delegate.

- **Contributor**: Can manage everything except access.

- **Reader**: Can view resources, but cannot make changes.

- **User Access Administrator**: Can manage access but not resources.

Assigning Roles

To assign a role, you must have the appropriate permissions (typically **Owner** or **User Access Administrator** on the scope).

Portal:

- Navigate to the desired scope (e.g., subscription).

- Go to **Access Control (IAM) > Add role assignment**.

- Choose a role, assign access to a user or group, and select the identity.

CLI:

```
az role assignment create \
  --assignee <userOrGroupId> \
  --role "Contributor" \
  --scope
/subscriptions/<subscriptionId>/resourceGroups/<resourceGroupName>
```

PowerShell:

```
New-AzRoleAssignment -ObjectId <userOrGroupObjectId> `
                     -RoleDefinitionName "Reader" `
```

```
                        -Scope "/subscriptions/<subscriptionId>"
```

Custom Roles

If built-in roles don't meet your needs, you can define **custom roles** with a specific set of permissions.

Sample Custom Role JSON:

```
{
  "Name": "Billing Reader",
  "Description": "Can read billing data only.",
  "Actions": [
    "Microsoft.Billing/*/read"
  ],
  "NotActions": [],
  "AssignableScopes": ["/subscriptions/<subscriptionId>"]
}
```

Create Role via CLI:

```
az role definition create --role-definition @billingReaderRole.json
```

Group-Based Access Management

Instead of assigning roles directly to users, best practice is to:

1. Create a group (e.g., "AppX-Admins").

2. Assign the group a role at the appropriate scope.

3. Add/remove users from the group as needed.

This improves scalability and auditability.

Directory Roles (Azure AD Roles)

In contrast to RBAC roles for resource access, **Azure AD roles** govern permissions within the Azure AD tenant itself, such as managing users or groups.

Common roles include:

- **Global Administrator**: Full control over Azure AD.

- **User Administrator**: Can manage users and groups.

- **Groups Administrator**: Manages group settings and memberships.

- **Application Administrator**: Manages app registrations and permissions.

Assigning Azure AD Roles:

Portal:

- Go to **Azure AD > Roles and administrators**.

- Select a role > **Add assignments** > Choose user or group.

PowerShell:

```
Add-AzureADDirectoryRoleMember -ObjectId <roleObjectId> -RefObjectId
<userObjectId>
```

Lifecycle Management

Managing the lifecycle of users and groups includes:

- **Provisioning**: Automate user creation from HR systems.

- **Deprovisioning**: Automatically disable or delete users upon exit.

- **Group Expiration**: Set policies to auto-expire unused groups.

- **Access Reviews**: Regularly review group memberships and role assignments.

Azure AD integrates with identity governance features like **Access Reviews**, **Entitlement Management**, and **Terms of Use**.

Best Practices

- **Least Privilege**: Assign only the permissions users need.

- **Use Groups for Permissions**: Avoid direct role assignments to users.

- **Enable MFA for Admin Roles**: All administrative accounts should require MFA.

- **Review Roles Regularly**: Audit role assignments for accuracy.

- **Automate User Onboarding**: Use provisioning systems and scripts.

- **Implement Access Reviews**: Ensure memberships and access are still valid.

- **Name Groups and Roles Clearly**: Use consistent naming conventions to identify purpose and scope.

Conclusion

Effectively managing users, groups, and roles is essential for securing your Azure environment and ensuring operational efficiency. By leveraging Azure AD's built-in tools and best practices, you can enforce proper access control, streamline permissions management, and enhance the security posture of your organization. Whether you are setting up simple team collaboration groups or managing complex role hierarchies for a multi-region application, Azure AD provides the flexibility and control needed to do so reliably.

Azure Key Vault and Secrets Management

Modern applications often require secure access to sensitive information such as API keys, connection strings, passwords, certificates, and encryption keys. Hardcoding these secrets in application code or storing them in insecure locations exposes systems to a wide array of security vulnerabilities. To solve this challenge, Microsoft Azure provides **Azure Key Vault**, a secure, centralized cloud service for managing secrets, keys, and certificates.

Azure Key Vault helps safeguard cryptographic keys and secrets used by cloud applications and services. With Key Vault, you can maintain control over these sensitive assets while reducing the chances of accidental leaks, enforcing access policies, enabling audit logging, and integrating with identity and compliance services.

This section explores the architecture, capabilities, use cases, and best practices of Azure Key Vault and provides practical guidance for implementing secrets management in your Azure-based applications.

Overview of Azure Key Vault

Azure Key Vault is a multi-tenant service that allows secure storage and tight access control over:

- **Secrets**: Passwords, connection strings, API keys, etc.

- **Keys**: Cryptographic keys used for encryption/decryption or signing.

- **Certificates**: SSL/TLS certificates for securing communications.

- **Managed HSM (Hardware Security Module)**: For ultra-secure key storage.

Key Vault supports integration with Azure RBAC (Role-Based Access Control), Azure AD for authentication, and tools such as Azure CLI, PowerShell, SDKs, and REST APIs.

Creating a Key Vault

You can create a Key Vault using the Azure Portal, Azure CLI, or PowerShell.

Azure Portal:

1. Go to **Create a resource > Security + Identity > Key Vault**.

2. Provide a name, region, and resource group.

3. Choose access policy method: Azure RBAC or Access policies.

4. Enable features such as soft delete, purge protection, or managed HSM.

Azure CLI:

```
az keyvault create \
  --name MyKeyVault \
  --resource-group MyResourceGroup \
  --location westeurope \
  --sku standard
```

PowerShell:

```
New-AzKeyVault -Name "MyKeyVault" -ResourceGroupName
"MyResourceGroup" -Location "westeurope"
```

Storing and Retrieving Secrets

Secrets are values such as database credentials or API tokens that applications need at runtime. You can add, update, and retrieve secrets using CLI, PowerShell, or SDKs.

Add a Secret (CLI):

```
az keyvault secret set \
  --vault-name MyKeyVault \
  --name "DbConnectionString" \
```

```
  --value
"Server=tcp:myserver.database.windows.net;Database=mydb;User
Id=admin;Password=SecureP@ss123;"
```

Retrieve a Secret (CLI):

```
az keyvault secret show \
  --vault-name MyKeyVault \
  --name "DbConnectionString" \
  --query value
```

Access in Application (via Environment Variable): Many Azure services like App Service or Azure Functions support linking to secrets using @Microsoft.KeyVault(...) syntax in configuration settings.

```
{
  "ConnectionStrings:Database":
"@Microsoft.KeyVault(SecretUri=https://mykeyvault.vault.azure.net/se
crets/DbConnectionString/)"
}
```

This setup ensures secrets never live in source code or app configs.

Access Control

Azure Key Vault supports two models of access control:

1. Access Policies

Classic access model where you define:

- Who (user, group, app) can perform

- What actions (get, list, set, delete) on

- Which objects (keys, secrets, certs)

You can configure access policies in the portal or via PowerShell.

Example (PowerShell):

```
Set-AzKeyVaultAccessPolicy `
  -VaultName "MyKeyVault" `
```

```
-ObjectId "user-or-app-object-id" `
-PermissionsToSecrets get,list,set,delete
```

2. Azure RBAC (Recommended)

Modern approach using built-in roles like:

- **Key Vault Reader**

- **Key Vault Secrets User**

- **Key Vault Administrator**

You assign these roles at the vault, resource group, or subscription scope.

Example (CLI):

```
az role assignment create \
  --assignee <user-or-app-id> \
  --role "Key Vault Secrets User" \
  --scope /subscriptions/<sub-
id>/resourceGroups/<rg>/providers/Microsoft.KeyVault/vaults/MyKeyVau
lt
```

Using RBAC simplifies governance and integrates better with other Azure security features.

Keys and Cryptographic Operations

Key Vault lets you manage keys used for encryption, signing, and key wrapping. Keys can be software-based or stored in HSM-backed storage.

Supported key types:

- RSA (2048, 3072, 4096)

- EC (P-256, P-384, P-521)

You can perform operations like:

- Encrypt / Decrypt

- Sign / Verify

- Wrap / Unwrap

Create a Key:

```
az keyvault key create \
  --vault-name MyKeyVault \
  --name MyEncryptionKey \
  --protection software
```

Encrypt Data Using Key:

```
az keyvault key encrypt \
  --vault-name MyKeyVault \
  --name MyEncryptionKey \
  --algorithm RSA-OAEP \
  --value "SensitiveData"
```

These operations are often used in client apps, Azure Storage, or integration scenarios with custom encryption.

Managing Certificates

Azure Key Vault can manage certificates, including:

- Importing existing certs

- Creating certs with policies

- Auto-renewing with trusted Certificate Authorities

Create a Certificate:

```
az keyvault certificate create \
  --vault-name MyKeyVault \
  --name MySSLCert \
  --policy "$(az keyvault certificate get-default-policy)"
```

Certs can also be auto-synced with Azure App Services for SSL binding.

Soft Delete and Purge Protection

To prevent accidental or malicious deletion:

- **Soft Delete**: Deleted secrets, keys, and vaults can be recovered within the retention period (default 90 days).

- **Purge Protection**: Prevents permanent deletion unless explicitly enabled and confirmed.

These features are highly recommended for production workloads.

Enable Purge Protection (CLI):

```
az keyvault update \
  --name MyKeyVault \
  --enable-purge-protection true
```

Audit Logging

Audit logs for Key Vault are stored in **Azure Monitor** or **Log Analytics**, showing operations like:

- Secret/key creation and retrieval

- Access policy changes

- Failed access attempts

Enable diagnostic settings:

Portal:

- Go to **Key Vault > Diagnostic Settings**

- Choose destination (Log Analytics, Event Hub, Storage)

- Select logs (AuditEvent, KeyVaultAuditEvents)

CLI:

```
az monitor diagnostic-settings create \
  --resource-id <vault-resource-id> \
  --name "keyvault-logs" \
  --workspace <log-analytics-workspace-id> \
  --logs '[{"category": "AuditEvent", "enabled": true}]'
```

Integration with Azure Services

Many Azure services natively integrate with Key Vault:

- **Azure App Service / Functions**: Load secrets as app settings

- **Azure Kubernetes Service (AKS)**: Use CSI driver for secret injection

- **Azure DevOps / GitHub Actions**: Fetch secrets at runtime

- **Azure Automation**: Access secrets for runbook tasks

Example: Using Secret in Azure App Service:

1. Go to **Configuration > Application Settings**

2. Add new setting:

   - Name: `Database__ConnectionString`

   - Value:
     `@Microsoft.KeyVault(SecretUri=https://mykeyvault.vault.azure.net/secrets/DbConnectionString/)`

This automatically resolves and injects the secret securely into your application runtime.

Programmatic Access via SDKs

Azure SDKs support secure programmatic access to Key Vault.

C# Example:

```
var client = new SecretClient(new
Uri("https://mykeyvault.vault.azure.net/"), new
DefaultAzureCredential());
KeyVaultSecret secret = await
client.GetSecretAsync("DbConnectionString");
string connectionString = secret.Value;
```

Node.js Example:

```
const { SecretClient } = require("@azure/keyvault-secrets");
const { DefaultAzureCredential } = require("@azure/identity");
```

```
const client = new
SecretClient("https://mykeyvault.vault.azure.net/", new
DefaultAzureCredential());
const latestSecret = await client.getSecret("DbConnectionString");
console.log(latestSecret.value);
```

These libraries support token-based authentication using **Managed Identity**, eliminating the need for secrets in code.

Best Practices

- Use **Managed Identity** for services to access Key Vault.

- Enable **soft delete** and **purge protection**.

- Use **Azure RBAC** for consistent role management.

- Avoid hardcoding secrets in code or configuration files.

- Rotate secrets and keys regularly using automation.

- Monitor access with logs and enable alerts for abnormal access patterns.

- Use **private endpoint** to restrict network access to Key Vault.

- Separate development, test, and production secrets into different vaults.

Conclusion

Azure Key Vault is a cornerstone of secure cloud application design. By managing your secrets, keys, and certificates through Key Vault, you reduce risk, increase automation, and align with industry best practices for secure development and operations. Whether you're working on a microservice architecture, deploying AI workloads, or running classic web apps, integrating Key Vault ensures your sensitive data is protected, accessible only to the right people and services, and governed according to modern security standards.

Network Security Groups and Firewalls

Securing Azure network infrastructure is a vital part of defending against unauthorized access, data exfiltration, and lateral movement across workloads. Two core elements used in Microsoft Azure to secure traffic flow are **Network Security Groups (NSGs)** and **Azure Firewalls**. These tools allow granular control over inbound and outbound traffic for resources deployed in virtual networks (VNets), ensuring compliance, minimizing the attack surface, and preventing unauthorized communication within or outside the cloud environment.

This section explores the architecture, configuration, and best practices for using NSGs and Azure Firewalls effectively, along with advanced usage scenarios to support enterprise-grade network security.

What Are Network Security Groups?

A **Network Security Group (NSG)** is a stateful, Layer 3–Layer 4 virtual firewall used to control network traffic in and out of Azure resources. NSGs contain security rules that allow or deny inbound or outbound traffic based on five-tuple information:

- **Source IP**

- **Source Port**

- **Destination IP**

- **Destination Port**

- **Protocol (TCP/UDP)**

NSGs can be associated with:

- **Subnets**: Controls traffic entering or exiting an entire subnet.

- **Network Interfaces (NICs)**: Controls traffic to or from individual VMs.

NSG Security Rule Structure

Each security rule has the following components:

- **Name**: Unique identifier

- **Priority**: Integer (100–4096); lower numbers are evaluated first

- **Direction**: Inbound or outbound

- **Access**: Allow or deny

- **Protocol**: TCP, UDP, or Any

- **Source / Destination**: IP range, service tag, or application security group

- **Port Ranges**: Single or multiple ports

Example Inbound Rule:

Name	Priority	Direction	Access	Protocol	Source	Source Port	Destination	Dest Port	Action
Allow-SSH	100	Inbound	Allow	TCP	Internet	*	10.0.0.4	22	Allow

Default Rules:

NSGs come with default rules (lowest priority) that allow VNet-internal communication, allow Azure load balancer probes, and deny all other traffic.

These defaults can't be deleted but are overridden by custom rules with higher priority.

Creating an NSG

Azure Portal:

1. Go to **Create a resource > Networking > Network Security Group**

2. Name the NSG and assign it to a resource group.

3. After creation, define inbound/outbound rules.

4. Associate with a subnet or NIC.

Azure CLI:

```
az network nsg create \
  --resource-group MyResourceGroup \
  --name MyNSG
```

Adding Rules:

```
az network nsg rule create \
  --nsg-name MyNSG \
  --resource-group MyResourceGroup \
  --name AllowSSH \
  --priority 100 \
  --direction Inbound \
  --access Allow \
  --protocol Tcp \
  --source-address-prefix Internet \
```

```
  --source-port-range '*' \
  --destination-address-prefix '*' \
  --destination-port-range 22
```

Associating NSGs

To a Subnet:

```
az network vnet subnet update \
  --vnet-name MyVNet \
  --name MySubnet \
  --resource-group MyResourceGroup \
  --network-security-group MyNSG
```

To a NIC:

```
az network nic update \
  --name MyNIC \
  --resource-group MyResourceGroup \
  --network-security-group MyNSG
```

Application Security Groups (ASGs)

ASGs let you group VMs and reference them in NSG rules. This provides abstraction over IP addresses, enabling dynamic management of workloads.

Create an ASG:

```
az network asg create \
  --name WebServers \
  --resource-group MyResourceGroup \
  --location westeurope
```

Use in NSG Rule:

```
az network nsg rule create \
  --nsg-name MyNSG \
  --resource-group MyResourceGroup \
  --name AllowHTTPToWeb \
  --priority 200 \
  --direction Inbound \
  --access Allow \
```

```
--protocol Tcp \
--source-address-prefix '*' \
--destination-asg WebServers \
--destination-port-range 80
```

Azure Firewall

Azure Firewall is a managed, cloud-native, stateful firewall offering high availability and scalability. Unlike NSGs, which are local to VNets and NICs, Azure Firewall provides a **centralized control plane** and supports:

- Network and Application rules

- FQDN filtering

- Threat intelligence filtering

- DNAT/SNAT

- TLS inspection

- Logging to Azure Monitor

Azure Firewall sits at the network edge, acting as a security boundary for all ingress/egress traffic.

Deploying Azure Firewall

1. **Create a dedicated subnet** in your VNet named **AzureFirewallSubnet**.

2. **Deploy the Firewall** using the portal or CLI.

3. **Configure Route Tables** to send traffic through the firewall.

4. **Define Rules** for allowed/denied traffic.

Example CLI:

```
az network firewall create \
  --name MyFirewall \
  --resource-group MyResourceGroup \
  --location westeurope

az network firewall ip-config create \
```

```
  --firewall-name MyFirewall \
  --resource-group MyResourceGroup \
  --name FWConfig \
  --public-ip-address MyFirewallPublicIP \
  --vnet-name MyVNet
```

Define Application Rule:

```
az network firewall application-rule create \
  --firewall-name MyFirewall \
  --resource-group MyResourceGroup \
  --collection-name AppRules \
  --name AllowWeb \
  --rule-type ApplicationRule \
  --action Allow \
  --priority 100 \
  --protocols Http=80 Https=443 \
  --source-addresses 10.0.0.0/24 \
  --target-fqdns '*.microsoft.com'
```

Firewall vs. NSG

Feature	Network Security Group	Azure Firewall
Scope	NIC/Subnet	Centralized (VNet-wide)
Layer	Network (L3/L4)	Network & Application (L3–L7)
Stateful	Yes	Yes
FQDN Filtering	No	Yes
DNAT/SNAT	No	Yes
TLS Inspection	No	Yes
Cost	Free	Paid (based on usage)
Logging	Limited	Full (Azure Monitor)

Use both in tandem: NSGs for internal micro-segmentation and basic rules, Firewall for advanced inspection and edge control.

Using Route Tables (UDRs)

To force all traffic through Azure Firewall, define **User Defined Routes (UDRs)**.

Create a Route:

```
az network route-table create \
  --name MyRouteTable \
  --resource-group MyResourceGroup

az network route-table route create \
  --resource-group MyResourceGroup \
  --route-table-name MyRouteTable \
  --name SendToFirewall \
  --address-prefix 0.0.0.0/0 \
  --next-hop-type VirtualAppliance \
  --next-hop-ip-address 10.0.1.4
```

Attach the route table to the subnet hosting your workloads:

```
az network vnet subnet update \
  --vnet-name MyVNet \
  --name MySubnet \
  --resource-group MyResourceGroup \
  --route-table MyRouteTable
```

Threat Intelligence

Azure Firewall integrates with Microsoft Threat Intelligence feeds. You can configure it to:

- **Alert only** (log potential threats)

- **Deny and alert** (block known malicious traffic)

Enable Threat Intelligence:

```
az network firewall update \
  --name MyFirewall \
  --resource-group MyResourceGroup \
  --threat-intel-mode Alert
```

This proactive filtering helps reduce attack surface and detect anomalies.

Logging and Monitoring

Both NSGs and Azure Firewalls can emit logs to Azure Monitor, Event Hubs, or Storage Accounts.

Enable NSG Flow Logs:

```
az network watcher flow-log configure \
  --resource-group MyResourceGroup \
  --nsg MyNSG \
  --enabled true \
  --workspace <LogAnalyticsWorkspaceID>
```

Azure Firewall Diagnostic Settings:

- Navigate to the firewall instance.

- Go to **Diagnostic settings** > **Add diagnostic setting**.

- Choose logs: `AzureFirewallApplicationRule`, `NetworkRule`, `ThreatIntel`, etc.

Query logs using **Kusto Query Language (KQL)**:

```
AzureDiagnostics
| where ResourceType == "AZUREFIREWALLS"
| where Category == "AzureFirewallApplicationRule"
| project TimeGenerated, msg_s, SourceIP_s, DestinationIP_s,
Action_s
```

Best Practices

- **Apply NSGs to subnets and NICs** for layered defense.

- **Use ASGs** for dynamic and scalable rules.

- **Use Azure Firewall** for centralized traffic inspection, logging, and governance.

- **Use UDRs** to ensure traffic flows through inspection points.

- **Restrict traffic by default**, allow only required sources/destinations.

- **Log and review** flow and rule logs regularly.

- **Enable Threat Intelligence** in alert or block mode.

- **Separate workloads** in different subnets with specific rules.

- **Use private endpoints and service endpoints** to restrict traffic to Azure PaaS services.

Conclusion

Securing network traffic in Azure is a multifaceted task requiring layered defense, centralized inspection, and detailed logging. Network Security Groups provide a lightweight, flexible way to segment traffic at the subnet or NIC level, while Azure Firewall delivers enterprise-grade perimeter protection with application-level intelligence.

By combining these tools effectively and applying the principle of least privilege, organizations can confidently deploy secure cloud-native applications and services in Azure. Proper use of NSGs and Azure Firewalls not only strengthens your security posture but also ensures compliance with regulatory and internal governance standards.

Chapter 6: Monitoring, Logging, and Diagnostics

Azure Monitor and Log Analytics

Monitoring is an essential component of any production-grade application and infrastructure. In the dynamic and distributed world of cloud computing, the ability to observe, measure, and respond to the behavior of systems in real-time is fundamental for maintaining reliability, performance, and security. Microsoft Azure offers a robust suite of monitoring tools, with **Azure Monitor** and **Log Analytics** being at the core.

Azure Monitor is a unified platform for collecting, analyzing, and acting on telemetry from your Azure resources and applications. It helps you understand how your applications are performing and proactively identifies issues affecting them and the resources they depend on. Log Analytics, a feature of Azure Monitor, provides powerful querying and visualization capabilities over large volumes of telemetry data.

This section explores Azure Monitor and Log Analytics in detail, covering their architecture, configuration, data sources, querying language, visualization, alerting, and best practices.

Overview of Azure Monitor

Azure Monitor is a full-stack monitoring service designed to provide:

- **Infrastructure monitoring**: Track metrics and logs from Azure resources like VMs, storage, databases, and networking.

- **Application performance monitoring**: Gain insights into app behavior using Application Insights.

- **Network monitoring**: Assess network performance, flow, and availability.

- **Security monitoring**: Analyze security events and integrate with Microsoft Sentinel.

- **Custom telemetry**: Ingest custom logs and metrics from any source.

Key components of Azure Monitor include:

- **Metrics**: Numeric time-series data that provides near real-time performance statistics.

- **Logs**: Structured records of events, diagnostics, or usage data from Azure resources and applications.

- **Alerts**: Automated responses to data conditions.

- **Dashboards**: Visual representations of monitoring data.

- **Workbooks**: Interactive reports for combining data from multiple sources.

Data Sources for Azure Monitor

Azure Monitor collects data from a variety of sources:

- **Azure resources**: Platform logs, metrics, and diagnostics.

- **Virtual Machines**: OS-level logs and performance counters.

- **Applications**: Telemetry using Application Insights SDK.

- **Custom sources**: Custom APIs, containers, and hybrid on-premises setups.

To enable full telemetry, diagnostic settings must be configured on each resource.

Example – Enable diagnostics for a storage account:

```
az monitor diagnostic-settings create \
  --name "storage-logs" \
  --resource /subscriptions/<sub-
id>/resourceGroups/<rg>/providers/Microsoft.Storage/storageAccounts/
<account> \
  --workspace <log-analytics-workspace-id> \
  --logs '[{"category": "StorageRead", "enabled": true},
{"category": "StorageWrite", "enabled": true}]'
```

Log Analytics Workspaces

Log Analytics is a data analysis tool that queries collected logs using **Kusto Query Language (KQL)**. All logs are sent to a **Log Analytics workspace**, which acts as a central repository.

You can create one via the portal or CLI:

```
az monitor log-analytics workspace create \
  --resource-group MyResourceGroup \
  --workspace-name MyWorkspace \
  --location westeurope
```

Each workspace is bound to a region and pricing tier. It's advisable to centralize your logs for better correlation and cost optimization.

Writing KQL Queries

KQL is a rich, SQL-like query language designed for analyzing large datasets. A basic query filters data from a table, for example:

```
AzureActivity
| where ResourceGroup == "MyResourceGroup"
| where ActivityStatus == "Failed"
| project TimeGenerated, OperationName, Caller, ActivityStatus
```

More advanced operations include:

Aggregation:

```
Perf
| summarize avg(CounterValue) by bin(TimeGenerated, 5m), CounterName
```

*

Join:

```
Heartbeat
| join kind=inner (
    LogManagement
    | where Message contains "error"
) on Computer
```

*

Time Filtering:

```
AzureDiagnostics
| where TimeGenerated > ago(1h)
```

*

Use **Log Analytics** in the Azure Portal to experiment with these queries. The query interface provides IntelliSense, schema references, and visualization options.

Metrics in Azure Monitor

Metrics are lightweight and near real-time. Azure collects metrics such as CPU utilization, disk IO, and network throughput. These are typically used for real-time dashboards and threshold-based alerts.

Metrics can be accessed via:

- **Azure Portal**

- **Metrics REST API**

- **Azure CLI / PowerShell**

- **Metric Alerts**

Example CLI to view metric definitions:

```
az monitor metrics list-definitions \
  --resource /subscriptions/<sub-
id>/resourceGroups/<rg>/providers/Microsoft.Compute/virtualMachines/
MyVM
```

Retrieve a specific metric:

```
az monitor metrics list \
  --resource /subscriptions/<sub-
id>/resourceGroups/<rg>/providers/Microsoft.Compute/virtualMachines/
MyVM \
  --metric "Percentage CPU"
```

Metrics can be visualized on dashboards or used in autoscale rules.

Dashboards and Workbooks

Azure provides two ways to visualize monitoring data:

- **Dashboards**: Customizable canvas to pin metrics, logs, alerts, and more.

- **Workbooks**: Advanced reports that combine metrics, logs, parameters, and filters.

Creating a Workbook:

1. Go to **Azure Monitor > Workbooks > New**.

2. Choose a data source (e.g., Log Analytics).

3. Add tiles: Charts, Grids, Text blocks.

4. Save to a resource group for sharing.

Workbooks are ideal for building shareable reports for performance, usage, cost, and security data.

Alerts and Actions

Alerts are based on metric thresholds, log query results, or activity logs. Alerts include:

- **Metric Alerts**: Triggered by numerical data, e.g., CPU > 80%.

- **Log Alerts**: Based on KQL queries evaluated on a schedule.

- **Activity Log Alerts**: Triggered by Azure control plane operations.

Steps to create an alert:

1. Go to **Azure Monitor > Alerts > New alert rule**.

2. Choose a resource.

3. Define the condition (metric, log query, etc.).

4. Add an **action group** (email, SMS, webhook, Azure Function).

5. Review and create.

CLI Example:

```
az monitor metrics alert create \
  --name "HighCPUAlert" \
  --resource-group MyResourceGroup \
  --scopes /subscriptions/<sub-
id>/resourceGroups/<rg>/providers/Microsoft.Compute/virtualMachines/
MyVM \
  --condition "avg Percentage CPU > 80" \
  --window-size 5m \
  --evaluation-frequency 1m \
  --action-group MyActionGroup
```

Action Groups

Action groups define what happens when an alert fires. They can include:

- **Email/SMS/Push notifications**

- **Webhook**

- **Azure Function**

- **Logic App**

- **ITSM Connector**

Creating via CLI:

```
az monitor action-group create \
  --resource-group MyResourceGroup \
  --name MyActionGroup \
  --short-name AG1 \
  --email-receiver name=myadmin email=myadmin@example.com
```

Use **action groups** to integrate alerts with your DevOps or incident management pipelines.

Monitoring Non-Azure Resources

Azure Monitor also supports hybrid and multicloud environments:

- **On-premises VMs**: Via Log Analytics Agent.

- **Other clouds**: Using Azure Arc.

- **Containers**: Monitor Kubernetes clusters via Azure Monitor for containers.

Install Log Analytics Agent (Linux):

```
wget https://raw.githubusercontent.com/Microsoft/OMS-Agent-for-
Linux/master/installer/scripts/onboard_agent.sh
sh onboard_agent.sh -w <workspace-id> -s <workspace-key>
```

With Azure Arc, you can onboard physical or virtual machines outside Azure into Azure Monitor.

Integration with Other Services

Azure Monitor integrates with:

- **Application Insights**: For deep application performance telemetry.

- **Azure Security Center**: For security-related events and posture management.

- **Azure Policy**: To enforce diagnostic settings at scale.

- **Microsoft Sentinel**: For SIEM and advanced security analysis.

- **Power BI**: Connect Log Analytics queries as a dataset for dashboards.

This unified ecosystem allows consistent observability across infrastructure, application, and security layers.

Best Practices

- **Centralize logs** in a shared Log Analytics workspace per region.

- **Use Workbooks** for rich, interactive dashboards.

- **Filter logs at source** to control data ingestion costs.

- **Use KQL functions** to simplify complex queries.

- **Set up alerts** for both proactive and reactive monitoring.

- **Tag resources** for better searchability and analytics grouping.

- **Enable diagnostic settings** for all production-grade resources.

- **Periodically audit** alert rules and retention policies.

- **Integrate with CI/CD** pipelines to validate monitoring as part of deployment.

Conclusion

Azure Monitor and Log Analytics offer a comprehensive monitoring solution capable of handling diverse workloads and environments. By collecting telemetry from across your Azure infrastructure and applications, these tools provide the visibility needed to maintain performance, detect anomalies, resolve issues quickly, and ensure compliance. Mastery of Azure Monitor and KQL empowers operations teams and developers to gain real-time insights and make data-driven decisions across the entire cloud landscape.

Setting Up Alerts and Dashboards

In cloud environments, proactive monitoring and rapid incident response are essential for maintaining availability, performance, and security. Azure provides powerful mechanisms for building observability through **alerts** and **dashboards**, allowing teams to be informed about critical events in real time and visualize data in a meaningful way.

This section will walk through how to design and implement alerts for both metric and log data, organize them with **action groups**, and leverage dashboards for a unified view of infrastructure and application telemetry. By the end of this section, you will understand how to create a complete alerting and visualization strategy in Azure that scales with your workload.

Types of Alerts in Azure

Azure supports multiple alert types, each tailored to a specific source of data:

- **Metric Alerts**: Triggered when numeric performance indicators cross thresholds.

- **Log Alerts**: Triggered when a log query condition is met.

- **Activity Log Alerts**: Triggered by control-plane events (e.g., VM creation, deletion).

- **Prometheus Alerts**: For Azure Monitor-managed Kubernetes clusters.

- **Smart Detection Alerts**: AI-based detection for anomalies in Application Insights.

Metric Alerts

Metric alerts monitor resource-level performance counters such as CPU usage, disk I/O, memory availability, and network throughput. They are ideal for immediate infrastructure monitoring.

Creating a Metric Alert (Azure CLI)

```
az monitor metrics alert create \
  --name "HighCPU" \
  --resource-group MyResourceGroup \
  --scopes /subscriptions/<sub-
id>/resourceGroups/MyResourceGroup/providers/Microsoft.Compute/virtu
alMachines/MyVM \
  --condition "avg Percentage CPU > 80" \
  --window-size 5m \
  --evaluation-frequency 1m \
  --action-group MyActionGroup
```

Portal Steps

1. Go to **Azure Monitor > Alerts > Create > Alert rule**.

2. Select the target resource (VM, App Service, etc.).

3. Define the condition based on available metrics.

4. Link an action group.

5. Set the severity and alert details.

Log Alerts

Log alerts use **Kusto Query Language (KQL)** to evaluate log data collected in **Log Analytics Workspaces**. These are useful for high-level anomaly detection, application behavior, and custom telemetry.

Example Log Alert Query

```
Heartbeat
| where TimeGenerated > ago(5m)
| summarize LastSeen = max(TimeGenerated) by Computer
| where LastSeen < ago(5m)
```

This detects when a VM hasn't sent a heartbeat in the last 5 minutes — a potential downtime indicator.

Creating a Log Alert via CLI

```
az monitor scheduled-query create \
  --name "VM-Down-Alert" \
  --resource-group MyResourceGroup \
  --workspace MyWorkspace \
  --description "Alert when VM stops sending heartbeats" \
  --severity 2 \
  --enabled true \
  --scopes /subscriptions/<sub-
id>/resourceGroups/<rg>/providers/Microsoft.OperationalInsights/work
spaces/MyWorkspace \
```

```
--condition-query "Heartbeat | where TimeGenerated > ago(5m) |
summarize LastSeen=max(TimeGenerated) by Computer | where LastSeen <
ago(5m)" \
  --condition-time-aggregation Count \
  --condition-failed-count 1 \
  --frequency 5m \
  --time-window 5m \
  --action MyActionGroup
```

Activity Log Alerts

Activity log alerts monitor **control-plane operations** such as resource creation, deletion, and modification. These are particularly useful for auditing and security monitoring.

Example Use Case:

- Alert when a network security group (NSG) is deleted.

- Alert when someone assigns the Owner role to a user.

Steps (Portal):

1. Go to **Monitor > Alerts > Create > Alert rule**.

2. Select the subscription as the resource.

3. Choose an event category (e.g., Administrative).

4. Select operation name (e.g., `Delete Network Security Group`).

5. Add action group and configure details.

Action Groups

Action groups define what happens when an alert is triggered. They can notify personnel or trigger automation.

Supported Actions:

- **Email**

- **SMS**

- **Push Notifications**

- **Voice**

- **Webhooks**

- **Azure Functions**

- **Logic Apps**

- **ITSM Connectors**

- **Azure Automation Runbooks**

Creating an Action Group (CLI)

```
az monitor action-group create \
  --resource-group MyResourceGroup \
  --name DevOpsTeamAlert \
  --short-name DevOps \
  --email-receiver name=DevOpsAlerts email=devops@example.com \
  --action webhook name=DevOpsWebhook
uri=https://hooks.myapp.com/alert
```

Suppression and Alert Rules

To avoid alert fatigue, Azure supports **alert suppression** and **alert rule states**:

- **Suppression**: Delay or pause alerts after triggering to avoid duplicates.

- **State Management**: Alerts can be automatically resolved or remain active until user action.

Use suppression when monitoring highly volatile metrics like CPU bursts that self-correct quickly.

Alert Severity Levels

Azure alerts support five severity levels:

Level	Description
0	Critical
1	Error
2	Warning
3	Informational
4	Verbose / Debug

Assign these based on business impact to help prioritize response.

Dashboards in Azure

Dashboards allow visual representation of metrics, logs, and other telemetry across your Azure environment.

Azure Dashboard Features

- **Tiles**: Visual blocks like charts, grids, KPIs, and markdown.

- **Sharing**: Dashboards can be shared with roles or made public within the organization.

- **Templates**: Import/export JSON definitions for dashboard reuse.

- **Pinning**: Pin charts directly from Log Analytics or Metrics.

Creating a Dashboard (Portal)

1. Go to **Dashboard > New Dashboard**.

2. Add tiles:

   - Metrics Chart

   - Log Analytics Query

   - Text/Markdown

3. Save and assign RBAC permissions.

Using Azure CLI to Create Dashboard

```
az portal dashboard create \
  --name DevOpsDashboard \
  --resource-group MyResourceGroup \
  --input-path ./dashboard.json
```

Example of a simple dashboard JSON snippet:

```
{
  "lenses": {
    "0": {
      "order": 0,
      "parts": {
        "0": {
          "position": {
            "x": 0,
            "y": 0,
            "rowSpan": 2,
            "colSpan": 3
          },
          "metadata": {
            "inputs": [],
            "type": "Extension/HubsExtension/PartType/MarkdownPart"
          },
          "settings": {
            "content": "### Production Dashboard\nOverview of all
critical systems"
          }
        }
      }
    }
  },
  "metadata": {
    "model": {
      "timeRange": {
        "value": {
          "relative": "24h"
        }
      }
```

```
      }
    }
  }
```

Workbooks vs Dashboards

Feature	Dashboards	Workbooks
Flexibility	Moderate (visual only)	High (interactive + queries)
Data Sources	Metrics, Logs, Alerts	Logs, Metrics, APIs
Target Users	Operations Teams	Engineers, Analysts
Parameters	Limited	Rich support for filters

Workbooks are preferred when building dynamic, filterable reports using multiple telemetry streams.

Best Practices for Alerts and Dashboards

- **Avoid alert storms**: Use suppression and composite alerts.
- **Consolidate alerts**: Use log queries for high-level condition checks.
- **Integrate into workflows**: Send alerts to ITSM or ticketing tools.
- **Tag resources**: Use Azure tags to scope alerts by environment or team.
- **Use managed identities**: For secure automation via alerts.
- **Separate environments**: Create different alert rules for dev, test, and production.
- **Tune thresholds**: Adjust over time based on real usage patterns.
- **Visual clarity**: Keep dashboards readable, avoid overcrowding.
- **Auto-deploy dashboards**: Include them in infrastructure-as-code (IaC) templates.

Conclusion

Alerts and dashboards are essential tools for any Azure monitoring strategy. They empower teams to detect anomalies, respond to incidents, and maintain visibility across distributed applications and infrastructure. By leveraging metric and log-based alerts alongside customizable dashboards, organizations can create intelligent observability frameworks that scale with their operations and provide actionable insight into system health. A well-configured alerting and visualization setup is not just a luxury — it is a foundational requirement for operating reliably in the cloud.

Diagnosing Issues with Application Insights

Diagnosing issues in modern cloud-native applications requires visibility beyond just infrastructure metrics. It demands a deep understanding of how code behaves under varying conditions, how dependencies perform, and how user experience is impacted. **Azure Application Insights**, a feature of Azure Monitor, delivers comprehensive application performance monitoring (APM) for web applications, microservices, APIs, and background workers.

Application Insights automatically detects application failures, performance bottlenecks, response time outliers, and dependency issues. It provides developers and operations teams with powerful tools to track requests, trace failures, monitor usage patterns, and improve application reliability and user experience.

This section explores how to integrate, configure, and effectively use Application Insights to detect, diagnose, and resolve application issues in real-time.

Core Concepts of Application Insights

Application Insights captures telemetry data such as:

- **Request telemetry**: HTTP requests and responses

- **Dependency telemetry**: External calls to databases, APIs, or services

- **Exception telemetry**: Unhandled exceptions or crashes

- **Trace telemetry**: Developer-added logs and custom events

- **Performance counters**: CPU, memory, response times, etc.

- **Availability tests**: Simulated requests to test uptime

Each of these data types helps paint a picture of what your app is doing and where it might be failing or slowing down.

Application Insights supports .NET, Java, JavaScript, Python, Node.js, and more, making it applicable across tech stacks.

Enabling Application Insights

There are multiple ways to enable Application Insights for your application, depending on where it's hosted.

Azure App Services

If your app is hosted in App Service:

1. Go to **App Service > Application Insights**.

2. Click **Turn on Application Insights**.

3. Select or create a new Application Insights resource.

4. Enable auto-instrumentation (no code changes required).

.NET Core or .NET Framework Applications

Install the SDK via NuGet:

```
Install-Package Microsoft.ApplicationInsights.AspNetCore
```

Configure in `Startup.cs`:

```
public void ConfigureServices(IServiceCollection services)
{
    services.AddApplicationInsightsTelemetry();
}
```

Add your instrumentation key in `appsettings.json`:

```
{
  "ApplicationInsights": {
    "InstrumentationKey": "your-instrumentation-key"
  }
}
```

JavaScript (Browser-Based Apps)

```
<script type="text/javascript">
  var appInsights=window.appInsights||function(config){
    function r(config){t[config]=function(){var
i=arguments;t.queue.push(function(){t[config].apply(t,i)})}}
    var
t={config:config},u=document,e=window,o="script",s=u.createElement(o
),i,f;

for(t.queue=[],f=["trackPageView","trackEvent","trackException","tra
ckMetric","trackDependencyData","setAuthenticatedUserContext","clear
AuthenticatedUserContext"],i=0;i<f.length;i++)r(f[i]);

s.src=config.url||"https://az416426.vo.msecnd.net/scripts/a/ai.0.js"
;
    u.getElementsByTagName("head")[0].appendChild(s);
    e.appInsights=t;return t
  }({
    instrumentationKey:"your-instrumentation-key"
  });

  window.appInsights=appInsights;
  appInsights.trackPageView();
</script>
```

Real-Time Monitoring Dashboard

Once data starts flowing in, the **Application Insights Overview** dashboard will populate with key telemetry:

- Server response time

- Server requests and failure rates

- Availability tests and success rates

- Dependency calls

- Exceptions

You can access this from:

Azure Portal > Application Insights > Overview

This dashboard gives at-a-glance insights into whether the app is operating normally.

Investigating Failures

When users experience errors, failures are logged in Application Insights, allowing you to pinpoint root causes.

Failure Pane:

- Shows breakdown of failed requests by response code and operation.

- Lists top exceptions with stack traces and frequency.

- Correlates failures with performance or dependency bottlenecks.

You can drill into a failure instance to see:

- Request and response headers

- Stack trace

- Correlated dependency call logs

- Custom telemetry attached to the request

KQL Query Example – Failed Requests:

```
requests
| where success == false
| project timestamp, name, url, resultCode, performanceBucket,
operation_Name, cloud_RoleName
```

Diagnosing Performance Issues

The **Performance Pane** shows the slowest operations, average response time, and percentile breakdowns.

- Identify slow dependencies

- Compare regions or endpoints

- Detect latency from external APIs

Example – Slowest Operations:

```
requests
| summarize avg(duration) by name
| top 10 by avg_duration desc
```

This helps detect whether the slowness is due to application code, downstream services, or networking.

Distributed Tracing with Application Map

The **Application Map** visualizes the entire topology of your application:

- Each node represents a component or service.

- Arrows show dependencies and direction of traffic.

- Red or yellow indicators highlight performance or availability problems.

Hovering over a node shows metrics like:

- Average response time

- Request count

- Failure rate

You can click into a node to view traces and logs.

This is particularly helpful in microservices architectures, where diagnosing issues between services becomes challenging.

Availability Tests

Availability tests simulate user traffic to monitor uptime from global locations. There are three types:

1. **URL ping tests**: Check if a site responds.

2. **Multi-step tests**: Execute custom scripts using Visual Studio.

3. **Custom TrackAvailability API**: Trigger availability from your own code.

Creating a URL Ping Test (CLI):

```
az monitor app-insights web-test create \
  --resource-group MyResourceGroup \
  --name "HomePageTest" \
  --location westeurope \
  --kind ping \
  --enabled true \
  --frequency 300 \
  --timeout 30 \
  --web-test-kind standard \
  --request-url "https://myapp.com"
```

These help ensure that your critical endpoints are reachable and performant globally.

Live Metrics Stream

Live Metrics provides a real-time view into:

- Incoming requests

- Dependencies

- Exception rates

- Server CPU and memory

This is especially useful during a deployment or incident when immediate feedback is needed.

Go to **Application Insights > Live Metrics Stream** to view:

- A rolling feed of requests and telemetry

- Drill-down into individual instances

- Visual correlation between metrics and errors

You can also filter by specific roles, instances, or operations.

Custom Events and Metrics

You can track business logic, feature usage, and application state through custom events and metrics.

.NET Example – Track Custom Event:

```
var telemetryClient = new TelemetryClient();
telemetryClient.TrackEvent("UserSignup",
    new Dictionary<string, string> { { "Plan", "Pro" } },
    new Dictionary<string, double> { { "SignupDuration", 12.3 } });
```

KQL Query:

```
customEvents
| where name == "UserSignup"
| summarize count() by tostring(customDimensions.Plan)
```

This lets you answer questions like:

- Which features are most used?
- How long do users take to complete signup?
- Are premium users experiencing more errors?

Smart Detection and Anomaly Detection

Application Insights includes built-in **Smart Detection** features:

- **Failure Anomalies**: Sudden spikes in failed requests.
- **Performance Anomalies**: Sudden changes in response time.
- **Degradation Patterns**: Persistent performance drops over time.

These detections trigger alerts even without manually defined rules.

Enable or configure them in:

Application Insights > Smart Detection Settings

Integration with DevOps and Incident Response

Application Insights integrates with:

- **Azure DevOps Pipelines**: View telemetry during and after deployment.

- **GitHub Actions**: Alert engineers directly in pull requests.

- **ServiceNow / PagerDuty**: Automate incident creation.

- **Slack / Teams**: Send alerts to collaboration platforms.

You can connect alert rules from Application Insights to an **action group** for downstream automation.

Exporting Data

You can export Application Insights data to:

- **Log Analytics**: For long-term retention and advanced queries.

- **Event Hubs**: For stream processing or ingestion into third-party tools.

- **Storage Accounts**: For raw telemetry archive.

Export to Log Analytics:

1. Go to **Application Insights > Diagnostic Settings**.

2. Add a new setting.

3. Choose your Log Analytics Workspace.

4. Select data types to forward (requests, dependencies, exceptions, etc.).

This allows for centralized logging and dashboarding across multiple applications.

Best Practices

- **Enable Application Insights during development** to catch early-stage issues.

- **Use distributed tracing** across services with the same operation ID.

- **Set up availability tests** for critical endpoints.

- **Use Smart Detection** as a fallback for missed alert conditions.

- **Filter and sample data** in production to control telemetry volume and cost.

- **Use Live Metrics during deployments** to validate performance and stability.

- **Correlate telemetry with user context** to understand impact on real users.

- **Build Workbooks** to visualize specific application KPIs and health.

Conclusion

Application Insights provides a rich set of tools for monitoring the performance, availability, and usage of your applications. It empowers developers and operations teams with real-time telemetry, powerful diagnostics, and visual tools to quickly identify and resolve issues. From simple web apps to complex microservices, integrating Application Insights into your architecture is a vital step toward achieving full-stack observability, improving user experience, and reducing mean time to resolution (MTTR).

Leveraging Azure Advisor

Optimizing cloud infrastructure for performance, reliability, security, and cost-effectiveness is an ongoing challenge. Microsoft Azure provides a built-in recommendation engine called **Azure Advisor** to help with this. Azure Advisor analyzes your deployed resources and configurations and offers actionable recommendations based on best practices.

This intelligent tool evaluates your subscriptions and provides personalized suggestions to improve high availability, security, performance, operational excellence, and cost optimization. Whether you're operating a few services or managing enterprise-scale environments, Azure Advisor helps guide your decisions and streamline your operational strategy.

This section explores how to use Azure Advisor effectively, interpret its recommendations, and integrate its insights into your DevOps, FinOps, and SecOps workflows.

What is Azure Advisor?

Azure Advisor is a free service that scans your Azure environment and provides **recommendations** in five major categories:

1. **Reliability** – Ensure and improve the continuity of your business-critical applications.

2. **Security** – Detect potential vulnerabilities and strengthen your security posture.

3. **Performance** – Enhance the speed and responsiveness of your applications.

4. **Cost Optimization** – Eliminate unnecessary spending and improve cost-efficiency.

5. **Operational Excellence** – Improve governance, management, and monitoring.

Advisor evaluates both platform services (e.g., Azure SQL, VMs, App Services) and infrastructure (e.g., networking, storage) to generate recommendations tailored to your specific resource usage.

Accessing Azure Advisor

You can access Azure Advisor in several ways:

Azure Portal

1. Go to the **Azure Portal**.

2. Search for **Advisor** in the global search bar.

3. Open **Azure Advisor** to view an overview dashboard of all recommendations.

4. Filter by category, resource group, or subscription.

Azure CLI
```
az advisor recommendation list --output table
```

PowerShell
```
Get-AzAdvisorRecommendation
```

This allows you to automate the collection of Advisor insights or integrate them into a continuous monitoring script.

Understanding Advisor Categories

1. Reliability

This category focuses on preventing service disruptions and ensuring continuity.

Common Recommendations:

- Enable **Azure Backup** for virtual machines.

- Configure **Availability Sets** or **Availability Zones**.

- Implement **Geo-redundant storage (GRS)**.

- Increase replication or fault tolerance for data stores.

Example:

> Your VM is not in an availability set. Consider placing it in an availability set to improve reliability during planned or unplanned maintenance.

You can act on this by redeploying your VM into a properly configured availability set or scaling set.

2. Security

Azure Advisor pulls in security recommendations from **Microsoft Defender for Cloud**.

Common Recommendations:

- Enable **MFA** for all administrator accounts.

- Apply **Just-in-Time VM Access**.

- Use **Key Vault** for secret management.

- Secure public-facing endpoints.

- Implement **Network Security Groups (NSGs)**.

KQL to find exposed ports from logs:

```
AzureDiagnostics
| where Category == "NetworkSecurityGroupRuleCounter"
| where RemotePort_s in ("22", "3389")
```

This query complements Advisor's security recommendations by showing real-time port usage.

3. Performance

Performance recommendations target bottlenecks and inefficiencies.

Common Recommendations:

- Resize underperforming or overutilized VMs.

- Upgrade storage tiers for I/O-heavy workloads.

- Scale out App Services.

- Enable **read replicas** for databases.

Example:

> Your VM is consistently using more than 90% of its CPU. Consider scaling to a larger size.

You can respond by selecting a VM SKU that offers better performance for your workload, using the **Resize** feature in the VM blade.

4. Cost Optimization

This is one of the most used categories. Advisor helps reduce costs by identifying inefficient or unnecessary spending.

Common Recommendations:

- Shut down underutilized VMs.

- Purchase **Reserved Instances** for long-running workloads.

- Remove unattached disks and idle public IPs.

- Use **Auto-shutdown** policies for dev/test environments.

- Move infrequently accessed storage to **cool** or **archive** tiers.

CLI Example – View cost savings:

```
az advisor recommendation list \
  --category Cost \
  --query "[].{Resource:resourceMetadata.resourceName,
Recommendation:shortDescription.problem,
Savings:extendedProperties.annualSavingsAmount}" \
  --output table
```

You can act on cost recommendations via Azure Cost Management + Billing or automation scripts.

5. Operational Excellence

These recommendations focus on improving monitoring, deployment, and lifecycle practices.

Common Recommendations:

- Enable **diagnostic logs** for all resources.

- Set up **alerts** on critical resources.

- Use **resource tags** for governance.

- Define **naming conventions**.

- Implement **deployment pipelines** for consistent releases.

Advisor encourages alignment with the **Azure Well-Architected Framework** pillars.

Implementing Advisor Recommendations

Each recommendation in Azure Advisor includes:

- **Description** of the issue.

- **Recommended action**.

- **Estimated impact** (e.g., cost savings, security improvement).

- **Affected resources**.

- **Potential savings** or benefits.

Clicking a recommendation takes you to the relevant Azure resource blade to take action.

Exporting Recommendations

You can export all recommendations to a CSV for further analysis.

```
az advisor recommendation list --output csv > advisor_report.csv
```

Or using PowerShell:

```
Get-AzAdvisorRecommendation | Export-Csv -Path advisor.csv -
NoTypeInformation
```

This is helpful for sharing with stakeholders or tracking changes over time.

Integrating Advisor into DevOps

Advisor recommendations can be checked during CI/CD workflows.

1. Use **Azure CLI** tasks in Azure Pipelines to pull recommendations.

2. Fail builds if critical recommendations (e.g., security misconfigurations) are present.

3. Create work items in Azure Boards or GitHub Issues automatically.

4. Send recommendations to Slack or Teams using webhooks.

Example GitHub Action Workflow:

```
jobs:
  check-advisor:
    runs-on: ubuntu-latest
    steps:
    - name: Login to Azure
      uses: azure/login@v1
      with:
        creds: ${{ secrets.AZURE_CREDENTIALS }}

    - name: Get Advisor Recommendations
      run: |
        az advisor recommendation list --output table
```

Programmatic Filtering

Use filters to narrow down high-impact or critical recommendations.

Filter by category and severity:

```
az advisor recommendation list \
```

```
--category Security \
--query "[?impact=='High']"
```

Filter for cost savings above a threshold:

```
az advisor recommendation list \
  --category Cost \
  --query "[?to_number(extendedProperties.annualSavingsAmount) >
`1000`]"
```

This helps prioritize recommendations for quarterly planning or sprint backlogs.

Tagging and Governance

Advisor also suggests enforcing **tagging standards** and **resource organization**:

- Use policies to require environment, owner, costCenter tags.

- Apply tagging at deployment using ARM templates or Bicep.

Example Bicep Tag Block:

```
resource myVM 'Microsoft.Compute/virtualMachines@2022-08-01' = {
  name: 'myVM'
  location: resourceGroup().location
  tags: {
    environment: 'production'
    owner: 'ops-team'
    costCenter: 'IT123'
  }
}
```

Best Practices

- **Review Advisor weekly**: Integrate into team rituals like backlog grooming.

- **Act on high-impact items first**: Use filtering to isolate top priorities.

- **Automate cleanups**: Use Logic Apps or scripts for recurring cost savings.

- **Create reports**: Share Advisor insights with management.

- **Combine with Defender for Cloud**: For unified security and compliance posture.

- **Monitor changes**: Use Azure Policy to prevent new issues.

Conclusion

Azure Advisor is more than a passive suggestion tool—it's a powerful ally in optimizing your cloud environment. By surfacing actionable insights across cost, security, performance, reliability, and operations, Advisor helps you ensure your Azure workloads remain healthy, secure, and efficient. Integrating its recommendations into your development and operations workflows allows you to build a more proactive, intelligent, and governed cloud ecosystem that continuously improves over time.

Chapter 7: Scaling and Performance Optimization

Autoscaling Strategies

In cloud computing, **autoscaling** refers to the process of dynamically adjusting computing resources based on current demands. Azure provides robust autoscaling capabilities that help maintain application performance while optimizing costs. In this section, we will dive deep into the different autoscaling strategies available in Azure, explore their configuration, best practices, and real-world scenarios.

Why Autoscaling Matters

Applications hosted in the cloud often experience variable loads. For example, an e-commerce site might receive traffic spikes during sales events. Without autoscaling, you'd need to provision resources for the worst-case scenario, which can be expensive and inefficient. Conversely, underprovisioning leads to poor user experiences during traffic peaks. Autoscaling ensures you always have the right amount of resources at the right time.

Azure Autoscale Options

Azure provides multiple ways to autoscale resources:

1. **Virtual Machine Scale Sets (VMSS)**

2. **App Service Autoscaling**

3. **Azure Kubernetes Service (AKS) Autoscaling**

4. **Functions and Logic Apps (Serverless Autoscaling)**

We will cover each of these with configuration steps and best practices.

Virtual Machine Scale Sets (VMSS)

Virtual Machine Scale Sets allow you to deploy and manage a set of identical VMs. Azure automatically increases or decreases the number of VM instances based on predefined rules.

Key Features:

- Integrated load balancing

- Automatic scaling based on metrics

- Support for custom VM images and extensions

Creating a VMSS

You can create a VMSS from the Azure Portal, Azure CLI, ARM templates, or Terraform. Here's how to do it using Azure CLI:

```
az vmss create \
  --resource-group myResourceGroup \
  --name myScaleSet \
  --image UbuntuLTS \
  --upgrade-policy-mode automatic \
  --custom-data cloud-init.txt \
  --admin-username azureuser \
  --generate-ssh-keys
```

Configuring Autoscaling Rules

```
az monitor autoscale create \
  --resource-group myResourceGroup \
  --resource myScaleSet \
  --resource-type Microsoft.Compute/virtualMachineScaleSets \
  --name myAutoScaleSetting \
  --min-count 2 \
  --max-count 10 \
  --count 2
```

Add scale-out and scale-in rules:

```
az monitor autoscale rule create \
  --resource-group myResourceGroup \
  --autoscale-name myAutoScaleSetting \
  --condition "Percentage CPU > 70 avg 5m" \
  --scale out 1

az monitor autoscale rule create \
  --resource-group myResourceGroup \
```

```
--autoscale-name myAutoScaleSetting \
--condition "Percentage CPU < 30 avg 5m" \
--scale in 1
```

App Service Autoscaling

Azure App Services are platform-as-a-service (PaaS) offerings. Autoscaling for App Services is typically simpler and more UI-driven.

Configuration via Azure Portal:

1. Go to your App Service

2. Select "Scale out (App Service plan)"

3. Choose **Custom autoscale**

4. Set the **Instance limits** (min/max)

5. Add a rule based on metrics like CPU, Memory, HTTP queue length

Example:

*   Scale out by 1 instance if CPU > 80% for 10 minutes

*   Scale in by 1 instance if CPU < 40% for 15 minutes

Autoscale with Azure Monitor

You can use Azure Monitor to define rules that trigger autoscaling, similar to VMSS. This works well in enterprise environments where infrastructure as code is preferred.

Azure Kubernetes Service (AKS) Autoscaling

In Kubernetes, autoscaling can occur at both the **node** and **pod** level.

Cluster Autoscaler (Node Scaling)

Automatically adds or removes nodes in the cluster when pods cannot be scheduled or when nodes are underutilized.

Enable it using ARM or Azure CLI:

```
az aks create \
  --resource-group myResourceGroup \
  --name myAKSCluster \
  --node-count 3 \
  --enable-cluster-autoscaler \
  --min-count 3 \
  --max-count 10 \
  --node-vm-size Standard_DS2_v2
```

Horizontal Pod Autoscaler (HPA)

Automatically scales the number of pod replicas based on CPU or custom metrics.

Apply an HPA to a deployment:

```
kubectl autoscale deployment myapp-deployment \
  --cpu-percent=50 \
  --min=2 \
  --max=10
```

Serverless Autoscaling

Serverless offerings like Azure Functions and Logic Apps handle scaling automatically. You only pay for actual usage, and Azure handles provisioning behind the scenes.

Azure Functions Scaling

Functions scale based on the number of incoming events:

- HTTP requests

- Queue messages

- Timer triggers

Under the **Consumption Plan**, Azure automatically manages instances. For more control, use **Premium Plan** which supports VNETs and longer execution times.

Configuration Tips:

- Use application insights to monitor cold starts

- Minimize dependencies and startup time

- Break down monolithic functions into smaller units

Best Practices for Autoscaling

1. **Set Reasonable Minimums and Maximums**

   - Don't set min/max values too aggressively. You want to avoid both excessive costs and degraded performance.

2. **Use Metrics That Reflect User Experience**

   - CPU is common, but consider queue length, request latency, and memory usage for better accuracy.

3. **Avoid Flapping (Oscillations)**

   - Add cool-down periods to prevent frequent scaling in/out actions that cause instability.

4. **Test Autoscaling in QA**

   - Simulate high loads and ensure autoscale rules trigger as expected before going to production.

5. **Use Application Insights and Azure Monitor**

   - Track how scaling affects performance and costs. Tweak rules accordingly.

6. **Plan for Scaling Limits**

   - Each service has documented limits (e.g., max instances). Know them and design accordingly.

Real-World Scenario: E-Commerce Application

An e-commerce platform experiences high traffic on weekends and holidays. The application is hosted on App Services with a backend on Azure SQL and Redis Cache.

Solution:

- Set autoscale rules to increase instances during peak hours.

- Monitor HTTP request queue length and CPU usage.

- Use Azure Front Door to route traffic efficiently and reduce latency.

- Implement caching to reduce backend load, delaying the need for scale-out.

Summary

Autoscaling is a critical capability in Azure that ensures your application remains responsive under varying loads while controlling costs. Whether you're using VMSS for infrastructure-level scaling, App Services for PaaS workloads, AKS for container orchestration, or Azure Functions for serverless execution, Azure provides rich tools and mechanisms to meet your scaling needs.

Understanding when and how to use these different strategies — and integrating them into your deployment pipelines — will enable you to build robust, resilient, and cost-effective applications.

Load Balancing Techniques

Load balancing is a crucial part of building scalable, resilient applications in the cloud. As demand grows, distributing incoming traffic across multiple instances ensures availability, responsiveness, and fault tolerance. In Azure, various load balancing services cater to different workloads and scenarios, from low-level infrastructure setups to platform-level applications and even global traffic routing.

This section explores the major Azure load balancing options, their use cases, configuration, and best practices for implementing them across different architectures.

Why Load Balancing Is Essential

Applications without proper load balancing are prone to:

- **Single points of failure**: If one instance goes down, the entire app might be unavailable.

- **Poor performance under load**: Without traffic distribution, one server can be overwhelmed.

- **Inefficient resource utilization**: Load might not be evenly distributed across servers.

Effective load balancing helps mitigate these issues by distributing traffic intelligently, handling spikes in demand, and increasing availability.

Azure Load Balancing Solutions Overview

Azure provides a spectrum of load balancing services, including:

1. **Azure Load Balancer (Layer 4)**

2. **Azure Application Gateway (Layer 7)**

3. **Azure Front Door (Global Load Balancing)**

4. **Traffic Manager (DNS-based Load Balancing)**

5. **Azure API Management (for APIs)**

Let's explore each in depth.

Azure Load Balancer

Azure Load Balancer operates at Layer 4 (TCP, UDP) and is ideal for scenarios where you want to distribute traffic across VMs or VM Scale Sets.

Key Features:

- High availability and low latency

- Supports inbound and outbound NAT rules

- Health probes for instance monitoring

- Two tiers: **Basic** and **Standard**

Use Case:

Distribute traffic across a pool of backend VMs for a stateless web app or API.

Configuration Example (Using Azure CLI):

```
# Create a public IP
az network public-ip create \
  --resource-group MyResourceGroup \
  --name MyPublicIP
```

```
# Create a load balancer
az network lb create \
  --resource-group MyResourceGroup \
  --name MyLoadBalancer \
  --public-ip-address MyPublicIP \
  --frontend-ip-name MyFrontEnd \
  --backend-pool-name MyBackEndPool

# Create a health probe
az network lb probe create \
  --resource-group MyResourceGroup \
  --lb-name MyLoadBalancer \
  --name MyHealthProbe \
  --protocol tcp \
  --port 80

# Create a load balancing rule
az network lb rule create \
  --resource-group MyResourceGroup \
  --lb-name MyLoadBalancer \
  --name MyHTTPRule \
  --protocol tcp \
  --frontend-port 80 \
  --backend-port 80 \
  --frontend-ip-name MyFrontEnd \
  --backend-pool-name MyBackEndPool \
  --probe-name MyHealthProbe
```

This setup routes TCP traffic on port 80 to healthy backend instances.

Azure Application Gateway

Azure Application Gateway is a Layer 7 load balancer, meaning it operates at the HTTP/HTTPS level and understands application protocols.

Features:

- SSL termination and end-to-end SSL

- URL-based routing

- Web Application Firewall (WAF)

- Session affinity (cookie-based)

Use Case:

You want to route traffic based on URL paths or host headers, or protect your app using WAF.

Path-Based Routing Example:

- `/api/*` → backend pool 1 (API service)

- `/images/*` → backend pool 2 (media service)

Creating with Azure CLI:

```
az network application-gateway create \
  --name MyAppGateway \
  --location eastus \
  --resource-group MyResourceGroup \
  --capacity 2 \
  --sku WAF_v2 \
  --frontend-port 80 \
  --http-settings-cookie-based-affinity Enabled \
  --routing-rule-type PathBasedRouting
```

App Gateway is ideal for microservices or any app needing intelligent routing.

Azure Front Door

Azure Front Door provides global Layer 7 load balancing using Microsoft's edge network. It improves performance by routing requests to the closest available backend, reducing latency and enabling high availability across regions.

Features:

- Global HTTP/HTTPS load balancing

- SSL offloading

- Application acceleration via caching and split TCP

- URL path-based routing and rewrite rules

- Automatic failover between regions

Use Case:

You have users across the world and want low-latency, fault-tolerant routing to multi-region backend services.

Configuration in Portal:

1. Define your backend pools (e.g., US West App Service, Europe App Service)

2. Create routing rules (match all traffic or specific paths)

3. Enable health probes and WAF policies if needed

You can use Azure Resource Manager (ARM) templates or Bicep to automate this configuration.

Azure Traffic Manager

Unlike Application Gateway or Front Door, **Traffic Manager** works at the **DNS level**, using policies to resolve DNS queries to the most appropriate endpoint.

Routing Methods:

- Priority (failover)

- Weighted (load distribution)

- Performance (latency)

- Geographic (location-based)

- Multivalue

- Subnet

Use Case:

You want DNS-level routing across Azure or non-Azure endpoints. Useful for hybrid cloud or global applications.

Example: Performance-Based Routing

```
az network traffic-manager profile create \
  --name mytmprofile \
  --resource-group MyResourceGroup \
  --routing-method Performance \
  --unique-dns-name mytmexample \
  --ttl 30 \
  --protocol HTTP \
  --port 80 \
  --path "/"
```

Then register your web app endpoints to the profile.

Comparing Azure Load Balancing Solutions

Service	Layer	Use Case	Global	Smart Routing	WAF Support
Azure Load Balancer	4	Basic traffic distribution	No	No	No
Application Gateway	7	Web apps with complex routing needs	No	Yes	Yes
Azure Front Door	7	Global web apps	Yes	Yes	Yes
Traffic Manager	DNS	Hybrid or external endpoints	Yes	Yes	No

Load Balancing in Real Architectures

Scenario 1: High-Traffic Web App in Single Region

- Use **App Gateway** for path-based routing and SSL termination

- Enable **WAF** for protection

- Backend pool contains multiple **App Services** or VMs with autoscale

Scenario 2: Multi-Region Web App

- Deploy instances in East US and West Europe

- Use **Azure Front Door** for global routing

- Backend pools include regional App Gateways

- Traffic is routed to the closest healthy endpoint

Scenario 3: Hybrid App with Azure and On-Premises

- Use **Traffic Manager** with weighted or priority routing

- Endpoints include Azure App Service and on-prem server exposed via VPN

- Use **Application Gateway** for Azure-side routing

Best Practices for Load Balancing

1. **Health Probes Are Critical**
   Always configure health probes to ensure only healthy instances receive traffic.

2. **Combine Services Strategically**
   Use Front Door + App Gateway + Load Balancer when needed. Each layer solves a different problem.

3. **Use CDN Where Appropriate**
   Azure CDN can offload static content and reduce load on backend servers.

4. **Secure Your Endpoints**
   Use WAF with Application Gateway or Front Door to block common web attacks.

5. **Test Failover Scenarios Regularly**
   Validate how your system behaves during failures. Simulate outages and monitor traffic redirection.

6. **Use Monitoring Tools**
   Track metrics using Azure Monitor and Application Insights. Set up alerts on probe failures and high latency.

7. **Optimize for Performance**
   Enable compression, caching, and keep-alive connections. Choose the right SKUs and tune capacity settings.

Summary

Azure offers a powerful set of load balancing solutions that can be tailored to match virtually any application architecture — from simple VM-based backends to globally distributed microservices. Choosing the right load balancer involves understanding your application needs, traffic patterns, geographic distribution, and security requirements.

By mastering Azure's load balancing tools and applying best practices, you can build scalable, resilient, and performant cloud-native applications that handle traffic spikes gracefully and deliver consistent user experiences worldwide.

Cost Management and Optimization

Managing and optimizing cloud costs is a fundamental aspect of running scalable and sustainable applications in Azure. While the cloud offers immense flexibility and on-demand scalability, it also introduces the risk of unchecked resource sprawl, unused services, and spiraling expenses. This section explores cost management strategies, Azure-native tools, policies, governance models, and real-world practices to help you take full control of your Azure spending.

Understanding Azure Pricing

Before diving into cost optimization, it's crucial to understand how Azure pricing works. Azure charges based on consumption, which varies by resource type:

- **Compute**: Billed per second/minute/hour, depending on SKU

- **Storage**: Charged by capacity (GB), transaction volume, and redundancy options

- **Networking**: Egress data transfer costs more than ingress

- **Licensing**: Services like SQL Database may include license-included or bring-your-own-license (BYOL) models

Every Azure resource has a **SKU**, which defines its pricing tier. Choosing the right SKU can significantly reduce costs.

Core Cost Optimization Principles

1. **Right-size resources** – Avoid over-provisioning. Use performance metrics to match resources to workloads.

2. **Deallocate unused services** – Shut down or scale down resources during off-hours.

3. **Use Reserved Instances (RIs)** – Commit to 1- or 3-year terms to get deep discounts (up to 72%).

4. **Implement tagging and chargeback** – Track spending by department, team, or project.

5. **Monitor and analyze usage regularly** – Prevent budget surprises with early detection of unusual spend.

Azure Cost Management + Billing

Azure provides a comprehensive set of tools under **Cost Management + Billing**, accessible from the Azure Portal.

Key Features:

*   **Cost analysis**: Visualize spend trends and drill down by resource, location, or tag.

*   **Budgets**: Set monthly/quarterly/yearly budgets with email alerts when thresholds are crossed.

*   **Recommendations**: Get AI-driven cost-saving suggestions (e.g., unused VMs, underutilized disks).

*   **Exports and APIs**: Export billing data to storage or retrieve it programmatically for integration with your own BI tools.

Example: Setting a Budget

From Azure Portal:

1. Navigate to **Cost Management + Billing**

2. Select **Budgets** > **Add**

3. Name your budget, set scope (subscription/resource group), and choose time period

4. Add alert thresholds (e.g., 80%, 100%)

5. Define action groups for notifications

Cost-Saving Features by Service

Virtual Machines

- Use **Azure Spot VMs** for workloads that can tolerate interruptions (up to 90% cheaper).

- Apply **auto-shutdown policies** to dev/test environments.

- Monitor with Azure Advisor to identify oversized VMs.

```
az vm auto-shutdown --resource-group MyRG --name MyVM --time 1900
```

- Consider **VM Reserved Instances** for production workloads.

App Services

- Use **deployment slots** only when needed (they consume resources).

- Scale down to lower tiers (e.g., from Premium to Standard) if traffic is low.

- Consider **consumption plans** for Functions instead of always-on services.

Storage

- Choose appropriate storage tiers: **Hot**, **Cool**, or **Archive**.

- Delete or archive unused blobs.

- Use **lifecycle management policies** to automate data tiering.

```json
{
  "rules": [
    {
      "name": "archive-old-logs",
      "enabled": true,
```

```json
      "definition": {
        "filters": {
          "blobTypes": [ "blockBlob" ],
          "prefixMatch": [ "logs/" ]
        },
        "actions": {
          "baseBlob": {
            "tierToArchive": {
              "daysAfterModificationGreaterThan": 30
            }
          }
        }
      }
    }
  ]
}
```

Apply this rule using ARM templates or Azure CLI for Blob Storage.

Databases

- Use **serverless SQL databases** where workloads are intermittent.

- Configure **automatic pause/resume** for cost savings.

- Scale **Cosmos DB** throughput dynamically using autoscale.

```
az cosmosdb update \
  --name mycosmosdb \
  --resource-group myRG \
  --max-throughput 4000
```

Tagging for Cost Visibility

Tagging resources is essential for organizing and allocating costs. Example tags:

- Environment: Production

- Department: Finance

- Project: Migration2025

- Owner: jdoe

Use Azure Policy to **enforce tagging**:

```
{
  "if": {
    "field": "[concat('tags[', parameters('tagName'), ']')]",
    "equals": ""
  },
  "then": {
    "effect": "deny"
  }
}
```

You can also create auto-tagging policies to apply tags based on resource group or owner.

Governance Through Azure Policy and Blueprints

Governance is key to long-term cost control. Azure provides:

- **Azure Policy**: Automate and enforce cost-related rules (e.g., only allow specific VM SKUs).

- **Azure Blueprints**: Define environments with predefined resources, policies, and permissions.

Example: Enforce usage of only B-series VMs:

```
{
  "policyRule": {
    "if": {
      "field": "Microsoft.Compute/virtualMachines/sku.name",
      "notIn": [ "Standard_B1s", "Standard_B2s" ]
    },
    "then": {
      "effect": "deny"
    }
  }
}
```

}

Deploy these policies across subscriptions or management groups for enterprise-level governance.

Real-World Optimization Scenario

Scenario: Mid-sized SaaS App Hosting in Azure

A SaaS company runs multiple environments (dev, staging, production) using App Services, SQL Database, Redis Cache, and Azure Front Door.

Problems Identified:

- Dev/staging environments run 24/7

- Unused App Insights instances are active

- Large data stored in hot tier unnecessarily

- No tagging — unclear cost attribution

Actions Taken:

1. Enabled auto-shutdown on dev/test VMs and App Services

2. Scheduled archiving of old blob data using lifecycle policies

3. Moved rarely accessed SQL databases to serverless tier

4. Applied mandatory tags and built Power BI reports using exported cost data

5. Configured budget alerts for each environment

Outcome: 28% reduction in monthly Azure spend and improved team accountability

---

Cost Forecasting and Trend Analysis

Use **Cost Analysis** in the Azure Portal or Power BI to visualize:

- Forecasted vs. actual spend

- Spend by tag or resource group

- Cost by service over time

Automated exports enable integration with tools like Power BI, Excel, and your own dashboards.

```
az costmanagement export create \
  --name monthlyExport \
  --type ActualCost \
  --time-frame MonthToDate \
  --dataset-configuration file \
  --storage-account-id
"/subscriptions/.../resourceGroups/.../providers/Microsoft.Storage/s
torageAccounts/myStorage" \
  --storage-container mycontainer \
  --recurrence Weekly
```

Leveraging Azure Advisor

Azure Advisor provides personalized, actionable recommendations across five areas:

- **Cost**

- **Security**

- **Reliability**

- **Performance**

- **Operational Excellence**

For cost, it highlights:

- Idle VMs

- Underutilized databases

- Expired RIs

- Overprovisioned disks

You can access Azure Advisor via the portal or API and integrate it into weekly ops reviews.

Summary

Effective cost management in Azure is not a one-time task, but a continuous process involving visibility, optimization, governance, and accountability. Azure's native tools — from Cost Management + Billing to Policy and Advisor — provide a powerful ecosystem for gaining control over your cloud budget.

Key takeaways:

- Regularly monitor and audit your resources

- Use tags and scopes for accountability

- Right-size, deallocate, and automate where possible

- Use pricing tiers, reservations, and spot instances to optimize cost

- Educate teams and enforce policies for sustainable cloud usage

By embedding cost management practices into your DevOps and operations workflows, you'll not only reduce expenses but also increase your team's efficiency and alignment with business goals.

Designing for High Availability

High Availability (HA) is a cornerstone of modern cloud architecture. It refers to the ability of a system or component to remain operational and accessible for a high percentage of time— often measured as uptime percentages like 99.9% (three nines), 99.99% (four nines), or higher. Designing for high availability in Azure requires careful planning across compute, storage, networking, and application layers, using redundancy, fault tolerance, and failover strategies.

In this section, we will explore how to design Azure-based systems for high availability, cover key Azure services and architectural patterns, and walk through real-world scenarios and implementation strategies.

Core Principles of High Availability

To achieve high availability, consider the following foundational principles:

1. **Eliminate Single Points of Failure**: Duplicate critical components.

2. **Fail Fast and Recover Gracefully**: Detect and recover from failures quickly.

3. **Design for Redundancy**: Use multiple instances, zones, or regions.

4. **Automate Recovery**: Use Azure-native automation and orchestration.

5. **Implement Health Monitoring**: Constantly assess the system's state and route traffic only to healthy endpoints.

6. **Use Managed Services Where Possible**: Azure PaaS services often offer built-in HA.

Azure Regions and Availability Zones

Azure Region: A set of datacenters deployed within a geographic area. Azure has dozens of regions across the globe.

Availability Zones (AZs): Physically separate locations within a region, each with independent power, cooling, and networking. By deploying across AZs, you can protect your app from data center-level failures.

Example: Multi-Zone Deployment

- Deploy App Service instances or VMs in Zone 1, Zone 2, and Zone 3.

- Use a Zone-redundant load balancer (Standard SKU) to distribute traffic.

- Azure guarantees 99.99% uptime when using multiple zones.

```
az network lb create \
  --resource-group MyRG \
  --name MyZonalLB \
  --sku Standard \
  --frontend-ip-name myFrontEnd \
  --backend-pool-name myBackEndPool \
  --public-ip-address myPublicIP
```

High Availability for Compute Resources

Virtual Machines

To ensure HA for VMs:

- **Availability Sets**: Group VMs to distribute them across multiple fault and update domains.

- **Availability Zones**: Place VMs in different zones to protect against data center failure.

- **VM Scale Sets**: Use for automatic instance distribution and autoscaling across zones.

```
az vm availability-set create \
  --name MyAvailabilitySet \
  --resource-group MyRG \
  --platform-fault-domain-count 2 \
  --platform-update-domain-count 5
```

When using Availability Sets, Azure guarantees 99.95% uptime; with Availability Zones, it's 99.99%.

App Services

Azure App Services are built on high-availability infrastructure. For improved resilience:

- Use **Premium plans** with zone redundancy

- Deploy to **multiple regions** using deployment slots and traffic manager

- Enable **auto-healing** to restart instances on anomalies

High Availability for Data and Storage

Azure Storage

- **Locally Redundant Storage (LRS)**: 3 copies within one data center.

- **Zone-Redundant Storage (ZRS)**: 3 copies across different AZs.

- **Geo-Redundant Storage (GRS)**: Replication to a secondary region.

- **Read-Access Geo-Redundant Storage (RA-GRS)**: Adds read access to the secondary region.

For mission-critical data, use ZRS or GRS based on latency and durability requirements.

Azure SQL Database

- **Active Geo-Replication**: Create up to four readable secondaries in different regions.

- **Auto-failover groups**: Enable automatic failover and geo-load balancing.

```
az sql failover-group create \
  --name myFailoverGroup \
  --partner-server mySecondarySQLServer \
  --resource-group myRG \
  --server myPrimarySQLServer \
  --failover-policy Automatic
```

These options provide high resilience for transactional systems.

Networking for High Availability

Load Balancers

- Use **Azure Load Balancer (Standard)** for regional layer 4 load balancing.

- Use **Azure Application Gateway** for layer 7 with built-in WAF and SSL termination.

- Use **Azure Front Door** for global layer 7 traffic distribution with health probes and failover.

Each service plays a role:

- Front Door: Global traffic routing and acceleration.

- Application Gateway: Internal routing, SSL offload, and app-level routing.

- Load Balancer: Distributes TCP/UDP traffic to backend VMs or containers.

DNS and Traffic Manager

Azure Traffic Manager operates at the DNS level to route users to the most appropriate endpoint based on performance, geography, or priority.

Example: Primary region with failover to secondary:

```
az network traffic-manager profile create \
  --name myProfile \
  --resource-group myRG \
  --routing-method Priority \
  --unique-dns-name myappdns \
  --ttl 30
```

Then, add endpoints with priority levels and health probes.

Automation and Recovery

Azure Site Recovery

Azure Site Recovery (ASR) enables disaster recovery and orchestrated failover for:

- VMs

- Physical servers

- Azure-to-Azure replication

It supports RPOs and RTOs with configurable recovery plans.

```
az backup vault create \
  --resource-group MyRG \
  --name MyBackupVault \
  --location eastus
```

Combine ASR with Azure Backup for complete protection of your workloads.

Auto-healing

Configure auto-healing for App Services by setting rules for unhealthy responses or long server response times.

- Navigate to App Service > Diagnose and Solve Problems > Auto-Heal

- Set trigger conditions (e.g., memory limit, response code)

- Choose actions (recycle process, log dump, etc.)

HA for Serverless and Containers

Azure Functions

Under the **Premium Plan**, Azure Functions can run in multiple zones, with guaranteed availability and VNET integration. Avoid using Consumption Plan for mission-critical systems due to cold starts.

Azure Kubernetes Service (AKS)

AKS can be configured for zone redundancy:

- Use multiple agent pools spread across zones

- Deploy the control plane in a zone-redundant configuration (if supported in the region)

```
az aks create \
  --resource-group myRG \
  --name myAKSCluster \
  --location eastus \
  --node-count 3 \
  --zones 1 2 3 \
  --enable-managed-identity
```

Use **PodDisruptionBudgets**, **ReplicaSets**, and **Horizontal Pod Autoscalers** to ensure workloads remain available.

Multi-Region High Availability

Deploying across regions offers protection from region-wide outages. This requires:

- **Geo-replication of data** (e.g., SQL, Blob Storage)

- **Global load balancing** with Azure Front Door or Traffic Manager

- **Deployment automation** for cross-region updates

- **Failover orchestration** to redirect traffic automatically

Example Scenario:

- Web App in East US and West Europe

- Cosmos DB with geo-replication

- Azure Front Door routes users to the closest available backend

- App Insights tracks latency and errors per region

This setup provides not only HA but also performance benefits via edge routing.

Monitoring and Health Checks

High availability means being aware of issues before they affect users. Implement monitoring and alerting using:

- **Azure Monitor**: Tracks metrics and logs across services

- **Application Insights**: Real-time telemetry, exceptions, and usage patterns

- **Log Analytics**: Centralized queryable logging

- **Health Probes**: Automatically detect unresponsive endpoints

Sample Health Probe for Load Balancer:

```
az network lb probe create \
  --resource-group MyRG \
  --lb-name MyLB \
  --name MyProbe \
  --protocol Tcp \
  --port 80
```

Set up alerts for CPU spikes, disk failures, dropped connections, or service downtimes.

Real-World Architecture Example

Use Case: Highly Available E-commerce Platform

Requirements:

- 99.99% uptime

- Zero data loss

- Geo-redundancy

- Automatic failover

Solution:

- Frontend hosted on Azure App Services with Premium v3 plans across two zones

- Azure SQL Database with auto-failover group enabled

- Redis Cache in zone-redundant configuration

- Azure Front Door for global load balancing

- Cosmos DB with multi-region writes

- Application Gateway WAF in front of the frontend for app-level protection

- Azure Monitor and Alerts for operational visibility

Failover Strategy:

- App Insights detects spike in 5xx errors

- Health probe fails on App Gateway

- Azure Front Door routes traffic to secondary region

- SQL auto-failover group initiates failover

- DevOps team is alerted automatically

Summary

High availability is not a single feature, but a design mindset. It involves redundancy, intelligent traffic distribution, proactive monitoring, and failover planning. Azure provides all the tools necessary to build resilient systems, from zone-aware load balancers and region-paired storage to disaster recovery orchestration and serverless scaling.

To achieve high availability in Azure:

- Deploy across fault domains, update domains, and availability zones

- Use redundant networking and load balancing layers

- Implement geo-replication and automated failover

- Monitor, test, and continuously improve your HA strategy

By following these practices, you can ensure that your applications are always accessible, performant, and resilient to failures—delivering consistent value to your users and stakeholders.

Chapter 8: Advanced Azure Services and Scenarios

Serverless Architectures with Azure Functions

Serverless computing represents a major paradigm shift in application architecture. Rather than provisioning and maintaining infrastructure, developers can focus solely on writing and deploying code, allowing cloud providers like Azure to handle the rest. At the forefront of Azure's serverless offerings is **Azure Functions**, which lets you execute event-driven code without explicitly provisioning or managing servers.

In this section, we'll dive deep into serverless architecture on Azure using Azure Functions, exploring concepts, best practices, integration scenarios, real-world use cases, and step-by-step implementation strategies.

What is Serverless Computing?

Serverless doesn't mean there are no servers—it means the underlying infrastructure is abstracted away from the developer. In serverless models:

- You are only charged for the actual compute time your code consumes.

- Infrastructure provisioning and scaling are handled automatically.

- Code is triggered by events (HTTP requests, timers, messages, etc.).

Azure Functions is Azure's implementation of this model, designed for building microservices, APIs, scheduled tasks, and real-time data processing pipelines.

Azure Functions: Overview and Use Cases

Azure Functions supports multiple programming languages, including C#, JavaScript, TypeScript, Python, Java, and PowerShell. It is deeply integrated with the Azure ecosystem and can be triggered by over a dozen event sources.

Common Use Cases:

- **Web APIs**: Stateless endpoints handling HTTP requests

- **Data Processing Pipelines**: Triggered by changes in Blob Storage, Cosmos DB, or Event Hubs

- **Scheduled Tasks**: Replacing cron jobs or Windows Task Scheduler

- **IoT Processing**: Reacting to messages from IoT Hub

- **Microservice Orchestration**: Through Durable Functions

Hosting Plans for Azure Functions

Azure Functions supports several hosting options:

1. **Consumption Plan** (Default):

   o Auto-scales based on workload

   o Pay only for execution time and resource usage

   o Subject to cold starts and execution timeout limits

2. **Premium Plan**:

   o Eliminates cold starts

   o Supports VNET integration and longer execution times

   o Ideal for production workloads

3. **Dedicated (App Service) Plan**:

   o Fixed resource allocation

   o Suitable when Functions need to share compute with web apps

Example of creating a Function App using Azure CLI with Consumption Plan:

```
az functionapp create \
  --resource-group myResourceGroup \
  --consumption-plan-location westus \
  --runtime node \
  --functions-version 4 \
  --name myUniqueFunctionApp \
```

```
--storage-account mystorageaccount
```

Anatomy of an Azure Function

A typical Azure Function includes:

- **Trigger**: Specifies the event that causes the function to execute (e.g., HTTP request, queue message).

- **Input Bindings**: Optional. Data sources your function can read from.

- **Output Bindings**: Optional. Where your function sends output data.

- **Function Code**: The actual business logic.

Example: HTTP Trigger (JavaScript)

```
module.exports = async function (context, req) {
    context.log('HTTP trigger received a request.');

    const name = req.query.name || (req.body && req.body.name);
    context.res = {
        status: 200,
        body: name ? `Hello, ${name}` : "Please provide a name."
    };
};
```

This function runs when an HTTP GET or POST request is received and returns a simple message.

Triggers and Bindings

Azure Functions supports numerous triggers and bindings. Some examples:

Trigger Type	Description
HTTP	Responds to RESTful requests
Timer	Executes on a schedule (cron-like syntax)

Blob Storage	Runs when a blob is added/updated
Queue Storage	Reacts to messages in Azure Queue Storage
Event Hub	Processes event stream data
Service Bus	Handles messages from queues/topics
Cosmos DB	Runs on data changes in Cosmos DB

Example: Timer Trigger (C#)

```csharp
public static void Run([TimerTrigger("0 */5 * * * *")]TimerInfo
myTimer, ILogger log)
{
    log.LogInformation($"Timer triggered at: {DateTime.Now}");
}
```

Runs every 5 minutes.

Deploying Azure Functions

There are multiple deployment options:

1. **VS Code / Visual Studio** – Ideal for local development and publishing

2. **GitHub Actions / Azure DevOps** – CI/CD pipelines

3. **Zip Deploy** – Upload ZIP files via CLI or HTTP

4. **ARM Templates / Bicep / Terraform** – Infrastructure-as-code deployment

Deploy with GitHub Actions:

```yaml
name: Deploy Function App
on:
  push:
    branches:
      - main
jobs:
  build-and-deploy:
```

```
    runs-on: ubuntu-latest
    steps:
      - uses: actions/checkout@v2
      - name: Set up Node.js
        uses: actions/setup-node@v2
        with:
          node-version: '16'
      - run: npm install
      - run: npm run build
      - uses: Azure/functions-action@v1
        with:
          app-name: 'myFunctionApp'
          package: '.'
          publish-profile: ${{
secrets.AZURE_FUNCTIONAPP_PUBLISH_PROFILE }}
```

Monitoring and Troubleshooting

Monitoring Azure Functions is essential for understanding performance, diagnosing failures, and maintaining SLAs.

Tools:

- **Azure Monitor**: Aggregates metrics and logs

- **Application Insights**: Provides end-to-end telemetry and distributed tracing

- **Live Metrics**: Real-time monitoring of invocations and dependencies

Common metrics to monitor:

- Function execution count

- Average duration

- Failure rate

- Cold starts

- Throttled executions

Use alerts to detect anomalies:

```
az monitor metrics alert create \
  --name "FunctionErrors" \
  --resource-group myResourceGroup \
  --scopes /subscriptions/{sub-
id}/resourceGroups/myResourceGroup/providers/Microsoft.Web/sites/myF
unctionApp \
  --condition "total Requests >= 5" \
  --description "High error rate detected"
```

Durable Functions: Serverless Orchestration

Durable Functions extend Azure Functions by allowing stateful orchestrations. You can define workflows with:

- **Orchestrator Functions**: Control logic and sequencing

- **Activity Functions**: Execute tasks

- **Entity Functions**: Maintain state in a distributed fashion

Use cases:

- Chained workflows (e.g., order processing)

- Fan-out/fan-in operations

- Human interaction workflows with timeouts

Example: Chained Workflow (JavaScript)

```
const df = require("durable-functions");

module.exports = df.orchestrator(function* (context) {
    const x = yield context.df.callActivity("Add", 1);
    const y = yield context.df.callActivity("Multiply", x);
    return y;
});
```

Best Practices for Serverless Architectures

1. **Keep Functions Small and Focused**
   Follow the single-responsibility principle. Smaller functions are easier to test and scale independently.

2. **Avoid Long-Running Functions**
   Use Durable Functions for orchestrating lengthy tasks. The default timeout for HTTP functions in the consumption plan is 5 minutes.

3. **Implement Retry Logic and Idempotency**
   Azure Functions may retry failed executions. Ensure your functions can handle this gracefully.

4. **Secure Your Endpoints**
   Use authentication keys or integrate with Azure AD and API Management to secure access.

5. **Use Dependency Injection (DI)**
   Improve testability and manage shared resources like DB connections.

6. **Monitor Cold Starts**
   Use Premium Plan or pre-warmed instances to avoid performance degradation due to cold starts.

7. **Use Queue-Based Communication Between Functions**
   Decouple services and ensure reliability via Azure Storage Queues or Service Bus.

Real-World Example: Image Processing Pipeline

A real-world use case of serverless architecture is an image-processing pipeline for a media application.

Architecture:

1. **Blob Storage Trigger**: When a user uploads an image

2. **Function 1 (Validator)**: Validates file type/size

3. **Function 2 (Thumbnail Generator)**: Creates thumbnails and stores them

4. **Function 3 (Metadata Writer)**: Updates metadata in Cosmos DB

5. **Queue Messages**: Pass context between functions

Benefits:

- Highly scalable and cost-effective

- Parallel processing with fan-out

- Event-driven and fully automated

Summary

Serverless architectures, powered by Azure Functions, allow developers to build scalable, event-driven systems with minimal operational overhead. From simple HTTP APIs to complex orchestrations using Durable Functions, Azure provides a powerful and flexible platform to build next-gen cloud-native applications.

Key advantages include:

- No infrastructure management

- True pay-per-use pricing

- Instant scalability

- Seamless integration with other Azure services

By following best practices, leveraging the full set of triggers and bindings, and monitoring your functions effectively, you can build robust, efficient, and production-ready serverless solutions on Azure.

Containers and Kubernetes on Azure

Containerization is a transformative approach to software development that enables consistent deployment across environments, faster iterations, and efficient resource utilization. Azure offers a rich ecosystem for running and managing containers—from lightweight, serverless container instances to fully orchestrated Kubernetes environments.

This section delves into the use of containers and Kubernetes in Azure, including core concepts, architectural patterns, deployment options, tooling, best practices, and real-world scenarios.

Why Containers?

Containers package applications and their dependencies into a single unit that can run anywhere. This resolves the classic "it works on my machine" problem and facilitates microservices, DevOps practices, and CI/CD.

Key Benefits:

- **Portability**: Run anywhere—on-prem, cloud, or hybrid

- **Speed**: Fast startup times and efficient scaling

- **Isolation**: Each container runs independently

- **Consistency**: Identical environments from dev to prod

Docker is the most popular container runtime, and Kubernetes has become the de facto standard for container orchestration.

Azure Container Services Overview

Azure supports multiple options for running containers:

Service	Description	Best Use Case
Azure Container Instances	Fast, serverless container execution	Ephemeral workloads, testing, event-driven jobs
Azure Kubernetes Service	Fully managed Kubernetes cluster	Microservices, enterprise-grade workloads
App Service for Containers	Web apps running in Docker containers	Simple web apps in containerized form
Azure Container Apps	Serverless containers with Dapr support and autoscaling	Event-driven, microservices, minimal ops
Azure Functions w/ Custom Image	Serverless execution of code inside containers	Specific runtime or dependency needs

Azure Container Instances (ACI)

ACI is the simplest way to run containers in Azure. It allows you to spin up a container in seconds, without managing VMs or orchestrators.

Key Features:

- Billing per second

- VNET integration

- Secrets, volumes, and GPU support

- Linux and Windows containers

Deploying a Container with ACI:

```
az container create \
  --resource-group myResourceGroup \
  --name myContainer \
  --image mcr.microsoft.com/azuredocs/aci-helloworld \
  --cpu 1 --memory 1 \
  --dns-name-label myhelloworld \
  --ports 80
```

Use cases: batch processing, scheduled jobs, testing environments, CI/CD jobs.

Azure Kubernetes Service (AKS)

Azure Kubernetes Service (AKS) is a managed Kubernetes offering that abstracts away much of the complexity involved in running production-grade clusters.

AKS Highlights:

- Fully managed control plane (master nodes)

- Integrated monitoring and logging

- Built-in support for Helm, GitOps, and Azure Policy

- Auto-scaling of nodes and pods

- Supports Windows and Linux nodes

Creating an AKS Cluster

```
az aks create \
  --resource-group myResourceGroup \
  --name myAKSCluster \
  --node-count 3 \
  --enable-addons monitoring \
  --generate-ssh-keys
```

After creation:

```
az aks get-credentials --resource-group myResourceGroup --name
myAKSCluster
kubectl get nodes
```

You can now deploy workloads using standard Kubernetes manifests or Helm charts.

Deploying to AKS: Basic YAML Example

Here's a simple deployment for an NGINX pod:

```
apiVersion: apps/v1
kind: Deployment
metadata:
  name: nginx-deployment
spec:
  replicas: 3
  selector:
    matchLabels:
      app: nginx
  template:
    metadata:
      labels:
        app: nginx
    spec:
      containers:
      - name: nginx
        image: nginx:latest
        ports:
        - containerPort: 80
```

Apply it:

```
kubectl apply -f nginx-deployment.yaml
```

Expose with a service:

```
apiVersion: v1
kind: Service
metadata:
  name: nginx-service
spec:
  type: LoadBalancer
  selector:
    app: nginx
  ports:
    - protocol: TCP
      port: 80
      targetPort: 80
```

Helm: Kubernetes Package Management

Helm simplifies Kubernetes deployments by packaging related resources as charts.

Install Helm:

```
brew install helm
```

Example: Deploy WordPress to AKS:

```
helm repo add bitnami https://charts.bitnami.com/bitnami
helm install my-wordpress bitnami/wordpress
```

Helm enables versioned, reusable templates for deployment.

Container Registries

Azure provides a private registry with **Azure Container Registry (ACR)** for storing Docker images securely.

Create an ACR:

```
az acr create --resource-group myRG --name myRegistry --sku Basic
```

Build and push an image:

```
az acr build --registry myRegistry --image myapp:v1 .
```

Connect AKS to ACR:

```
az aks update \
  --name myAKSCluster \
  --resource-group myRG \
  --attach-acr myRegistry
```

Now you can pull private images from ACR into your AKS pods.

Networking and Ingress Controllers

Kubernetes provides **ClusterIP**, **NodePort**, and **LoadBalancer** services. For advanced routing, use **Ingress Controllers** like:

- NGINX Ingress Controller

- Azure Application Gateway Ingress Controller (AGIC)

Deploy NGINX Ingress Controller:

```
helm repo add ingress-nginx https://kubernetes.github.io/ingress-nginx
helm install ingress-nginx ingress-nginx/ingress-nginx
```

Define an Ingress resource:

```
apiVersion: networking.k8s.io/v1
kind: Ingress
metadata:
  name: my-ingress
spec:
  rules:
  - host: myapp.example.com
    http:
```

```
    paths:
    - backend:
        service:
          name: nginx-service
          port:
            number: 80
      path: /
      pathType: Prefix
```

Security and Identity

Kubernetes has rich support for role-based access control (RBAC). Integrate with Azure Active Directory for unified identity management.

Azure AD Integration:

- Use AAD-integrated clusters to authenticate users via Azure AD.

- Map users to Kubernetes roles using `RoleBinding` and `ClusterRoleBinding`.

```
kubectl create rolebinding dev-access \
  --clusterrole=view \
  --user "<user-object-id>" \
  --namespace dev
```

Also consider using **Azure Key Vault with CSI driver** to securely mount secrets.

Monitoring and Logging

AKS integrates natively with **Azure Monitor**, **Container Insights**, and **Log Analytics**.

Enable monitoring:

```
az aks enable-addons \
  --addons monitoring \
  --name myAKSCluster \
  --resource-group myRG
```

Key telemetry includes:

- Pod and node health

- CPU and memory usage

- Log search and alerting via Kusto Query Language (KQL)

- Prometheus and Grafana integration for detailed metrics

Best Practices for Containers and AKS

1. **Use Resource Requests and Limits**
   Define CPU and memory requests/limits to ensure fair scheduling.

2. **Isolate Workloads with Namespaces**
   Use namespaces to segregate environments or teams.

3. **Implement Auto-Scaling**
   Enable **Horizontal Pod Autoscaler (HPA)** to scale based on CPU or custom metrics.

```
kubectl autoscale deployment nginx-deployment \
  --cpu-percent=50 \
  --min=1 \
  --max=10
```

4. **Secure Images**
   Scan images for vulnerabilities using tools like Microsoft Defender for Containers or Trivy.

5. **Manage Secrets Securely**
   Avoid hardcoding secrets in YAML. Use Azure Key Vault or Kubernetes Secrets.

6. **CI/CD Integration**
   Use GitHub Actions or Azure DevOps for automated build/test/deploy pipelines.

7. **Disaster Recovery**
   Back up etcd, configuration files, and Helm releases regularly. Use multi-region deployment for critical workloads.

Real-World Scenario: Microservices on AKS

Architecture:

- Microservices in separate Docker containers

- Each service deployed via Helm chart

- NGINX Ingress Controller handling internal routing

- Azure Application Gateway + WAF in front of NGINX

- Azure Container Registry for storing private images

- Azure Monitor + Prometheus for observability

Benefits:

- Easy scalability of individual services

- Clear separation of concerns

- Secure and observable architecture

Challenges:

- Initial learning curve with Kubernetes

- Complexity increases with number of services

- Needs ongoing cost and performance tuning

Summary

Containers and Kubernetes are central to building modern, scalable, and portable cloud-native applications. Azure simplifies container adoption through services like Azure Kubernetes Service, Container Apps, and ACR, while offering deep integration with monitoring, security, and DevOps tooling.

Key takeaways:

- Start with ACI or Azure Container Apps for quick and simple workloads

- Use AKS for advanced, production-grade orchestration

- Automate deployment with Helm, CI/CD, and Infrastructure as Code

- Secure, monitor, and scale your containerized apps effectively

By mastering containers and Kubernetes on Azure, you'll be well-positioned to architect resilient, modular systems that meet the demands of today's fast-moving development landscape.

AI and Machine Learning with Azure Cognitive Services

Artificial Intelligence (AI) and Machine Learning (ML) are rapidly transforming every industry—from healthcare and finance to retail and logistics. Azure Cognitive Services enables developers to embed powerful AI capabilities into their applications without requiring deep expertise in data science or machine learning.

Azure's suite of Cognitive Services offers pre-built APIs for vision, speech, language, decision-making, and more. These services are backed by years of research from Microsoft and are continually updated to improve accuracy, scalability, and security.

In this section, we'll explore how to leverage Azure Cognitive Services, integrate AI features into real-world applications, understand pricing and deployment models, and apply best practices for performance, security, and governance.

What is Azure Cognitive Services?

Azure Cognitive Services is a collection of AI services and APIs that allow applications to see, hear, speak, understand, and interpret the needs of users.

The main categories are:

1. **Vision** – Analyze images and video content.

2. **Speech** – Convert speech to text, text to speech, and handle spoken language understanding.

3. **Language** – Understand and process text using NLP.

4. **Decision** – Provide recommendations and personalized content.

5. **Search** – Integrate web-scale search experiences into your app (Bing APIs).

These services offer both REST APIs and SDKs, supporting multiple programming languages including Python, C#, JavaScript, and Java.

Setting Up Cognitive Services in Azure

To get started:

Create a Cognitive Services resource:

```
az cognitiveservices account create \
  --name myCognitiveService \
  --resource-group myResourceGroup \
  --kind CognitiveServices \
  --sku S0 \
  --location westus \
  --yes
```

1.

Retrieve your API keys and endpoint:

```
az cognitiveservices account keys list \
  --name myCognitiveService \
  --resource-group myResourceGroup
```

2.

These keys are used to authenticate API requests.

Computer Vision

Computer Vision allows you to extract information from images and video, including:

- Object detection

- Face recognition

- Text extraction (OCR)

- Image tagging and categorization

- Spatial analysis

Example: Analyze an Image (Python)

```
import requests
```

```python
subscription_key = 'YOUR_KEY'
endpoint = 'https://your-
region.api.cognitive.microsoft.com/vision/v3.2/analyze'

image_url = 'https://example.com/image.jpg'
params = {'visualFeatures': 'Categories,Description,Objects'}
headers = {'Ocp-Apim-Subscription-Key': subscription_key}
data = {'url': image_url}

response = requests.post(endpoint, headers=headers, params=params,
json=data)
result = response.json()

for obj in result['objects']:
    print(f"Detected {obj['object']} with confidence
{obj['confidence']}")
```

Use cases: e-commerce (visual search), accessibility, security monitoring, content moderation.

Speech Services

Azure's Speech APIs support:

- **Speech to Text**: Real-time and batch transcription

- **Text to Speech**: Natural-sounding voice synthesis

- **Speech Translation**: Translate spoken language on the fly

- **Speaker Recognition**: Identify or verify speakers

Example: Real-time Speech Recognition (C#)

```csharp
var config = SpeechConfig.FromSubscription("YourKey", "YourRegion");
using var recognizer = new SpeechRecognizer(config);

Console.WriteLine("Say something...");
var result = await recognizer.RecognizeOnceAsync();

Console.WriteLine($"Recognized: {result.Text}");
```

Applications include virtual assistants, transcription services, voice-activated interfaces, and accessibility tools.

Language Services

Natural Language Processing (NLP) is essential for analyzing, interpreting, and generating text.

Key features include:

- **Text Analytics**: Sentiment analysis, key phrase extraction, entity recognition

- **Translator**: Translate between 90+ languages

- **Language Understanding (LUIS)**: Train custom models to interpret user intent

- **QnA Maker / Azure Question Answering**: Turn FAQs into conversational bots

Example: Sentiment Analysis (Python)

```python
import requests

key = 'YOUR_KEY'
endpoint = 'https://your-
region.api.cognitive.microsoft.com/text/analytics/v3.1/sentiment'

documents = {"documents": [{"id": "1", "language": "en", "text": "I
love Azure Cognitive Services!"}]}
headers = {'Ocp-Apim-Subscription-Key': key, 'Content-Type':
'application/json'}

response = requests.post(endpoint, headers=headers, json=documents)
sentiment = response.json()
print(sentiment)
```

Great for social media monitoring, customer feedback analysis, and chatbot conversations.

Decision Services

These services use machine learning to help applications make informed decisions.

Examples:

- **Personalizer**: Tailor content for each user using reinforcement learning

- **Content Moderator**: Detect offensive or inappropriate content in text, images, or videos

- **Anomaly Detector**: Detect patterns and anomalies in time series data

Example: Using Personalizer for Dynamic Recommendations

You define *rankable actions*, collect *reward scores* based on user feedback, and Personalizer adapts over time.

```
{
  "contextFeatures": [{"userType": "new", "device": "mobile"}],
  "actions": [
    {"id": "article1", "features": [{"topic": "sports"}]},
    {"id": "article2", "features": [{"topic": "tech"}]}
  ],
  "excludedActions": [],
  "eventId": "unique-event-id"
}
```

This kind of dynamic experience is critical for media apps, e-commerce, and personalization engines.

Deployment and Customization Options

Azure Cognitive Services offers:

- **Pre-trained models (as-a-service)** – Fast, simple, no training required

- **Custom models** – Train using your own labeled data (e.g., Custom Vision, LUIS)

- **Containers** – Deploy services on-premises or in your VNET for low latency and compliance

Running Cognitive Services in Containers:
Pull the container:

```
docker pull mcr.microsoft.com/azure-cognitive-
services/vision/computervision
```

1.

Run it locally:

```
docker run -it -p 5000:5000 \
  -e EULA=accept \
  -e ApiKey=your_key \
  mcr.microsoft.com/azure-cognitive-services/vision/computervision
```

2.

This provides flexibility to run services anywhere while maintaining control and meeting compliance requirements.

Integrating AI into Applications

Here are examples of how AI capabilities can be integrated into real-world apps:

- **Retail**: Product recommendation engine using Personalizer + Product Images with Custom Vision

- **Healthcare**: Medical transcription using Speech to Text, anomaly detection in patient vitals

- **Customer Support**: Chatbot powered by QnA Maker + LUIS + Text Analytics

- **Manufacturing**: Real-time defect detection with object detection from video streams

- **Education**: Real-time translation and closed captioning for multilingual classrooms

These integrations improve automation, efficiency, accessibility, and user engagement.

Monitoring, Governance, and Compliance

AI systems must be monitored, especially in regulated industries. Azure provides:

- **Metrics and Logs**: Usage stats, API latency, success/failure rates

- **Role-Based Access Control (RBAC)**: Secure access to models and endpoints

- **Private Endpoints and VNET Integration**: Prevent data exfiltration

- **Responsible AI Practices**: Transparency, bias detection, data anonymization

Use tools like **Azure Monitor**, **Azure Policy**, and **Microsoft Purview** for compliance tracking and auditing.

Best Practices

1. **Start with Pre-built APIs**
   Leverage Cognitive Services to prototype quickly before investing in custom models.

2. **Secure Your Keys and Endpoints**
   Use Key Vault to manage API keys and secrets.

3. **Evaluate Model Performance**
   Test AI features in your context. Use confidence scores and human-in-the-loop validation when needed.

4. **Use Containers for Isolation**
   Run models in containers when latency, compliance, or data residency is a concern.

5. **Monitor and Optimize**
   Track usage and retrain or refine models as your data changes over time.

6. **Combine Services**
   For richer applications, chain together multiple Cognitive Services (e.g., image captioning + language translation + speech synthesis).

Summary

Azure Cognitive Services democratize AI by making complex models accessible through simple APIs. Whether you're analyzing images, transcribing speech, understanding text, or personalizing content, these services offer a fast, scalable, and cost-effective way to add intelligence to your apps.

Key takeaways:

- Use pre-trained models for quick wins

- Explore containerized deployments for flexibility and control

- Integrate multiple services for rich, end-to-end experiences

- Prioritize governance and responsible AI practices

- Continually monitor and optimize your AI workflows

By mastering Azure Cognitive Services, developers and organizations can accelerate innovation, deliver smarter user experiences, and unlock the full potential of modern AI.

Hybrid Cloud with Azure Arc

As organizations increasingly operate in diverse environments—including on-premises data centers, multiple public clouds, and edge locations—there's a growing need for unified management, governance, and innovation across all infrastructure. Azure Arc is Microsoft's answer to this challenge, enabling a **hybrid and multicloud** approach with a single control plane for managing your entire digital estate.

Azure Arc extends Azure's management, security, and compliance capabilities beyond its native cloud to **any infrastructure**. It brings cloud-native capabilities to your on-premises servers, Kubernetes clusters, data services, and more—without requiring a full migration to Azure.

This section explores Azure Arc's architecture, capabilities, practical use cases, configuration steps, and integration strategies to help you build resilient, modern hybrid cloud solutions.

What is Azure Arc?

Azure Arc is a **bridge between Azure and external environments**. It lets you project non-Azure resources into the Azure Resource Manager (ARM) so they appear and behave like native Azure resources.

Azure Arc supports:

1. **Servers**: Windows and Linux machines outside Azure

2. **Kubernetes clusters**: Any CNCF-compliant cluster, including those on-premises or in AWS/GCP

3. **Azure data services**: Deploy and manage Azure SQL and PostgreSQL Hyperscale anywhere

4. **Applications**: Use GitOps, policy-driven deployments, and security for containerized apps

5. **VMware vSphere and Azure Stack HCI**: Extend Azure control over on-prem virtual machines

This unified model allows for centralized policy enforcement, security posture management, monitoring, and more.

Key Benefits of Azure Arc

- **Unified Operations**: Manage all resources from the Azure Portal, CLI, and APIs

- **Governance at Scale**: Apply Azure Policy, RBAC, and tagging to non-Azure resources

- **Consistent Security**: Integrate with Microsoft Defender, Azure Monitor, and Sentinel

- **Run Azure Services Anywhere**: Bring Azure SQL, Kubernetes, and ML services on-premises

- **DevOps-Ready**: Use GitOps for configuration and CI/CD across environments

Onboarding Machines to Azure Arc

Azure Arc for servers allows you to connect any physical or virtual machine to Azure for management.

Prerequisites

- Azure subscription

- Admin access to the machine

- Outbound HTTPS access

Onboarding a Linux Server

1. Generate the onboarding script from the Azure Portal or use CLI:

```
az connectedmachine onboarding \
  --resource-group ArcRG \
  --name arc-linux \
```

```
--location eastus
```

2. On the target server, install the Azure Connected Machine agent and run the onboarding script:

```
curl -o install.sh https://aka.ms/AzureConnectedMachineAgent
chmod +x install.sh
sudo ./install.sh

azcmagent connect \
  --resource-group ArcRG \
  --location eastus \
  --subscription-id <SUB_ID> \
  --tenant-id <TENANT_ID> \
  --resource-name arc-linux
```

After onboarding, the machine appears in the Azure Portal under "Azure Arc – Servers".

Azure Arc for Kubernetes

Arc enables you to manage Kubernetes clusters anywhere—whether in another cloud, on-premises, or at the edge.

Benefits:

- Apply Azure Policy to control configurations

- Monitor with Azure Monitor for containers

- Use GitOps to enforce desired state

- Central visibility and compliance tracking

Onboarding a Kubernetes Cluster

1. Register the provider:

```
az provider register --namespace Microsoft.Kubernetes
az provider register --namespace Microsoft.KubernetesConfiguration
```

2. Connect your cluster:

```
az connectedk8s connect \
  --name arc-k8s \
  --resource-group ArcRG \
  --location eastus \
  --cluster-type connectedClusters
```

3. Enable GitOps:

```
az k8sconfiguration create \
  --name config-policy \
  --cluster-name arc-k8s \
  --resource-group ArcRG \
  --cluster-type connectedClusters \
  --operator-instance-name flux \
  --operator-namespace flux-system \
  --repository-url https://github.com/myorg/arc-config \
  --scope cluster
```

Now, configuration changes pushed to your Git repo are automatically synced to the Kubernetes cluster via Flux.

Azure Arc-Enabled Data Services

With Azure Arc, you can run **Azure SQL Managed Instance** and **PostgreSQL Hyperscale** outside Azure while still benefiting from features like:

- Automated patching and backups

- Elastic scaling

- Built-in high availability

- Azure Portal and CLI integration

Prerequisites:

- Kubernetes cluster (AKS, OpenShift, or other supported platforms)

- Data controller deployed in connected or disconnected mode

Deploying SQL Managed Instance

1. Deploy the Arc Data Controller:

```
az arcdata dc create \
  --name arc-dc \
  --resource-group ArcRG \
  --k8s-namespace arc \
  --connectivity-mode indirect \
  --profile-name azure-arc
```

2. Create a SQL Managed Instance:

```
az arcdata sql mi create \
  --name arc-sql \
  --resource-group ArcRG \
  --k8s-namespace arc \
  --storage-class default \
  --cores-request 4 \
  --memory-request 16Gi
```

These services offer consistent database operations whether you're on-prem or in Azure.

Governance and Policy Management with Arc

Azure Arc enables you to extend Azure governance practices to your entire infrastructure.

Use Cases:

- Apply security baselines to on-prem VMs

- Enforce tag policies for external resources

- Monitor policy compliance across multicloud deployments

Example: Enforcing Tags on Arc-Connected Servers

```
{
```

```
  "if": {
    "allOf": [
      {
        "field": "type",
        "equals": "Microsoft.HybridCompute/machines"
      },
      {
        "field": "tags",
        "exists": "false"
      }
    ]
  },
  "then": {
    "effect": "audit"
  }
}
```

Deploy this policy using Azure Policy to maintain consistent metadata across your estate.

Security Integration

Arc-connected resources can be monitored and secured with Azure-native tools:

- **Microsoft Defender for Cloud**: Extended threat protection for Arc servers and Kubernetes

- **Azure Sentinel**: SIEM integration for incident detection and response

- **Azure Monitor**: Logs, metrics, and custom dashboards

Example: Enable Defender for Arc Machines

```
az security auto-provisioning-setting update \
  --name default \
  --auto-provision "On"
```

Ensure Arc-connected machines are enrolled in Microsoft Defender for advanced threat analytics.

DevOps and Automation with GitOps

Azure Arc integrates natively with **Flux**, a GitOps operator that maintains cluster state based on a Git repository.

GitOps Workflow:

1. Define Kubernetes manifests in Git

2. Connect Git repo to Arc-enabled cluster

3. Flux automatically syncs changes

4. Azure tracks configuration drift and compliance

This model aligns with infrastructure-as-code principles, allowing consistent CI/CD workflows across all environments.

Real-World Scenario: Hybrid Retail Infrastructure

Company: Global retailer with 1,000+ stores, each with local compute and legacy POS systems.

Challenges:

- Fragmented infrastructure

- Inconsistent security policies

- Lack of centralized monitoring

- High latency for cloud-only solutions

Azure Arc Solution:

- Arc-enabled servers for all store devices

- Arc-enabled Kubernetes on edge clusters for running containerized POS systems

- Centralized policy enforcement using Azure Policy

- GitOps for software updates

- Defender for Cloud for endpoint security

- Azure Monitor to visualize real-time health across all stores

Results:

- Unified visibility across hybrid environments

- Faster rollout of application updates

- Improved compliance and incident response

Best Practices

1. **Start with Pilot Projects**
   Onboard a small set of servers or clusters to validate architecture and governance.

2. **Use Tags and Management Groups**
   Organize resources logically for access control, billing, and policy enforcement.

3. **Automate Onboarding**
   Use scripts or infrastructure-as-code tools (ARM, Bicep, Terraform) to scale deployments.

4. **Monitor Compliance Continuously**
   Regularly audit connected resources using Azure Policy and Security Center.

5. **Secure API Access**
   Use managed identities and Key Vault to securely handle credentials and automation tokens.

6. **Document Everything**
   Maintain architecture diagrams, scripts, and policy definitions as part of your DevOps lifecycle.

Summary

Azure Arc unlocks the power of the Azure ecosystem for environments beyond Microsoft's cloud. By extending Azure management, security, and governance to on-premises and multicloud infrastructures, Arc enables a unified, modern operational model.

Key takeaways:

- Manage any resource, anywhere, from a single Azure control plane

- Apply consistent governance, security, and monitoring across your estate

- Run cloud-native services—like Azure SQL and Kubernetes—on your own infrastructure

- Accelerate innovation while maintaining compliance and control

In a world of increasingly complex and distributed systems, Azure Arc delivers the tools and flexibility required to embrace hybrid and multicloud strategies without compromise.

Chapter 9: Real-World Projects and Use Cases

Building a Serverless Web API

Serverless computing has redefined how developers build, deploy, and scale modern applications. In this real-world project, we'll walk through building a fully functional **serverless web API** using **Azure Functions**, integrated with **Azure Cosmos DB**, and secured using **Azure API Management**. This project serves as a foundational blueprint for building scalable, event-driven APIs without managing infrastructure.

The project will cover:

- Designing the architecture

- Setting up the environment

- Building the function-based endpoints

- Persisting data with Cosmos DB

- Securing access via API keys and optional Azure AD

- Monitoring and optimizing performance

- Deploying via CI/CD

Project Overview

We will build a simple task management API that allows users to:

- Create new tasks

- Retrieve all tasks

- Update a task

- Delete a task

The API will be stateless and exposed via HTTP triggers. Tasks will be stored in Cosmos DB as JSON documents. We'll use a RESTful pattern and deploy everything to Azure using CLI and optionally GitHub Actions.

Architecture

Components:

- **Azure Functions** – Stateless backend for handling API requests

- **Azure Cosmos DB** – NoSQL database for fast, scalable storage

- **Azure API Management** – Secure and expose APIs

- **Azure Monitor + Application Insights** – Observability and diagnostics

- **GitHub Actions** – CI/CD pipeline for automatic deployment

Step 1: Environment Setup

Create Resource Group

```
az group create --name taskApiRG --location eastus
```

Create Cosmos DB (SQL API)

```
az cosmosdb create \

  --name taskcosmosdb \

  --resource-group taskApiRG \

  --kind MongoDB
```

Create a Database and Collection

```
az cosmosdb mongodb database create \

  --account-name taskcosmosdb \

  --name tasksdb \

  --resource-group taskApiRG
```

```
az cosmosdb mongodb collection create \
  --account-name taskcosmosdb \
  --database-name tasksdb \
  --name tasks \
  --resource-group taskApiRG
```

Step 2: Create the Azure Function App

```
az functionapp create \
  --resource-group taskApiRG \
  --consumption-plan-location eastus \
  --runtime node \
  --functions-version 4 \
  --name taskserverlessapi \
  --storage-account taskapistorage
```

This creates a Node.js function app using the consumption plan, ideal for bursty HTTP traffic.

Step 3: Build Function Endpoints

We'll create four functions: CreateTask, GetTasks, UpdateTask, and DeleteTask.

CreateTask.js (HTTP POST)

```
module.exports = async function (context, req) {
    const task = req.body;
```

```javascript
if (!task || !task.title) {

    context.res = {

        status: 400,

        body: "Task title is required"

    };

    return;

}


task.id = new Date().getTime().toString(); // Unique ID


const cosmos = require("@azure/cosmos");

const { CosmosClient } = cosmos;


const client = new CosmosClient(process.env.COSMOS_CONN);

const container = client.database("tasksdb").container("tasks");


await container.items.create(task);


context.res = {

    status: 201,

    body: task

};

};
```

Set environment variable COSMOS_CONN using Azure CLI:

```
az functionapp config appsettings set \
  --name taskserverlessapi \
  --resource-group taskApiRG \
  --settings "COSMOS_CONN=<your-connection-string>"
```

GetTasks.js (HTTP GET)

```javascript
module.exports = async function (context, req) {
    const cosmos = require("@azure/cosmos");
    const { CosmosClient } = cosmos;


    const client = new CosmosClient(process.env.COSMOS_CONN);
    const container = client.database("tasksdb").container("tasks");


    const { resources } = await container.items.readAll().fetchAll();


    context.res = {
        status: 200,
        body: resources
    };
};
```

The `UpdateTask` and `DeleteTask` functions follow a similar pattern using the `container.item(id, partitionKey)` method.

Step 4: Test Locally and Deploy

Install dependencies

```
npm init -y

npm install @azure/cosmos
```

Deploy to Azure

```
func azure functionapp publish taskserverlessapi
```

Once deployed, test endpoints using Postman or curl:

```
curl -X POST
https://taskserverlessapi.azurewebsites.net/api/CreateTask \

  -H "Content-Type: application/json" \

  -d '{"title": "Finish writing book", "completed": false}'
```

Step 5: Secure the API

Enable Function-Level Authorization

Functions are private by default unless `authLevel` is set to `anonymous`. Add function keys for each endpoint:

```
az functionapp function keys list \

  --name taskserverlessapi \

  --resource-group taskApiRG \

  --function-name CreateTask
```

Add Azure API Management (Optional)

```
az apim create \

  --name taskapiapim \

  --resource-group taskApiRG \

  --publisher-email admin@example.com \

  --publisher-name MyCompany
```

Import the function endpoints as APIs. This allows:

- Centralized authentication (OAuth2, API Keys)

- Rate limiting and caching

- Versioning

Step 6: Monitor and Optimize

Enable Application Insights:

```
az monitor app-insights component create \

  --app taskapiinsights \

  --location eastus \

  --resource-group taskApiRG \

  --application-type web
```

```
az functionapp config appsettings set \

  --name taskserverlessapi \

  --resource-group taskApiRG \
```

```
--settings "APPINSIGHTS_INSTRUMENTATIONKEY=<your-key>"
```

Use the Azure Portal or `Log Analytics` to:

- View logs, traces, and custom events

- Create alerts on failure rates or latency

- Set performance budgets

Step 7: CI/CD with GitHub Actions

Create `.github/workflows/deploy.yml`:

```yaml
name: Azure Function CI/CD


on:
  push:
    branches:
      - main


jobs:
  build-deploy:
    runs-on: ubuntu-latest
    steps:
      - uses: actions/checkout@v2


      - name: Set up Node.js
        uses: actions/setup-node@v2
```

```
      with:

        node-version: '16'


    - run: npm install


    - name: Deploy to Azure Functions

      uses: Azure/functions-action@v1

      with:

        app-name: taskserverlessapi

        package: '.'

        publish-profile: ${{
secrets.AZURE_FUNCTIONAPP_PUBLISH_PROFILE }}
```

Store the publish profile as a GitHub Secret and commit the file to begin automatic deployments.

Summary and Learnings

By the end of this project, we've built and deployed a real-world serverless API using only Azure services. This project demonstrates:

- How to structure scalable, stateless APIs

- How to persist and query data with Cosmos DB

- How to use Functions for HTTP endpoints

- How to secure, monitor, and continuously deploy cloud applications

Scalability: The consumption plan ensures the backend auto-scales based on demand.

Cost-effectiveness: You only pay for what you use—ideal for startups and variable workloads.

Security: With managed identities and API Management, fine-grained access control is achievable.

Extensibility: New features can be added simply by creating more functions and endpoints.

This pattern forms a repeatable foundation for countless applications—from IoT and analytics backends to customer-facing mobile app APIs and beyond.

Migrating a Legacy App to Azure

Legacy applications often form the backbone of business operations, but they are typically limited by outdated infrastructure, inflexible architectures, and scalability challenges. Migrating these applications to Microsoft Azure unlocks modern capabilities such as global scalability, enhanced security, high availability, and integration with DevOps practices.

In this project, we will walk through the process of migrating a monolithic on-premises web application to Azure using a phased strategy. We'll explore architectural considerations, tooling, security, database migration, and cloud-native enhancement opportunities. This hands-on scenario is designed to reflect what many enterprises face during digital transformation initiatives.

Legacy App Overview

Let's assume the legacy application is a .NET Framework-based internal line-of-business (LOB) web application. It runs on IIS, uses an on-premises SQL Server database, stores files locally, and has minimal observability or scalability.

Our goal is to migrate it to Azure, modernize it incrementally, and maintain operational continuity.

Step 1: Assessment and Planning

Before any migration, we must assess the app and define a migration plan.

Tools:

- **Azure Migrate**: Discovery, assessment, and migration of on-prem servers and workloads

- **App Service Migration Assistant**: Analyze web apps and determine PaaS readiness

- **Data Migration Assistant (DMA)**: Assesses SQL Server compatibility with Azure SQL

Assessment Workflow:

1. Inventory components: web servers, databases, dependencies

2. Identify unsupported frameworks or libraries

3. Determine migration strategy (rehost, refactor, rearchitect)

4. Plan for DNS, authentication, integrations, and downtime

Example Azure Migrate setup:

```
az migrate project create \
  --resource-group LegacyMigrationRG \
  --name LegacyMigrateProject \
  --location eastus
```

Step 2: Choosing a Migration Strategy

There are multiple migration strategies depending on risk tolerance, timelines, and technical debt.

Strategy	Description	Azure Target
Rehost	"Lift and shift" without code changes	Azure VMs or App Service
Refactor	Modify parts to fit PaaS architecture	App Service, Azure SQL
Rearchitect	Break into microservices or modern patterns	AKS, Azure Functions

Rebuild   Complete rewrite on cloud-native stack   Azure App Services

For this example, we'll **rehost the web app** and **refactor the database**, a balanced approach.

Step 3: Migrating the Web Application

We will deploy the app to **Azure App Service**, a fully managed PaaS for web applications.

Web App Preparation

1. Clean up web.config (remove hardcoded connections, file paths)

2. Externalize app settings and connection strings

3. Verify .NET Framework version compatibility (App Service supports up to 4.8)

Use App Service Migration Assistant

Download from https://appmigration.microsoft.com and run it on the source server. It generates a compatibility report and guides you through migration.

Manual Deployment (Alternative)

1. Create App Service and plan:

```
az appservice plan create \
  --name LegacyPlan \
  --resource-group LegacyMigrationRG \
  --sku P1v2 \
  --is-linux false
```

2. Create the web app:

```
az webapp create \
```

```
--resource-group LegacyMigrationRG \

--plan LegacyPlan \

--name legacywebapp \

--runtime "DOTNET|4.8"
```

3. Deploy via ZIP:

```
az webapp deployment source config-zip \

  --resource-group LegacyMigrationRG \

  --name legacywebapp \

  --src legacyapp.zip
```

4. Configure app settings:

```
az webapp config appsettings set \

  --name legacywebapp \

  --resource-group LegacyMigrationRG \

  --settings "ConnectionStrings__DefaultConnection=your-azure-sql-
connection-string"
```

Step 4: Migrating the Database

Azure SQL Database is the preferred PaaS destination for SQL Server workloads. It offers high availability, backups, and automatic tuning.

Assess Compatibility with DMA

Run **Data Migration Assistant** to detect deprecated features or compatibility issues. Download from https://aka.ms/dma.

Use Azure Database Migration Service (DMS)

1. Create an Azure SQL Server and database:

```
az sql server create \

  --name legacysqlserver \

  --resource-group LegacyMigrationRG \

  --location eastus \

  --admin-user sqladmin \

  --admin-password YourPassword123!


az sql db create \

  --resource-group LegacyMigrationRG \

  --server legacysqlserver \

  --name legacydb \

  --service-objective S1
```

2. Create DMS instance and run migration steps via the Azure portal. Choose online or offline migration based on whether downtime is acceptable.

Step 5: Handling File Storage

Legacy apps often store files locally. In Azure, use **Azure Blob Storage**.

1. Create a storage account:

```
az storage account create \

  --name legacystorage \

  --resource-group LegacyMigrationRG \
```

```
--sku Standard_LRS \

--kind StorageV2
```

2. Update your app to use Blob APIs for file uploads/downloads.

Example (C#):

```
var blobServiceClient = new BlobServiceClient(connectionString);

var containerClient =
blobServiceClient.GetBlobContainerClient("files");

await containerClient.UploadBlobAsync("document.pdf", fileStream);
```

Step 6: Securing the Application

Security in Azure should be **layered** and leverage identity providers.

Azure Identity

- Use **Managed Identity** to access Azure SQL without passwords

- Integrate with **Azure AD** for user authentication

Networking

- Restrict access using **Access Restrictions**

- Place app behind **Azure Front Door** or **Application Gateway**

- Enforce HTTPS and redirect HTTP automatically

Secrets Management

Use **Azure Key Vault** for storing secrets like database connection strings or storage keys.

```
az keyvault create --name legacyvault --resource-group
LegacyMigrationRG
```

```
az keyvault secret set --vault-name legacyvault --name "StorageKey"
--value "abc123"
```

Step 7: Observability and Optimization

Legacy apps often lack monitoring. Azure provides:

- **Application Insights** for performance and error tracking
- **Azure Monitor** for platform metrics and logs
- **Log Analytics** for advanced queries

Enable Insights:

```
az monitor app-insights component create \

  --app legacyappinsights \

  --location eastus \

  --resource-group LegacyMigrationRG \

  --application-type web
```

Configure the Instrumentation Key in app settings or use the SDK.

Step 8: CI/CD Pipeline Integration

Use **GitHub Actions** or **Azure DevOps** to automate builds and deployments.

Sample GitHub Action:

```
name: Deploy Legacy App


on:

  push:
```

```yaml
    branches: [ main ]


jobs:

  deploy:

    runs-on: windows-latest

    steps:

      - uses: actions/checkout@v2


      - name: Publish App

        run: |

          dotnet build

          dotnet publish -c Release -o publish_output


      - name: Deploy to Azure

        uses: Azure/webapps-deploy@v2

        with:

          app-name: legacywebapp

          slot-name: production

          publish-profile: ${{ secrets.AZURE_WEBAPP_PUBLISH_PROFILE }}

          package: publish_output
```

Step 9: Post-Migration Enhancements

Once migrated, you can begin refactoring parts of the app to take advantage of cloud-native patterns:

- Migrate some components to **Azure Functions**

- Use **Event Grid** or **Service Bus** for decoupled communication

- Replace scheduled tasks with **Logic Apps** or **Durable Functions**

- Introduce **feature flags** with Azure App Configuration

This gradual modernization keeps business running while incrementally improving the codebase.

Summary and Lessons Learned

Migrating a legacy application to Azure is a high-impact modernization project. This real-world case showed how to transition from a monolithic, on-premises stack to a cloud-first environment using proven Azure services.

Key takeaways:

- Assess thoroughly before migrating; tooling like Azure Migrate and DMA reduces surprises.

- Start with rehosting, then refactor incrementally.

- Use Azure App Service, Azure SQL, Blob Storage, and Key Vault for a robust foundation.

- Layer in monitoring, security, and automation from day one.

- Embrace DevOps and CI/CD to accelerate future releases.

This migration approach allows organizations to unlock the full value of Azure while controlling risk and maintaining agility throughout their digital transformation journey.

Setting Up a Secure Multi-Region App

Designing and deploying a secure, highly available application that spans multiple Azure regions is a critical step for enterprises aiming to deliver global services with minimal downtime and data sovereignty compliance. This real-world project demonstrates how to set up a multi-region architecture in Azure that is resilient, secure, performant, and scalable.

In this walkthrough, we'll architect and implement a multi-region web application using Azure App Services, Azure Front Door, Azure SQL with geo-replication, and other supporting services. We'll also apply enterprise-grade security controls, monitoring, and automated failover.

Objectives

- Deploy application instances in multiple Azure regions

- Ensure automatic failover and traffic routing based on health and geography

- Protect resources using zero-trust security principles

- Comply with data residency requirements

- Automate deployment and recovery processes

High-Level Architecture

1. **Azure App Service (Web App)** in two regions: Primary and Secondary

2. **Azure SQL Database** with active geo-replication

3. **Azure Blob Storage** with Geo-Redundant Storage (GRS)

4. **Azure Front Door** for global traffic routing, WAF, SSL offload, and health checks

5. **Azure Key Vault** for secrets management

6. **Azure Monitor and Log Analytics** for centralized monitoring

7. **Azure Application Gateway** (optional) for internal routing

Regions: East US (Primary) and West Europe (Secondary)

Step 1: Create Resource Groups in Both Regions

```
az group create --name MultiRegionAppUSEast --location eastus

az group create --name MultiRegionAppWEU --location westeurope
```

Step 2: Deploy Web Apps

We'll deploy the same application to both regions using Azure App Service.

Create App Service Plans

```
az appservice plan create --name WebPlanUSEast --resource-group
MultiRegionAppUSEast --sku P1v2 --is-linux

az appservice plan create --name WebPlanWEU --resource-group
MultiRegionAppWEU --sku P1v2 --is-linux
```

Create Web Apps

```
az webapp create --name app-primary-east --plan WebPlanUSEast --
resource-group MultiRegionAppUSEast --runtime "DOTNET|6.0"

az webapp create --name app-secondary-weu --plan WebPlanWEU --
resource-group MultiRegionAppWEU --runtime "DOTNET|6.0"
```

Deploy your application package to both using Zip Deploy or CI/CD pipelines.

Step 3: Configure Azure SQL Geo-Replication

Create a primary SQL server and database:

```
az sql server create --name sqlservereast --resource-group
MultiRegionAppUSEast --location eastus --admin-user sqladmin --
admin-password 'YourPassword123!'

az sql db create --name appdb --server sqlservereast --resource-
group MultiRegionAppUSEast --service-objective S1
```

Create a secondary SQL server:

```
az sql server create --name sqlserverweu --resource-group
MultiRegionAppWEU --location westeurope --admin-user sqladmin --
admin-password 'YourPassword123!'
```

Enable geo-replication:

```
az sql db replica create --name appdb --partner-server sqlserverweu
--resource-group MultiRegionAppUSEast --server sqlservereast --
partner-resource-group MultiRegionAppWEU
```

Configure your app settings with primary and secondary connection strings. The application should detect failures and switch accordingly, or use retry logic.

Step 4: Setup Azure Front Door

Azure Front Door provides global HTTP load balancing and automatic failover.

Create Front Door Profile

```
az network front-door profile create --name AppFrontDoor --resource-
group MultiRegionAppUSEast --sku Premium_AzureFrontDoor --location
global
```

Create Origin Groups

```
az network front-door origin-group create \

  --resource-group MultiRegionAppUSEast \

  --profile-name AppFrontDoor \

  --origin-group-name appOrigins \

  --probe-request-type GET \

  --probe-protocol Http \

  --probe-interval 10 \

  --probe-path "/health" \
```

```
  --sample-size 4 \

  --successful-samples-required 3
```

Add Origins (Web Apps)

```
az network front-door origin create \

  --resource-group MultiRegionAppUSEast \

  --profile-name AppFrontDoor \

  --origin-group-name appOrigins \

  --origin-name eastOrigin \

  --host-name app-primary-east.azurewebsites.net \

  --priority 1


az network front-door origin create \

  --resource-group MultiRegionAppUSEast \

  --profile-name AppFrontDoor \

  --origin-group-name appOrigins \

  --origin-name weuOrigin \

  --host-name app-secondary-weu.azurewebsites.net \

  --priority 2
```

Add Route

```
az network front-door route create \

  --resource-group MultiRegionAppUSEast \

  --profile-name AppFrontDoor \

  --endpoint-name mainEndpoint \
```

```
--route-name appRoute \

--origin-group appOrigins \

--custom-domains myapp.example.com \

--https-redirect Enabled \

--protocols Https
```

Now, Front Door will route traffic to the East US app, and failover to the West Europe app if health checks fail.

Step 5: Secure with Key Vault and Managed Identity

Create a Key Vault in each region:

```
az keyvault create --name keyvaulteast --resource-group
MultiRegionAppUSEast --location eastus

az keyvault create --name keyvaultweu --resource-group
MultiRegionAppWEU --location westeurope
```

Add a secret:

```
az keyvault secret set --vault-name keyvaulteast --name
"DbConnection" --value "Server=..."
```

Assign managed identity to web app and grant access to Key Vault:

```
az webapp identity assign --name app-primary-east --resource-group
MultiRegionAppUSEast

az keyvault set-policy --name keyvaulteast --object-id <IDENTITY_ID>
--secret-permissions get list
```

In your code, retrieve secrets using Azure SDK with DefaultAzureCredential.

Step 6: Monitoring and Alerts

Enable Application Insights:

```
az monitor app-insights component create \

  --app myappinsights \

  --location eastus \

  --resource-group MultiRegionAppUSEast \

  --application-type web
```

Link Insights to both Web Apps and configure alerts:

- High response time

- Failed requests > threshold

- Backend health check failures (from Front Door)

Set up Log Analytics workspace for cross-region insights and query with KQL.

Step 7: Automate with GitHub Actions

Use separate deployment pipelines for each region. Add gates for manual approval or health checks.

```
name: Deploy Multi-Region WebApp


on:

  push:

    branches: [ main ]


jobs:

  deploy-east:
```

```yaml
    runs-on: ubuntu-latest

    steps:

      - uses: actions/checkout@v2

      - name: Azure Login

        uses: azure/login@v1

        with:

          creds: ${{ secrets.AZURE_CREDENTIALS }}

      - name: Deploy to East

        uses: azure/webapps-deploy@v2

        with:

          app-name: app-primary-east

          package: .


  deploy-weu:

    needs: deploy-east

    runs-on: ubuntu-latest

    steps:

      - uses: actions/checkout@v2

      - name: Deploy to West

        uses: azure/webapps-deploy@v2

        with:

          app-name: app-secondary-weu

          package: .
```

Use Azure DevOps if integrating into existing enterprise delivery pipelines.

Step 8: Enhancements

After initial setup, consider:

- **Geo-aware session state** with Azure Redis Cache

- **Read replicas** for regional data access

- **BGP-based DNS routing** using Traffic Manager for DNS-level failover

- **Compliance tooling** with Microsoft Purview for data governance

- **Security hardening** with Conditional Access and Defender for App Service

---

Summary

A secure, multi-region Azure app architecture ensures business continuity, low latency for global users, and compliance with regulatory demands. This solution leverages PaaS resources like App Service, SQL, and Front Door to deliver robust HA/DR capabilities with minimal operational overhead.

Key Learnings:

- Azure Front Door is critical for real-time global failover and traffic steering.

- Active geo-replication enables high availability for mission-critical databases.

- Securing secrets with Key Vault and managed identity eliminates key sprawl.

- Centralized monitoring gives you unified control over global operations.

- CI/CD enables consistent and repeatable deployments across regions.

This design can be scaled and adapted for enterprise SaaS apps, public APIs, content portals, and any critical system requiring global availability and resilience.

Hosting a Scalable E-commerce Platform

Building a scalable e-commerce platform on Azure involves integrating a wide range of cloud-native services to handle dynamic workloads, ensure high availability, maintain security, and deliver fast, seamless shopping experiences globally. This real-world project focuses on deploying an enterprise-grade e-commerce application using microservices, distributed data, caching, and resilient architecture across the Azure ecosystem.

In this walkthrough, we'll design, implement, and secure a modern e-commerce stack on Azure that supports modularity, global traffic, and peak-season surges while remaining maintainable and cost-effective.

Key Requirements

- Scalable product catalog and checkout system

- User authentication and profile management

- Shopping cart and session handling

- Payment gateway integration

- Order history and inventory management

- Resilient, low-latency front end

- Multi-region failover and CDN

- Real-time monitoring and automated deployments

Architecture Overview

Core Components:

1. **Frontend**: Static web app (React/Angular/Vue) hosted via Azure Static Web Apps or Front Door + Blob Storage

2. **Backend APIs**: Azure App Services or Azure Kubernetes Service (AKS)

3. **Authentication**: Azure Active Directory B2C

4. **Database**: Azure SQL Database (relational) + Azure Cosmos DB (NoSQL product catalog)

5. **Queueing**: Azure Service Bus or Azure Event Grid for order processing

6. **Caching**: Azure Cache for Redis

7. **Storage**: Azure Blob Storage for images, invoices, etc.

8. **Search**: Azure Cognitive Search for product discovery

9. **Monitoring**: Azure Monitor + Application Insights

10. **DevOps**: GitHub Actions or Azure DevOps Pipelines for CI/CD

Step 1: Create the Frontend

Option 1: Azure Static Web Apps

```
az staticwebapp create \

  --name ecommercefrontend \

  --resource-group ecommerceRG \

  --source https://github.com/your-org/ecommerce-frontend \

  --location "East US" \

  --app-location "/" \

  --output-location "build"
```

Option 2: Azure Blob + CDN

Upload static files to Blob Storage and link with Azure CDN:

```
az storage account create --name ecomstorage --resource-group
ecommerceRG --location eastus

az storage container create --account-name ecomstorage --name \$web
--public-access blob

az storage blob upload-batch --source ./dist --destination \$web --
account-name ecomstorage
```

Step 2: Set Up Authentication

Use **Azure AD B2C** for customer authentication:

```
az ad b2c directory create --display-name "EComB2C"
```

Configure sign-up/sign-in policies, social logins (Google, Facebook), and MFA.

Frontend will use MSAL.js or equivalent to authenticate users and retrieve access tokens.

Step 3: Deploy Backend Microservices

Split backend into services like:

- Product Catalog
- Cart Service
- Order Service
- Payment Service
- User Service

Option 1: Azure App Service

Each service can be a separate Function App or App Service:

```
az webapp create --resource-group ecommerceRG \

  --plan ecommercePlan \

  --name cartserviceapi \

  --runtime "DOTNET|6.0"
```

Option 2: Azure Kubernetes Service (AKS)

Use AKS for containerized microservices:

```
az aks create \

  --resource-group ecommerceRG \
```

```
--name ecommerceaks \

--node-count 3 \

--enable-addons monitoring \

--generate-ssh-keys
```

Deploy using Helm or manifests.

Step 4: Database Design and Setup

Azure SQL (Transactional Data)

```
az sql server create --name sqlserverecom --resource-group
ecommerceRG \

  --location eastus --admin-user sqladmin --admin-password
P@ssword123


az sql db create --resource-group ecommerceRG --server sqlserverecom
\

  --name ecommerceorders --service-objective S1
```

Store transactional data like orders, payments, users.

Cosmos DB (Product Catalog)

```
az cosmosdb create --name productcatalogdb --resource-group
ecommerceRG --kind MongoDB

az cosmosdb mongodb database create --account-name productcatalogdb
--name products

az cosmosdb mongodb collection create --account-name
productcatalogdb --database-name products --name catalog
```

Store semi-structured product data for fast access and flexible schema.

Step 5: Integrate Queueing for Resilient Workflows

Use **Azure Service Bus** to decouple operations like order placement and inventory updates.

```
az servicebus namespace create --resource-group ecommerceRG --name
ecommercebus

az servicebus queue create --resource-group ecommerceRG --namespace-
name ecommercebus --name orders
```

Backend services listen to events and handle processing asynchronously.

Step 6: Enable Caching

Use Azure Redis to cache product details and shopping cart data.

```
az redis create \

  --name ecommercecache \

  --resource-group ecommerceRG \

  --location eastus \

  --sku Basic \

  --vm-size C1
```

Services use Redis to store session state and reduce database load.

Step 7: Add Search Capability

Use **Azure Cognitive Search** for product search and filtering.

```
az search service create --name ecomsearch --resource-group
ecommerceRG --sku Basic --location eastus
```

```
az search index create --service-name ecomsearch --name products \

  --fields
name:string,description:string,price:double,available:bool
```

Populate from Cosmos DB or via ETL pipelines. Provide autocomplete, filtering, and relevance tuning.

Step 8: Secure the Platform

API Protection

- Use **Azure API Management** for rate limiting and central policy enforcement.

- Enable **JWT validation** for B2C-issued tokens.

- Use **private endpoints** for database and storage.

Key Vault

Store secrets, keys, and certificates securely:

```
az keyvault create --name ecomkv --resource-group ecommerceRG

az keyvault secret set --name SqlPassword --vault-name ecomkv --
value 'P@ssword123'
```

Backend services authenticate via Managed Identity.

Step 9: Monitoring and Observability

Enable Application Insights for each service:

```
az monitor app-insights component create \

  --app ecomappinsights \

  --location eastus \

  --resource-group ecommerceRG \
```

```
--application-type web
```

Set up dashboards, alerts for:

- High response time

- Shopping cart abandonment

- Order processing delays

- Queue length and dead-letter messages

Use Log Analytics to correlate telemetry and analyze root causes.

Step 10: Automate CI/CD with GitHub Actions

Use GitHub Actions to deploy both frontend and backend.

Sample deploy-backend.yml

```yaml
name: Deploy Cart Service


on:

  push:

    paths:

      - 'services/cart/**'


jobs:

  deploy:

    runs-on: ubuntu-latest

    steps:

      - uses: actions/checkout@v2
```

```
    - name: Deploy to App Service

      uses: Azure/webapps-deploy@v2

      with:

        app-name: cartserviceapi

        package: services/cart/

        publish-profile: ${{ secrets.CART_SERVICE_PUBLISH_PROFILE
}}
}}
```

Deploy static frontend via similar action using azure/static-web-apps-deploy.

Step 11: Scaling and Global Distribution

Autoscaling

Enable autoscale on App Service or AKS:

```
az monitor autoscale create \

  --resource-group ecommerceRG \

  --resource cartserviceapi \

  --resource-type Microsoft.Web/sites \

  --min-count 1 --max-count 10 --count 2
```

Front Door + CDN

Accelerate and secure global access:

```
az network front-door create \

  --resource-group ecommerceRG \

  --name ecomfrontdoor \

  --backend-address ecommercefrontend.z22.web.core.windows.net
```

Summary

This project demonstrates how to architect and deploy a full-scale, production-ready e-commerce platform on Azure. With microservices, event-driven communication, distributed databases, and cloud-native security, the solution is designed for agility and growth.

Key Takeaways:

- Use App Services or AKS for backend services depending on scale

- Store structured data in Azure SQL and flexible catalogs in Cosmos DB

- Decouple workflows with Service Bus for resilience

- Accelerate search with Azure Cognitive Search

- Leverage API Management, Key Vault, and Azure AD B2C for security

- Integrate CI/CD pipelines for continuous deployment and scaling

By combining these services, developers can build performant, reliable, and secure e-commerce platforms that support modern expectations and global demand.

Chapter 10: Preparing for Azure Certification

Overview of Azure Certification Tracks

Microsoft Azure certifications have become one of the most respected and in-demand credentials in the cloud computing world. These certifications validate your skills in designing, deploying, managing, and securing cloud solutions using Microsoft Azure technologies. Whether you're a beginner looking to enter the industry or a seasoned professional aiming to advance your career, there's an Azure certification tailored to your goals.

This section provides a comprehensive overview of the Microsoft Azure certification tracks, from fundamentals to expert levels, including how they align with various roles in the tech industry. We'll examine the purpose, audience, prerequisites, exam structure, and real-world value of each certification path.

Certification Levels and Roles

Microsoft organizes its certifications into **three primary levels**:

1. **Fundamentals** – For beginners with limited or no cloud experience

2. **Associate** – For professionals with some hands-on experience

3. **Expert** – For advanced professionals and architects

Each certification corresponds to specific **job roles**, such as:

- Azure Administrator

- Developer

- Solution Architect

- Security Engineer

- DevOps Engineer

- Data Engineer

- AI Engineer

- Network Engineer

Azure Fundamentals (Beginner Level)

Certification: AZ-900: Microsoft Certified: Azure Fundamentals

Who it's for: Anyone new to cloud computing or Azure. Ideal for salespeople, marketers, project managers, and junior IT staff.

Skills measured:

- Cloud concepts (IaaS, PaaS, SaaS)

- Core Azure services and products

- Azure pricing, SLAs, and lifecycle

- Governance, compliance, and trust

- Azure identity, access, and security

Exam format: ~40–60 questions; multiple-choice, drag-and-drop, case studies

Preparation time: 1–2 weeks with 10–15 hours of study

Value: AZ-900 is not a prerequisite for other exams but provides a solid foundation and confidence boost.

Role-Based Associate Certifications

Microsoft offers several associate-level certifications targeting hands-on practitioners.

AZ-104: Microsoft Certified: Azure Administrator Associate

Target role: System administrators, cloud administrators, DevOps engineers

Key skills:

- Managing Azure identities and governance

- Deploying and managing Azure compute resources

- Configuring virtual networks and connectivity

- Monitoring and backing up resources

- Implementing storage solutions

Exam tips:

- Focus on the Azure Portal, CLI, and ARM templates

- Get hands-on with deploying VMs, configuring VNets, and setting up NSGs

- Practice setting up Azure Monitor and alerts

AZ-204: Microsoft Certified: Azure Developer Associate

Target role: Software developers building cloud-based applications

Key skills:

- Developing Azure compute solutions (App Services, Functions)

- Integrating storage (Blob, Cosmos DB, SQL)

- Securing apps with identity and access control

- Monitoring, logging, and troubleshooting

- Connecting to Azure services via APIs and SDKs

Recommended experience:

- 1–2 years of development experience

- Familiarity with REST, HTTP, and JSON

- Some experience with authentication (OAuth, OpenID Connect)

AZ-400: Microsoft Certified: DevOps Engineer Expert

Target role: DevOps engineers who manage pipelines and continuous delivery processes

Prerequisites: Must first earn AZ-104 or AZ-204

Key skills:

- Designing CI/CD pipelines using GitHub Actions and Azure DevOps

- Implementing security and compliance

- Managing infrastructure as code (ARM, Bicep, Terraform)

- Monitoring and feedback loops

- Container orchestration (AKS, Docker)

Highly recommended: Automate deployments using YAML and GitHub repositories; work with Azure Repos and Boards.

AZ-500: Microsoft Certified: Azure Security Engineer Associate

Target role: Cybersecurity professionals and cloud security architects

Skills measured:

- Managing identity and access

- Securing networks and workloads

- Managing security operations and threat protection

- Implementing secure data solutions

Tools to study:

- Microsoft Defender for Cloud

- Azure Sentinel (SIEM)

- Azure Security Center

- Key Vault, RBAC, and Conditional Access

Expert-Level Certifications

Expert-level certifications demonstrate deep architectural and strategic knowledge.

AZ-305: Microsoft Certified: Azure Solutions Architect Expert

Prerequisites: No mandatory prerequisite, but AZ-104 is highly recommended.

Ideal for: Senior cloud architects and consultants who design end-to-end Azure solutions

Key focus areas:

- Designing infrastructure, networking, security, and identity solutions

- Planning for high availability, DR, and scalability

- Integrating governance and cost optimization

- Making design decisions based on customer requirements

Real-world value: The AZ-305 is one of the most respected certifications for cloud architects in enterprise environments.

DP-203: Microsoft Certified: Azure Data Engineer Associate

Target role: Data engineers responsible for building and managing data pipelines

Core skills:

- Ingesting data with Azure Data Factory and Azure Synapse

- Designing data storage and analytics solutions

- Implementing data security and compliance

- Optimizing data processing performance

Hands-on requirements:

- Familiarity with SQL, Python, and big data concepts

- Experience with Azure Databricks, Synapse, and ADLS Gen2

Specialized Certifications

Additional certifications are available for specialized domains:

- **AI-102** – Azure AI Engineer

- **DP-100** – Azure Data Scientist

- **SC-300** – Identity and Access Administrator

- **SC-200** – Security Operations Analyst

- **MB-260** – Customer Data Platform Specialist (Dynamics + Azure)

These certifications are excellent for professionals working in niche areas of Azure.

Certification Benefits

- **Career growth**: Certifications enhance your resume and visibility to employers

- **Validation**: Proves your hands-on Azure experience and knowledge

- **Confidence**: Improves your ability to design and deliver real-world cloud solutions

- **Community**: Join the Microsoft Learn and Tech Community to network with peers and mentors

- **Perks**: Discounts on future exams, LinkedIn badge, and recognition in the Microsoft ecosystem

Choosing the Right Path

Use this decision tree as a guide:

- **New to cloud?** → AZ-900 (Fundamentals)

- **System admin or IT Pro?** → AZ-104 (Administrator)

- **Developer?** → AZ-204 (Developer)

- **Security-focused?** → AZ-500 (Security Engineer)

- **Want to become an architect?** → AZ-305 (Solutions Architect)

- **Interested in data?** → DP-203 (Data Engineer) or DP-100 (Data Scientist)

- **DevOps engineer?** → AZ-400 (DevOps Expert)

Once you choose your track, build a study plan and register through Microsoft's Certification Dashboard.

Summary

Microsoft Azure offers a structured certification path for every professional level and job role. Whether you're validating foundational knowledge or proving your expertise in architecting enterprise solutions, there is a certification designed to fit your journey.

Key takeaways:

- Start with fundamentals to build confidence

- Associate-level exams test hands-on ability and are often role-specific

- Expert certifications are highly valuable for senior and strategic roles

- Use labs, sandbox environments, and practice tests for effective preparation

- Stay current—certifications are updated regularly to reflect Azure's evolving platform

Certifications are not just milestones; they're stepping stones in your continuous Azure learning path.

Study Resources and Practice Exams

Preparing for an Azure certification exam requires more than just reading documentation. It involves structured study, hands-on practice, simulated exams, and regular assessment of your progress. This section presents a curated list of resources, platforms, strategies, and practical steps you can follow to prepare effectively for any Microsoft Azure certification— from AZ-900 to AZ-305 and beyond.

We will cover official resources, community contributions, third-party training platforms, hands-on labs, certification sandboxes, exam simulators, books, and tips on how to build a study schedule that works for you.

Microsoft Learn: The Official Starting Point

Microsoft Learn is the most comprehensive and official source of learning material for Azure. It's completely free, interactive, and includes assessments and guided exercises.

Features:

- Self-paced modules organized by certification

- Interactive browser-based environments (no setup required)

- Progress tracking and achievements

- Integrated with your Microsoft account and certifications

How to Use:

1. Visit https://learn.microsoft.com/training/azure

2. Search for your target certification (e.g., "AZ-104 learning path")

3. Bookmark relevant learning paths

4. Complete each module and track progress

5. Earn badges and XP as you go

Each certification exam has a dedicated **collection** of modules aligned with the skills measured in the exam guide.

Microsoft Documentation and Exam Guides

The official documentation is essential for in-depth understanding and clarity on topics such as:

- Azure CLI and PowerShell commands

- Resource Manager templates

- Service limitations and pricing

- Troubleshooting and diagnostics

Every certification exam has a corresponding **exam skills outline** PDF which can be found on the Microsoft Learn site (e.g., https://learn.microsoft.com/certifications).

Example: AZ-204 skills outline includes:

- Implement IaaS solutions

- Develop for Azure Storage

- Implement Azure Security

- Monitor, troubleshoot, and optimize Azure solutions

Tip: Print or save the PDF and check off each topic as you master it.

Hands-On Labs and Sandboxes

Azure exams are practical by design, and passing them requires more than theoretical knowledge. You must be comfortable using the Azure Portal, CLI, ARM templates, and Azure DevOps.

Free Tools and Labs:

- **Microsoft Learn sandbox**: Included in most modules. No Azure subscription required.

- **GitHub Labs by Microsoft**: Repositories such as `Azure/azure-quickstart-templates` and `Azure-Samples` offer real-world ARM/Bicep/Function examples.

- **Cloud Academy**: Offers interactive playgrounds with built-in cloud environments.

- **Whizlabs Labs**: Simulated Azure environments for realistic practice tasks.

Tip: Create a free Azure account at https://azure.microsoft.com/free which gives you:

- $200 credit for 30 days

- 12 months of popular services free

- Always free tier for select services

Use this account to deploy virtual networks, app services, function apps, Cosmos DB, storage accounts, and more.

Video Courses and Bootcamps

If you prefer visual and structured content, video courses are an excellent way to supplement your reading.

Recommended Platforms:

- **Pluralsight**

    - Offers complete Azure certification paths

    - Courses taught by Microsoft MVPs and cloud architects

    - Free access often provided during Microsoft events

- **LinkedIn Learning**

    - High-quality courses on AZ-900, AZ-104, AZ-204, AZ-500, and more

    - Includes practice quizzes and course certificates

- **Udemy**

    - Popular for affordability and depth

    - Look for instructors like Scott Duffy, Alan Rodrigues, and Nick Colyer

    - Many courses include downloadable study guides and bonus quizzes

- **A Cloud Guru / Linux Academy**

    - Excellent for immersive, hands-on labs and real-world scenarios

    - Expensive but enterprise-grade content

Books and Study Guides

Books remain valuable for in-depth study, especially if you prefer structured learning.

Top Picks:

- *Exam Ref AZ-104 Microsoft Azure Administrator* by Harshul Patel – Official Microsoft Press

- *Exam Ref AZ-305 Microsoft Azure Solutions Architect* by Santiago Fernandez Munoz – Great for expert-level prep

- *Microsoft Azure Fundamentals Certification and Beyond* by Steve Miles – Comprehensive AZ-900 guide

- *Cloud Adoption Framework for Azure* – Free eBook from Microsoft for governance and strategy

Tip: Use books to cover theory and then reinforce with hands-on labs.

Practice Exams and Simulators

Practice exams help you test your readiness, identify weak spots, and get comfortable with the format and pressure of a timed exam.

Recommended Platforms:

- **MeasureUp** – Official Microsoft partner for practice tests

  - Mimics the real exam environment closely

  - Offers feedback and explanations

  - Expensive, but very accurate

- **Whizlabs**

  - Large pool of questions

  - Timed tests and topic-wise quizzes

  - Affordable, but sometimes less accurate to real exams

- **Tutorials Dojo / Jon Bonso**

  - Highly rated practice sets for AZ-900, AZ-104, AZ-204, AZ-500

  - Detailed explanations and reference links

- **ExamTopics**

    - Community-contributed questions (use with caution)

    - Not always up-to-date, but helpful for checking concepts

How to Use Practice Tests:

1. Take a baseline practice test before studying.

2. Review all incorrect answers and learn why.

3. Revisit documentation on weak areas.

4. Retake the test weekly to measure improvement.

Building a Study Plan

A successful study plan balances reading, practice, review, and testing. Use this simple weekly model for 4–6 weeks of preparation:

Week	Focus Area	Actions
1	Core Concepts & Services	Read documentation, complete Learn modules
2	Hands-on Lab Setup	Deploy real resources (VMs, App Services, Storage)
3	Security, Monitoring, and Identity	Practice with Key Vault, RBAC, Azure Monitor
4	Architecture and Cost Optimization	Study Well-Architected Framework + Pricing Calculator

| 5 | Practice Tests + Notes Review | Take 2–3 practice tests, review and reinforce weaknesses |
| 6 | Final Prep + Booking Exam | Light review, rest, and register via Microsoft Dashboard |

Learning Communities and Forums

Joining communities enhances motivation and provides support:

- **TechCommunity.Microsoft.com** – Official community forums

- **Reddit** – r/AzureCertification, r/AzureDev

- **Discord Groups** – Search for Azure certification servers

- **LinkedIn Groups** – Connect with others studying for the same exam

Attend Microsoft-hosted events like **Learn Live**, **Cloud Skills Challenges**, and **MS Ignite** for live demos, free exam vouchers, and networking.

Summary

Effective Azure exam preparation requires a strategic blend of resources: official documentation, hands-on experience, practice exams, and community support. The more varied your study inputs, the better your retention and real-world understanding.

Key takeaways:

- Microsoft Learn is your foundational, free resource

- Use sandboxes and labs to get hands-on with every topic

- Practice exams help validate your readiness and reduce surprises

- Books and video courses fill in conceptual gaps

- Commit to a structured, consistent study schedule

- Leverage the community for support, tips, and updates

Whether you're preparing for your first Azure certification or your fifth, the tools and guidance outlined here will equip you to study smarter, build confidence, and pass your exam with ease.

Tips for Exam Success

Achieving certification in Microsoft Azure is a significant accomplishment and a testament to your skills in cloud technologies. However, passing the exam requires more than just studying—success involves strategic preparation, mental readiness, test-taking techniques, and post-exam reflection. Whether you're attempting your first Azure certification or aiming for an expert-level credential, the following tips will help you prepare effectively and walk into your exam with confidence.

This section compiles practical, field-tested strategies from certified professionals who have passed Microsoft exams with high scores. We'll cover pre-exam routines, memory aids, time management, tackling case studies and labs, and ways to manage stress on exam day.

Understand the Exam Format

Before diving into your preparation, familiarize yourself with the structure and types of questions that will appear in the exam.

Common Question Types:

- **Multiple Choice**: Single or multiple correct answers

- **Drag-and-Drop**: Matching scenarios with actions or components

- **Scenario-Based**: Case studies followed by multiple questions

- **Hot Area**: Click to configure a setting or choose from GUI-based options

- **Labs (for select exams)**: Hands-on configurations within a simulated Azure environment

Important: Not every exam includes labs, but when they do (e.g., AZ-104, AZ-500), they are scored based on task completion, not necessarily the method used.

Pre-Exam Preparation Tips

1. Use the Official Skills Outline

Microsoft publishes a detailed exam outline for each certification. Print it or use it as a checklist.

Actionable Tip: Create a spreadsheet from the PDF and add a column for:

- Study complete? ✓

- Lab practiced? ✓

- Notes taken? ✓

- Confidence level (1–5)

2. Practice in Azure Portal

Theory alone isn't enough. You must navigate the portal fluently and know how to:

- Create and configure resources (VMs, storage, web apps)

- Apply access controls

- Monitor and troubleshoot

- Use diagnostic settings and metrics

- Automate with the CLI or PowerShell

Even if you're not using paid services, simulate workflows using the free tier.

3. Know the Pricing and SLAs

Questions on pricing tiers, service limits, and SLAs are common, especially in AZ-900 and AZ-305.

Quick facts to memorize:

- App Service SLA: 99.95% (Standard tier and above)

- Azure SQL Database SLA: 99.99%

- Azure Storage redundancy options (LRS, ZRS, GRS, RA-GRS)

- Reserved Instances vs. Spot Instances

Use the Azure Pricing Calculator to experiment and learn.

Memory and Study Techniques

1. The "Why, What, How" Method

For every topic, ask:

- **Why** does this feature/service exist?

- **What** problem does it solve?

- **How** is it configured or implemented?

This structure aids deeper understanding and retention.

2. Create Acronyms and Mnemonics

Examples:

- **CIA** – Confidentiality, Integrity, Availability (Security Principles)

- **FAIR** – Front Door, App Gateway, Internal Load Balancer, Routing

- **PVTN** – Policy, Virtual Network, Tags, NSGs (Governance checklist)

Create your own to remember port numbers, service names, or SLA numbers.

3. Flashcards

Use apps like Anki or Quizlet to create digital flashcards for:

- Commands (az CLI)

- Storage account tiers

- VM families (B-series = burstable, D-series = general purpose, etc.)

- Key vault access policies vs. RBAC

Practice Tests: Use Wisely

Practice tests are essential, but they must be approached as a learning tool, not just a score tracker.

Strategy:

- Start with an untimed test to gauge your baseline

- Don't memorize answers—instead, understand *why* they are correct

- After each test, review every question, especially the ones you got right by guessing

- Take at least 3–5 full-length mock exams

Simulate real exam conditions: find a quiet room, set a timer (usually 90–120 minutes), and avoid looking up answers until the test ends.

Exam Day Tips

1. Get a Good Night's Sleep

Avoid cramming the night before. Resting your brain ensures better focus and decision-making under pressure.

2. Arrive Early or Set Up Early (Remote Exams)

- For test centers: Arrive 30 minutes early

- For remote exams: Set up 15–20 minutes before the check-in window

- Test your webcam, microphone, lighting, and internet connection in advance

Have a government-issued ID ready and ensure your workspace is clean and free from distractions.

3. Manage Exam Time Wisely

If your exam includes labs or case studies, these can consume large chunks of time.

Time management tips:

- Spend no more than 90 seconds on difficult multiple-choice questions—mark and revisit

- Read case studies quickly but thoroughly—focus on constraints, goals, and requirements

- Labs usually appear at the end and may be time-boxed or locked once started

Some exams prevent you from returning to case study questions after you've moved on. Watch for warnings.

4. Read Every Word

Exam questions often contain critical keywords:

- "Best" or "most appropriate" vs. "first" or "initial"

- "Minimize cost" or "maximize availability"

- "Publicly accessible" vs. "private access"

Don't fall into the trap of selecting the first familiar-sounding answer.

During the Exam: Mindset and Focus

- **Take deep breaths** to stay calm

- **Don't panic** if a few questions seem unfamiliar—Azure evolves rapidly, and Microsoft may test future-previewed features

- **Use the mark for review feature** liberally

- **Use all the time given**, even if you finish early—review your marked questions

If you feel stuck, eliminate clearly wrong answers and choose the best among the rest. Trust your prep.

After the Exam: Review and Reflect

You'll receive a provisional pass/fail immediately, along with a score breakdown by domain.

If you pass:

- Celebrate, update your resume and LinkedIn

- Download your digital badge from Credly

- Share your success in the community

If you don't pass:

- Don't be discouraged. Reflect on the score report

- Note your weakest areas and focus your study there

- Schedule a retake after additional practice (wait period is typically 24 hours, then longer if multiple failures)

Common Mistakes to Avoid

- Relying solely on video courses without hands-on practice

- Underestimating soft topics like pricing, SLA, or governance

- Memorizing CLI syntax instead of understanding concepts

- Skipping case study practice

- Taking the exam before you're consistently scoring 80%+ on mock tests

---

Summary

Success in Azure exams is achievable for anyone with a structured approach, a hands-on mindset, and strong study discipline. Combine reading, labs, practice, and review with a confident, focused mindset, and you'll be well-prepared to tackle any Azure certification.

Key tips to remember:

- Understand the exam blueprint thoroughly

- Practice hands-on tasks regularly

- Use mock exams to refine your knowledge

- Build confidence with spaced repetition and flashcards

- Stay calm, focused, and strategic during the exam

Passing your Azure exam is not just about earning a badge—it's about developing real-world skills that make you a better engineer, architect, or developer in today's cloud-first world.

Continuing Your Azure Learning Path

Earning a Microsoft Azure certification is a major accomplishment, but it's only the beginning of your journey. The world of cloud computing is dynamic, with new services, updates, and best practices emerging constantly. To remain effective and competitive in your career, you must continue learning long after the exam. In this section, we'll explore how to build a sustainable learning path after certification, align learning with real-world projects, engage with the community, stay up to date with Azure innovations, and prepare for future roles in cloud engineering, architecture, data, security, and beyond.

Embrace Lifelong Learning in Cloud

Cloud is not a static field. Azure services evolve continuously, with hundreds of updates each month. After your certification, shift your focus from exam preparation to **real-world mastery** and **career growth**.

Key post-certification goals:

- Strengthen skills in areas you didn't cover deeply during exam prep

- Learn emerging Azure services like OpenAI, Azure Arc, and Azure Container Apps

- Apply knowledge to real-world projects (professional or personal)

- Contribute to open-source or community learning

- Explore adjacent roles: DevOps, AI/ML, Security, Data

Create a Personalized Learning Map

After certification, it's time to build your **Azure learning roadmap** based on your career goals, interests, and job responsibilities.

Common tracks to consider:

Track	Focus Areas	Suggested Services

Cloud Developer	App Services, Functions, APIs, Storage	App Service, Cosmos DB, Key Vault, Azure DevOps
DevOps Engineer	CI/CD, IaC, Monitoring, GitOps	Azure DevOps, GitHub Actions, ARM/Bicep, Monitor
Data Engineer	ETL pipelines, data lakes, analytics	Data Factory, Synapse, ADLS, Databricks
AI Engineer	NLP, computer vision, bots, ML pipelines	Azure AI, Cognitive Services, ML, Bot Framework
Security Engineer	Identity, governance, threat detection, compliance	Azure AD, Defender for Cloud, Key Vault
Architect	High availability, cost optimization, hybrid solutions	Front Door, Arc, Policy, Advisor, Blueprints

Create a 6-month or 12-month learning plan, divided into weekly goals such as:

- Week 1–2: Review Azure Advisor and optimize an existing resource group

- Week 3–4: Build a CI/CD pipeline using GitHub Actions for a serverless app

- Week 5–6: Create a Logic App or Durable Function for automation

- Week 7–8: Experiment with Azure OpenAI service or deploy a GPT-powered chatbot

Use Microsoft Learn for Continued Growth

Microsoft Learn continues to offer **advanced, scenario-driven content** for post-certification growth. Examples:

- **Architecting Cloud-Native Apps**: Explore distributed design, API gateways, queues, and microservices

- **Implementing Azure Governance**: Deep dive into RBAC, Policy, Blueprints, and Cost Management

- **Managing Hybrid Infrastructure**: Practice with Azure Arc, Azure Stack HCI, and on-prem extensions

Search for **Learning Paths** beyond certification collections. Bookmark or schedule recurring learning time weekly.

Join Cloud Communities and Stay Engaged

Joining communities is one of the most effective ways to grow faster and stay motivated.

Community platforms:

- **Microsoft Tech Community** – Participate in discussions and webinars

- **LinkedIn** – Follow Azure MVPs, engineers, and Microsoft leaders

- **Reddit** – Join r/AZURE, r/AzureCertification, r/DevOps

- **GitHub** – Star and contribute to repositories from `Azure`, `MicrosoftDocs`, and independent developers

- **Twitter/X** – Follow hashtags like #Azure, #CloudNative, #DevOps

Attend **Azure meetups**, **local user groups**, and **conferences** such as Microsoft Ignite or Build. These provide exposure to current trends, direct learning from experts, and even job leads.

Build and Share Real-World Projects

One of the best ways to reinforce your learning is to **build projects** and **share your knowledge**. Projects can be personal or professional, simple or complex, and published publicly on GitHub or as blog posts.

Project ideas:

- Deploy a static website with CDN, Blob Storage, and Azure Front Door

- Build a serverless REST API using Azure Functions and Cosmos DB

- Create a hybrid Kubernetes solution using Azure Arc and AKS

- Configure an end-to-end DevSecOps pipeline with Azure DevOps

- Use Azure Cognitive Services to detect sentiment in real-time tweets

Document your approach. Explain architecture decisions. Write blog posts or record short videos.

Benefits:

- Reinforces learning through real-world implementation

- Builds your public portfolio for hiring managers

- Helps others who are learning

- Positions you as an Azure advocate or thought leader

Maintain and Renew Certifications

Most Azure certifications are now valid for **one year**, with **free online renewal exams** available through Microsoft Learn.

Renewal tips:

- Microsoft notifies you 6 months before expiration

- Visit the Certification Dashboard to renew

- The renewal is an open-book assessment focused on **what's changed**

- Review the "What's new" sections on Microsoft Learn before attempting

Even if you're not required to renew (e.g., no longer in that role), it's a great way to stay current with platform changes.

Explore Advanced Topics and Emerging Tech

Stay ahead of the curve by exploring advanced or emerging areas in Azure.

Topics to explore:

- **Azure OpenAI Service** – Build generative AI applications

- **Azure Chaos Studio** – Run fault injection for resilience testing

- **Azure Load Testing** – Load-test APIs and apps before go-live

- **Azure Container Apps** – Explore serverless containers with KEDA autoscaling

- **Confidential Computing** – Run secure workloads with hardware-based encryption

Subscribe to the **Azure Updates Blog** or use Azure Updates to track new service releases and previews.

Build Toward Expert Roles and Multi-Cloud Skills

As your Azure skills mature, consider broadening your scope:

- **Prepare for Expert-Level Certifications** like AZ-305 (Architect) or AZ-400 (DevOps Expert)

- **Learn Infrastructure as Code** with Bicep, Terraform, or Pulumi

- **Understand FinOps and cost governance** to advise business leaders

- **Experiment with Azure integrations** with AWS, GCP, GitHub, and third-party SaaS

- **Learn scripting and automation** with PowerShell and the Azure CLI

Give Back: Teach, Mentor, and Lead

The highest form of mastery is the ability to teach. Sharing your experience helps others and reinforces your knowledge.

Ways to give back:

- Mentor colleagues preparing for exams

- Deliver a presentation at work or a local meetup

- Start a YouTube channel or blog about your Azure learning journey

- Answer questions on Microsoft Q&A or Stack Overflow

- Contribute to Azure documentation (MicrosoftDocs is on GitHub!)

Becoming a community contributor opens doors to MVP nominations, speaking engagements, and new job opportunities.

Summary

Earning an Azure certification is not the end—it's the launchpad for lifelong growth in the cloud industry. By continuing to learn, building real-world projects, engaging with the community, and exploring new technologies, you'll keep your skills sharp and stay ahead in your career.

Key actions to take next:

- Build a post-certification learning roadmap based on your role or interests

- Continue using Microsoft Learn and explore advanced paths

- Join and participate in global and local Azure communities

- Practice building and sharing real projects on GitHub or blogs

- Stay current with Azure service updates and roadmap previews

- Teach others to deepen your understanding and amplify your impact

In the cloud world, the only constant is change. Embrace it, and keep growing. Your journey with Azure is just beginning.

Chapter 11: Appendices

Glossary of Terms

Understanding the terminology used in Microsoft Azure is essential for both newcomers and seasoned professionals. Azure includes a wide range of services and technologies that often come with specific jargon. This glossary serves as a comprehensive reference for key terms, acronyms, and phrases commonly encountered throughout your Azure learning journey and professional use.

Terms are listed alphabetically for quick reference.

A

AAD (Azure Active Directory)
Microsoft's cloud-based identity and access management service. Used to manage users, groups, and access to resources.

ARM (Azure Resource Manager)
The deployment and management service for Azure. ARM allows users to manage resources via templates (ARM templates), the portal, CLI, and SDKs.

AKS (Azure Kubernetes Service)
A managed Kubernetes service that simplifies container orchestration, scaling, and monitoring.

App Service
A platform-as-a-service (PaaS) for hosting web apps, REST APIs, and mobile backends.

B

Blob Storage
Object storage for unstructured data such as images, videos, documents, and backups. Includes access tiers: hot, cool, and archive.

Bicep
A domain-specific language (DSL) for deploying Azure resources declaratively. A more concise alternative to JSON ARM templates.

Backup Vault
Stores and manages backup data for Azure virtual machines and workloads.

C

CLI (Command-Line Interface)
The Azure CLI is a cross-platform tool used to create, configure, and manage Azure resources from the command line.

Cosmos DB
A globally distributed, multi-model NoSQL database service designed for high availability and low latency.

Content Delivery Network (CDN)
A distributed network of servers that deliver content to users based on geographic proximity. Azure CDN reduces latency for static assets.

Container Instance
A lightweight and fast way to run containers in Azure without managing servers or orchestration.

D

Databricks
An analytics platform optimized for Azure that supports Apache Spark and machine learning workflows.

DevOps
A set of practices and tools that combine software development (Dev) and IT operations (Ops) to shorten the development lifecycle.

Durable Functions
An extension of Azure Functions that enables writing stateful workflows in serverless applications.

E

Event Grid
A fully managed event routing service that enables event-based architectures across Azure services and custom applications.

Elastic Pool
A resource allocation model in Azure SQL Database that allows multiple databases to share a pool of resources.

ExpressRoute
A private connection between on-premises networks and Microsoft Azure data centers, offering greater reliability and lower latency than public internet connections.

F

Functions (Azure Functions)
Serverless compute service for running small pieces of code (functions) in response to events or triggers without managing infrastructure.

Firewall (NSG / Azure Firewall)
Azure offers network security through Network Security Groups (NSG) and centralized firewall capabilities with Azure Firewall.

G

Geo-redundant Storage (GRS)
An Azure Storage redundancy option that replicates data to a secondary region for disaster recovery.

GitOps
A DevOps practice that uses Git as the source of truth for infrastructure and application deployments.

Guided Learning Paths
Microsoft Learn's structured courses that guide users through mastering specific Azure roles or services.

H

Hybrid Cloud
A computing model that combines on-premises infrastructure with cloud services. Azure supports hybrid models via services like Azure Arc.

High Availability (HA)
A design principle that ensures systems continue operating with minimal downtime. Achieved in Azure using Availability Zones and Sets.

I

IaaS (Infrastructure as a Service)
A cloud computing model providing virtualized computing resources over the internet, such as virtual machines and storage.

Identity Provider (IdP)
A system that creates, maintains, and manages user identities and authentication. Azure AD is an example of an IdP.

Ingress Controller
A Kubernetes component that manages external access to services within a cluster, typically via HTTP/HTTPS.

J

JSON (JavaScript Object Notation)
A lightweight data-interchange format commonly used in Azure ARM templates and configuration files.

K

Key Vault
Azure service for storing and accessing secrets, encryption keys, and certificates securely.

Kubernetes
An open-source platform for automating container deployment, scaling, and operations.

L

Load Balancer
Distributes incoming traffic among healthy instances of services. Azure supports Basic and Standard Load Balancer SKUs.

Log Analytics
A service within Azure Monitor used to collect and analyze telemetry from cloud and on-premises environments.

M

Managed Identity
A feature of Azure Active Directory that provides Azure services with an automatically managed identity to access other resources securely.

Marketplace
Azure's catalog of third-party software, services, and solutions that can be deployed directly into an Azure environment.

Metrics
Numerical data collected about the performance and health of Azure resources. Used in monitoring and alerting.

N

NSG (Network Security Group)
A firewall-like service that controls inbound and outbound traffic at the network interface and subnet level.

NoSQL
A type of non-relational database designed for distributed data stores. Cosmos DB is Azure's NoSQL solution.

O

OAuth 2.0
An open standard for access delegation, often used for token-based authentication in Azure apps.

OMI (Open Management Infrastructure)
A lightweight CIM server designed for managing resources in heterogeneous environments.

P

PaaS (Platform as a Service)
A cloud service model that provides a platform allowing customers to develop, run, and manage applications without handling infrastructure.

Private Link
Allows access to Azure PaaS services over a private endpoint in your virtual network, enhancing security.

Public IP
An IP address that is reachable over the internet. Used for Azure resources requiring public connectivity.

Q

Queue Storage
A service that provides message queuing for large workloads and decoupling application components.

R

RBAC (Role-Based Access Control)
A system for managing user permissions based on roles. Ensures least privilege access in Azure environments.

Resource Group
A container that holds related Azure resources for an application. Allows collective management and deployment.

Replication
Process of copying data to ensure redundancy and availability across regions or zones.

S

Storage Account
A top-level Azure resource that allows you to store blobs, files, queues, and tables.

Serverless
A computing model where the cloud provider automatically manages the infrastructure. Azure Functions is a serverless service.

Security Center (Microsoft Defender for Cloud)
A unified infrastructure security management system for strengthening the security posture of your environments.

T

Terraform
An open-source infrastructure-as-code tool that lets you define cloud resources in declarative configuration files.

Tags
Metadata applied to Azure resources for organizing and tracking billing, ownership, environment, and more.

U

Update Domain
 A mechanism used by Azure to ensure high availability during updates. VMs in different update domains are not rebooted at the same time.

User-Assigned Managed Identity
 A managed identity created as a standalone Azure resource, which can be assigned to multiple services.

V

Virtual Machine (VM)
 A scalable computing resource provided by Azure for running Windows or Linux workloads.

VNet (Virtual Network)
 A logically isolated network in Azure where you can run your VMs and services securely.

W

Web App
 A managed platform for hosting web applications with auto-scaling and built-in security.

WAF (Web Application Firewall)
 A firewall specifically designed to protect web applications from common exploits and vulnerabilities.

X

X.509 Certificate
 A standard format for public key certificates used in SSL/TLS encryption. Azure Key Vault stores and manages certificates.

Y

YAML (YAML Ain't Markup Language)
 A human-readable configuration format used in Azure DevOps pipelines, Kubernetes manifests, and Bicep definitions.

Z

Zone Redundant Storage (ZRS)
Stores multiple copies of data across different Availability Zones in a region for high availability.

Zero Trust
A security model that assumes breach and verifies each request as though it originates from an open network.

Summary

This glossary serves as a quick reference for the most important Azure-related terms you'll encounter while studying, working, or architecting solutions on the Microsoft Cloud platform. Bookmark this section as your go-to companion when revisiting key concepts, exploring new services, or preparing for interviews and certifications.

Understanding the language of Azure is essential to communicating effectively, troubleshooting efficiently, and navigating the cloud ecosystem with confidence. As Azure evolves, so too will its vocabulary—keep learning, and stay curious.

Resources for Further Learning

Continuing your Azure education after completing this book is essential for staying up to date with evolving cloud technologies and expanding your expertise into new areas. Microsoft Azure is vast and constantly changing, and there are hundreds of high-quality resources available to help you maintain momentum on your learning journey.

This section covers a comprehensive list of learning platforms, documentation, blogs, YouTube channels, newsletters, GitHub repositories, conferences, certifications, and tools that can support and guide your continued education. Whether you're deepening existing knowledge or branching into AI, DevOps, Data, or Security, these resources are your next step.

Microsoft Learn

URL: https://learn.microsoft.com/training

Microsoft Learn is the **official and free** platform from Microsoft. It includes:

- Self-paced learning modules

- Role-based learning paths

- Hands-on exercises with the sandbox environment

- Certification preparation collections

- Real-world scenario-based tutorials

You can log in with a Microsoft account to track progress, earn XP, and display your learning history.

Pro Tip: Bookmark your target certification page (e.g., "AZ-104 learning path") and review it monthly for new modules or updates.

Microsoft Documentation

URL: https://learn.microsoft.com/azure

Azure's official documentation is continually updated and includes:

- Conceptual overviews

- Quickstarts and how-to guides

- API references

- CLI and PowerShell examples

- Architecture center articles and patterns

You can also contribute to the docs via GitHub if you find errors or want to add improvements.

Sample CLI command:

```
az webapp create --resource-group myRG --plan myAppServicePlan --
name mywebapp --runtime "DOTNET|6.0"
```

GitHub Repositories

Microsoft and the community maintain a wide array of open-source projects and sample codebases for Azure.

Recommended Repos:

- [Azure Samples](#) – Code samples for almost every Azure service

- [Azure Quickstart Templates](#) – 1,000+ ARM/Bicep templates

- [Microsoft Learning Paths](#) – Labs and learning resources aligned with certifications

- [Awesome Azure](#) – Curated list of Azure tools and resources

---

YouTube Channels

Visual learners benefit from tutorials, walkthroughs, and conference sessions. These channels are goldmines:

Official:

- **Microsoft Azure**: Demos, customer stories, and feature announcements

- **Azure Friday (Scott Hanselman)**: Weekly deep-dives into Azure services

- **Microsoft Developer**: Dev-focused sessions, events, and guides

Community:

- **John Savill's Technical Training** – Excellent certification prep and architecture guidance

- **CloudSkills.io (Mike Pfeiffer)** – Practical DevOps and automation tutorials

- **Stephane Maarek** – Focuses on cloud certifications and real-world tips

Tip: Subscribe and enable notifications to stay in sync with platform changes.

Books

Books provide depth that sometimes isn't possible in short-form content. These recommendations expand your understanding and can complement practical exercises.

Fundamentals:

- *Exam Ref AZ-900 Microsoft Azure Fundamentals* – Jim Cheshire

- *Microsoft Azure for Beginners* – Adney Ainsley

Intermediate to Advanced:

- *Azure for Architects* – Ritesh Modi

- *Azure Strategy and Implementation Guide* – Peter De Tender, Greg Leonardo

- *Designing Distributed Systems* – Brendan Burns (Microsoft Kubernetes expert)

DevOps & Security:

- *Infrastructure as Code* – Kief Morris

- *The Phoenix Project* – Gene Kim (DevOps culture)

- *Zero Trust Security on Azure* – Yuri Diogenes

Blogs and Newsletters

Stay informed and inspired by following expert blogs and curated newsletters.

Official Microsoft Blogs:

- Azure Blog

- IT Ops Talk Blog

- Azure DevOps Blog

Independent Blogs:

- Thomas Maurer (Microsoft MVP): https://www.thomasmaurer.ch

- Christos Matskas (Identity & Security): https://www.christosmatz.com

- Daniel Krzyczkowski (IoT and Edge): https://danielkrzyczkowski.blogspot.com

Newsletters:

- **Azure Weekly** – Curated weekly digest of news, tutorials, and videos

- **The Azure DevOps Community Newsletter** – DevOps-specific updates and tips

- **Cloud Skills Weekly** – Mike Pfeiffer's collection of advanced Azure/DevOps content

---

Learning Platforms

Free:

- **Microsoft Learn** (as above)

- **YouTube Channels**

- **edX (Microsoft courses)**

Paid (but worth the investment):

- **Pluralsight** – Role-based and service-specific courses

- **LinkedIn Learning** – Business and tech training, including Azure certification

- **Cloud Academy** – Labs, quizzes, and tracks

- **A Cloud Guru / Linux Academy** – Cloud playgrounds and project-based content

- **Udemy** – Inexpensive courses from experienced instructors like Scott Duffy and Alan Rodrigues

---

Events and Conferences

Attending events—virtually or in person—helps reinforce your knowledge and puts you in touch with the wider Azure ecosystem.

Major Microsoft Events:

- **Microsoft Ignite** – For IT professionals and decision-makers

- **Microsoft Build** – Developer-focused innovations

- **Microsoft Learn Live** – Live walkthroughs and interactive Q&A

Other Recommended Conferences:

- **Global Azure Bootcamp**

- **KubeCon (for AKS and containers)**

- **DevOpsDays**

- **Azure Summit**

- **MVP-led local user groups and meetups**

Most Microsoft events are recorded and available on-demand.

Certification Support and Communities

- Microsoft Certification Dashboard

- Reddit: r/AzureCertification

- Microsoft Q&A

- Stack Overflow

Ask questions, share progress, and get help when you're stuck. Participating in these communities can expose you to use cases and troubleshooting scenarios you may not encounter alone.

Developer and Architecture Tools

- **Azure CLI**: `az login`, `az vm create`, `az webapp deploy`

- **Azure Bicep**: For managing IaC (Infrastructure as Code)

- **Terraform**: Multi-cloud IaC tool

- **Postman**: Test REST APIs built with Azure Functions or Logic Apps

- **Visual Studio Code**: Azure extensions for quick deployments

- **Azure Architecture Center**: Diagrams, patterns, and best practices
  https://learn.microsoft.com/azure/architecture

Long-Term Learning Plans

Once you've completed one certification, consider mapping out your future path based on interest or job role:

- From AZ-900 to AZ-104 (Admin) or AZ-204 (Developer)

- From AZ-104/AZ-204 to AZ-305 (Architect)

- Add SC-300 or AZ-500 for Security and Compliance

- DP-203 or DP-100 for Data and AI professionals

- AZ-400 for DevOps Engineers

Plan for certifications every 6–12 months depending on your pace and workload. Pair each goal with projects, blog posts, or contributions to ensure the knowledge is applied, not just memorized.

Summary

Azure's ecosystem is growing faster than ever. Continuous learning is not just recommended—it's essential. The resources listed here provide everything you need to stay current, specialize further, and position yourself as a valuable cloud professional in any organization.

Key takeaways:

- Leverage Microsoft Learn, GitHub, and YouTube for ongoing, free learning

- Use certification guides and live sandboxes to gain hands-on experience

- Follow trusted blogs, newsletters, and documentation to stay up to date

- Attend events and conferences to learn directly from experts

- Create projects and share your journey publicly for deeper learning and networking

Your Azure journey is just getting started. Keep learning, keep building, and keep exploring.

Sample Projects and Code Snippets

Practical, hands-on experience is one of the most effective ways to solidify your understanding of Azure services. Building small- to medium-sized projects not only strengthens your technical skills but also gives you something to showcase on your resume or GitHub profile. This section contains sample project ideas, detailed breakdowns, and code snippets covering core Azure services, including web apps, databases, serverless functions, identity management, DevOps, and more.

These projects are structured to be modular and scalable, making them suitable for learners at all levels—from beginner to intermediate to advanced.

Project 1: Azure Web App with Continuous Deployment

Objective: Deploy a web application to Azure App Service with automatic deployment via GitHub Actions.

Tools and Services:

- Azure App Service

- Azure Resource Group

- GitHub

- GitHub Actions

Steps:

1. Create a resource group:

```
az group create --name WebAppRG --location eastus
```

2. Create an App Service Plan and Web App:

```
az appservice plan create --name WebAppPlan --resource-group
WebAppRG --sku FREE

az webapp create --name mywebappsample --resource-group WebAppRG --
plan WebAppPlan --runtime "NODE|16-lts"
```

3. Deploy using GitHub Actions (`.github/workflows/deploy.yml`):

```
name: Azure Node.js Deploy

on:
  push:
    branches:
      - main

jobs:
  build-and-deploy:
    runs-on: ubuntu-latest
    steps:
      - uses: actions/checkout@v2
      - name: 'Deploy to Azure Web App'
        uses: Azure/webapps-deploy@v2
        with:
          app-name: mywebappsample
          publish-profile: ${{ secrets.AZURE_WEBAPP_PUBLISH_PROFILE }}
          package: .
```

Project 2: Serverless API with Azure Functions and Cosmos DB

Objective: Build a simple CRUD API using Azure Functions and persist data to Azure Cosmos DB.

Tools and Services:

- Azure Functions (HTTP trigger)

- Azure Cosmos DB (Core SQL API)

- Azure CLI

Steps:

1. Create a Cosmos DB account:

```
az cosmosdb create --name mycosmosdbapi --resource-group
ServerlessRG --kind GlobalDocumentDB

az cosmosdb sql database create --account-name mycosmosdbapi --name
tododb --resource-group ServerlessRG

az cosmosdb sql container create --account-name mycosmosdbapi --
database-name tododb --name todos --partition-key-path /id
```

2. Create and initialize a function project:

```
func init myfunctions --worker-runtime node

cd myfunctions

func new --name AddTodo --template "HTTP trigger"
```

3. Add code to insert into Cosmos DB:

```
const { CosmosClient } = require("@azure/cosmos");


module.exports = async function (context, req) {

    const client = new
CosmosClient(process.env.COSMOS_DB_CONNECTION_STRING);

    const container = client.database("tododb").container("todos");
```

```
    const todoItem = req.body;

    const { resource: createdItem } = await
container.items.create(todoItem);


    context.res = {

        status: 201,

        body: createdItem

    };

};
```

4. Deploy and test your API using Postman or curl.

Project 3: Static Website Hosting with Blob Storage and CDN

Objective: Host a static website using Azure Blob Storage and deliver content via Azure CDN.

Tools and Services:

- Azure Storage Account

- Azure CDN

- Azure DNS (optional for custom domain)

Steps:

1. Create a storage account and enable static site hosting:

```
az storage account create --name mystaticwebstorage --resource-group
StaticSiteRG --location eastus --sku Standard_LRS
```

```
az storage blob service-properties update --account-name
mystaticwebstorage --static-website --index-document index.html
```

2. Upload files to the $web container:

```
az storage blob upload-batch --account-name mystaticwebstorage --
source ./site --destination \$web
```

3. Optional: Create and configure a CDN for faster global delivery.

Project 4: Securing a Web App with Azure AD Authentication

Objective: Add enterprise-level authentication to an Azure Web App using Azure Active Directory (Azure AD).

Tools and Services:

- Azure Web App

- Azure AD

- Microsoft Authentication Library (MSAL.js)

Steps:

1. Register your app in Azure AD:

```
az ad app create --display-name MyAuthWebApp --reply-urls
"https://mysecurewebapp.azurewebsites.net/.auth/login/aad/callback"
```

2. Update the Web App to enforce authentication:

```
az webapp auth update --name mysecurewebapp --resource-group
AuthWebRG --enabled true --action LoginWithAzureActiveDirectory \
```

```
--aad-client-id <your-client-id> --aad-allowed-token-audiences
"https://mysecurewebapp.azurewebsites.net"
```

3. Use MSAL.js on the frontend to handle login and token retrieval.

Project 5: Infrastructure as Code with Bicep

Objective: Use Bicep to declare and deploy infrastructure in a repeatable and automated way.

Tools and Services:

- Azure Bicep CLI
- Azure Resource Group
- Azure Storage Account

Sample Bicep file (`storage.bicep`):

```
param storageAccountName string

param location string = resourceGroup().location


resource storageAccount 'Microsoft.Storage/storageAccounts@2022-09-
01' = {

  name: storageAccountName

  location: location

  sku: {

    name: 'Standard_LRS'

  }

  kind: 'StorageV2'

  properties: {
```

```
    accessTier: 'Hot'

  }

}
```

Deploy using the CLI:

```
az deployment group create --resource-group InfraRG --template-file
./storage.bicep --parameters storageAccountName=demoaccount123
```

Project 6: Real-Time Notification System with SignalR

Objective: Create a real-time notification system using Azure SignalR and Azure Functions.

Tools and Services:

- Azure SignalR Service

- Azure Functions

- JavaScript client

Sample Code (Function binding):

```
{

  "type": "signalR",

  "name": "signalRMessages",

  "direction": "out",

  "hubName": "notifications",

  "connectionStringSetting": "AzureSignalRConnectionString"

}
```

Function Logic (JavaScript):

```
module.exports = async function (context, req) {

  context.bindings.signalRMessages = [{

    target: "newMessage",

    arguments: [ req.body ]

  }];

  context.res = { status: 202 };

};
```

Project 7: CI/CD Pipeline with Azure DevOps

Objective: Set up a full CI/CD pipeline for a Node.js app using Azure Repos and Azure Pipelines.

Tools and Services:

- Azure DevOps

- Azure Pipelines

- Azure App Service

YAML Pipeline Example (`azure-pipelines.yml`):

```
trigger:

  branches:

    include:

      - main


pool:

  vmImage: 'ubuntu-latest'
```

```
steps:

- task: NodeTool@0

  inputs:

    versionSpec: '16.x'

- script: npm install

- script: npm run build

- task: AzureWebApp@1

  inputs:

    azureSubscription: '<Service Connection>'

    appName: '<App Service Name>'

    package: '$(System.DefaultWorkingDirectory)'
```

Summary of Learning Outcomes

Each of these sample projects reinforces different areas of Azure expertise:

- **Web App Deployment**: PaaS basics, deployment automation

- **Serverless and NoSQL**: Event-driven architecture and Cosmos DB

- **Blob Storage and CDN**: Static content delivery

- **Security**: Identity-based access controls with Azure AD

- **Infrastructure as Code**: Repeatable, auditable deployment strategies with Bicep

- **Real-Time Apps**: Using SignalR for instant notifications

- **DevOps Pipelines**: Automating the build and release process

By working through these projects, you not only deepen your understanding but also build a valuable portfolio of demonstrable Azure skills. Don't just read—build, break, fix, and deploy. The Azure cloud is your playground.

API Reference Guide

As developers and architects build cloud-native solutions on Microsoft Azure, interacting with APIs becomes essential. Azure exposes RESTful APIs for nearly every service it offers—from managing resources to monitoring, identity, and automation. This section provides a comprehensive guide to working with Azure APIs, including authentication methods, request structure, key service endpoints, tools, SDKs, and best practices.

Whether you're writing a script to automate resource creation or building a SaaS product that integrates Azure services, understanding the Azure API landscape is crucial for delivering robust, secure, and maintainable solutions.

Azure REST API Basics

Azure APIs are built on standard **HTTP methods** (GET, POST, PUT, DELETE, PATCH) and use **JSON** as the primary data exchange format.

Base endpoint:

```
https://management.azure.com/
```

All resource-level calls are made under this root domain and require an API version parameter (`?api-version=`) to specify the schema.

Example: List Resource Groups

```
GET
https://management.azure.com/subscriptions/{subscriptionId}/resource
groups?api-version=2022-09-01
```

Headers:

```
Authorization: Bearer <access_token>

Content-Type: application/json
```

Authentication with Azure APIs

To call Azure APIs, you need to authenticate using **Azure Active Directory (Azure AD)**.

Steps:

1. Register an application in Azure AD (via portal or CLI)

2. Assign API permissions to the app

3. Obtain an access token using client credentials or user authentication

4. Include the token in the `Authorization` header

Token Request (Client Credentials Flow)

```
POST https://login.microsoftonline.com/{tenantId}/oauth2/v2.0/token

Content-Type: application/x-www-form-urlencoded


client_id=<app_id>&

client_secret=<secret>&

grant_type=client_credentials&

scope=https://management.azure.com/.default
```

Sample Access Token Retrieval (using cURL):

```
curl -X POST
https://login.microsoftonline.com/<tenant_id>/oauth2/v2.0/token \

 -H "Content-Type: application/x-www-form-urlencoded" \

 -d
"client_id=<app_id>&client_secret=<secret>&grant_type=client_credent
ials&scope=https://management.azure.com/.default"
```

Common Azure Management APIs

Create a Resource Group

```
PUT
https://management.azure.com/subscriptions/{subscriptionId}/resource
groups/myGroup?api-version=2022-09-01
```

```
{

  "location": "eastus"

}
```

Deploy a Virtual Machine (Simplified)

```
PUT
https://management.azure.com/subscriptions/{subscriptionId}/resource
Groups/myGroup/providers/Microsoft.Compute/virtualMachines/myVM?api-
version=2023-03-01
```

```
{

  "location": "eastus",

  "properties": {

    "hardwareProfile": {

      "vmSize": "Standard_DS1_v2"

    },

    "storageProfile": {

      "imageReference": {

        "publisher": "MicrosoftWindowsServer",

        "offer": "WindowsServer",

        "sku": "2019-Datacenter",

        "version": "latest"

      },
```

```json
    "osDisk": {

      "createOption": "FromImage"

    }

  },

  "osProfile": {

    "computerName": "myVM",

    "adminUsername": "azureuser",

    "adminPassword": "P@ssword1234"

  },

  "networkProfile": {

    "networkInterfaces": [

      {

        "id":
"/subscriptions/{subscriptionId}/resourceGroups/myGroup/providers/Microsoft.Network/networkInterfaces/myNic"

      }

    ]

  }

}
```

Using SDKs Instead of Raw HTTP

Azure provides official SDKs for several programming languages that abstract API calls and simplify development.

Available SDKs:

- **.NET** – `Azure.ResourceManager`, `Microsoft.Azure.Management.*`

- **JavaScript/TypeScript** – `@azure/arm-*`, `@azure/ms-rest-nodeauth`

- **Python** – `azure-mgmt-*`, `azure-identity`

- **Java** – `com.azure.resourcemanager`

- **Go** – `github.com/Azure/azure-sdk-for-go`

- **Terraform** and **Bicep** also translate to API calls under the hood

Example: Creating a Resource Group with Python

```python
from azure.identity import DefaultAzureCredential

from azure.mgmt.resource import ResourceManagementClient


credential = DefaultAzureCredential()

subscription_id = "your-subscription-id"

resource_client = ResourceManagementClient(credential,
subscription_id)


resource_group_params = { "location": "eastus" }

resource_client.resource_groups.create_or_update("myResourceGroup",
resource_group_params)
```

Monitoring and Logging APIs

You can access metrics and logs programmatically via the Azure Monitor REST APIs.

List Activity Logs:

```
GET
https://management.azure.com/subscriptions/{subscriptionId}/provider
```

```
s/microsoft.insights/eventtypes/management/values?api-version=2015-
04-01&$filter=eventTimestamp ge 2024-01-01T00:00:00Z and
eventTimestamp le 2024-04-01T00:00:00Z
```

Get Metrics for a VM:

```
GET
https://management.azure.com/subscriptions/{subscriptionId}/resource
Groups/myGroup/providers/Microsoft.Compute/virtualMachines/myVM/prov
iders/microsoft.insights/metrics?api-version=2018-01-
01&metricnames=Percentage CPU
```

Azure Graph API vs Azure REST API

- **Azure Resource Manager API** – Focused on managing Azure resources (VMs, storage, networking, etc.)

- **Microsoft Graph API** – Used for accessing Microsoft 365 services (users, groups, email, calendars, etc.)

To manage Azure AD users or groups, use Microsoft Graph:

```
GET https://graph.microsoft.com/v1.0/users
```

Requires a different scope (`https://graph.microsoft.com/.default`) and token endpoint.

Rate Limiting and Throttling

Azure APIs impose limits to prevent abuse and ensure fair use.

If throttled, you may receive a `429 Too Many Requests` response.

Response headers to inspect:

- `x-ms-ratelimit-remaining-subscription-reads`

- `x-ms-ratelimit-remaining-subscription-writes`

- `Retry-After`

Implement **exponential backoff** for retry logic in your code.

Automation with REST APIs

You can use REST APIs in:

- **PowerShell scripts**

- **Azure DevOps pipelines**

- **GitHub Actions**

- **Custom automation tools**

- **Bash/cURL-based shell scripts**

Example: Create Resource Group with Bash and REST

```
ACCESS_TOKEN=$(az account get-access-token --query accessToken -o
tsv)

curl -X PUT
https://management.azure.com/subscriptions/$SUBSCRIPTION_ID/resource
groups/myGroup?api-version=2022-09-01 \

  -H "Authorization: Bearer $ACCESS_TOKEN" \

  -H "Content-Type: application/json" \

  -d '{"location":"eastus"}'
```

API Best Practices

- Always use the latest API versions for new deployments

- Validate JSON payloads before sending requests

- Secure your API credentials using Azure Key Vault or environment variables

- Use retry logic and exponential backoff for transient errors

- Log every API interaction for debugging and compliance

- Use tools like **Postman** or **Insomnia** for testing

- Monitor API latency and error rates in Application Insights

Summary

Azure's APIs are powerful tools that allow you to automate, manage, and integrate with cloud services at scale. From provisioning infrastructure to monitoring performance and managing security, almost every aspect of Azure can be accessed programmatically.

Key takeaways:

- Use Azure REST APIs for fine-grained control and automation

- Authenticate using Azure AD and request scoped access tokens

- Prefer SDKs for productivity and readability where possible

- Be aware of rate limits and implement proper error handling

- Leverage logs and metrics endpoints for observability

- Practice secure API access using managed identities and secrets management

As your Azure experience matures, mastering the use of its APIs will unlock limitless potential for building reliable, scalable, and automated cloud solutions.

Frequently Asked Questions

In this section, we address the most common questions learners, developers, administrators, and architects ask when working with Microsoft Azure. These FAQs span a wide range of topics—from foundational concepts to best practices, troubleshooting tips, and strategic decision-making. Whether you're just starting your journey with Azure or managing enterprise workloads in production, this guide will help you find clarity and avoid common pitfalls.

General Azure Questions

Q: What is Microsoft Azure and how is it different from other cloud platforms?
Azure is Microsoft's cloud computing platform offering infrastructure as a service (IaaS), platform as a service (PaaS), and software as a service (SaaS). It competes with AWS and Google Cloud, and its biggest differentiators include deep integration with Microsoft tools (e.g., Active Directory, Office 365), strong hybrid support (e.g., Azure Arc), and a large enterprise ecosystem.

Q: Can I try Azure for free?
Yes. Azure offers a free tier that includes $200 in credit for 30 days and always-free services such as 750 hours of B1S VM, 5GB of Blob storage, and 250,000 monthly function executions.

```
az account list --output table  # View all available subscriptions
```

Q: What's the difference between a subscription and a resource group?
A subscription is a container for billing and permissions. A resource group is a logical container within a subscription that holds related resources (e.g., VMs, databases, storage accounts) that can be managed as a unit.

Services and Usage

Q: When should I use Azure App Service vs. Azure Functions?
Use **App Service** for long-running web apps, APIs, or applications with stateful sessions. Use **Functions** for short, event-driven tasks such as webhook processing or scheduled jobs.

Q: What are Availability Zones and why do they matter?
Availability Zones are physically separated data centers within a region. Deploying resources across zones improves fault tolerance and helps ensure high availability.

Q: How can I secure my application data in Azure?
Use services like **Azure Key Vault** to store secrets and keys, enforce **RBAC (Role-Based Access Control)** for access management, apply **NSGs (Network Security Groups)** to limit traffic, and encrypt data at rest and in transit.

Cost and Pricing

Q: How can I estimate the cost of a solution before deploying?
Use the Azure Pricing Calculator to model your architecture and estimate monthly costs.

Q: What is Azure Cost Management?
It's a suite of tools to track and manage your Azure spending. You can set budgets, analyze usage trends, and receive alerts when you exceed cost thresholds.

Q: How do I reduce Azure costs effectively?

- Use **Reserved Instances** for consistent workloads

- Set up **auto-shutdown** for dev/test VMs

- Scale down during off-hours using automation

- Clean up unused resources (e.g., orphaned disks or IPs)

- Leverage **Azure Advisor** recommendations

Identity and Security

Q: What's the difference between Azure AD and Active Directory?
Azure AD is Microsoft's cloud-based identity service, used for managing user access to Azure and Microsoft 365. Traditional Active Directory is an on-prem directory service. Azure AD supports modern protocols like OAuth2, OpenID Connect, and SAML.

Q: How can I enable MFA for users in Azure?
Use **Azure AD Conditional Access** policies to enforce multi-factor authentication for all or selected users and groups.

Q: What is a managed identity and when should I use it?
Managed identities allow your apps to access Azure services securely without storing credentials. Use them to authenticate to services like Key Vault, Storage, or SQL without hardcoded secrets.

Development and Deployment

Q: What's the best way to deploy infrastructure—Portal, CLI, ARM, Bicep, or Terraform?
For manual changes: Azure Portal
For scripting: Azure CLI or PowerShell
For automation and IaC: Use **Bicep** for native Azure IaC or **Terraform** for cross-cloud flexibility.

Q: How can I set up CI/CD for Azure apps?
Use **GitHub Actions**, **Azure DevOps Pipelines**, or third-party tools. Azure provides deployment slots, environment variables, and integration with multiple code repositories.

Example GitHub Action:

```
- name: Deploy to Azure Web App

  uses: Azure/webapps-deploy@v2

  with:

    app-name: myapp

    publish-profile: ${{ secrets.AZURE_WEBAPP_PUBLISH_PROFILE }}

    package: .
```

Q: What is Azure Container Apps and when should I use it?
Azure Container Apps is a serverless container service that supports KEDA-based autoscaling, Dapr integration, and microservice architectures. It's ideal for lightweight, containerized applications without managing a full Kubernetes cluster.

Monitoring and Troubleshooting

Q: How can I monitor the performance of my Azure services?
Use **Azure Monitor**, **Log Analytics**, and **Application Insights**. These tools provide logs, metrics, traces, and alerts across all your resources.

Q: What's the difference between Azure Monitor and Application Insights?
Azure Monitor provides a platform-wide view of metrics and logs. Application Insights focuses on performance monitoring for applications, including custom telemetry and end-to-end tracing.

Q: How do I set alerts for downtime or performance issues?
Create an **Alert Rule** in Azure Monitor based on metrics or log queries. You can route alerts to email, SMS, Azure mobile app, or external systems via webhooks or Logic Apps.

Networking and Access

Q: What is a Virtual Network (VNet) and why is it important?
A VNet is your private network in Azure. It provides IP addressing, DNS, routing, subnets, and network isolation. It's the foundation for secure and scalable cloud architectures.

Q: What's the difference between a Public IP and a Private IP in Azure?
Public IPs are accessible from the internet. Private IPs are internal to your VNet. Prefer private IPs for secure, internal communication between services.

Q: Can I connect on-prem networks to Azure?
Yes, using **VPN Gateway**, **ExpressRoute**, or **Azure Virtual WAN**, you can extend your datacenter into Azure with encrypted tunnels or dedicated links.

Governance and Policy

Q: What is Azure Policy and how does it help?
Azure Policy enforces governance by defining rules for resource configurations (e.g., allowed locations, tag requirements). It helps maintain compliance across your environment.

Q: What are tags in Azure?
Tags are key-value pairs applied to resources for cost tracking, automation, and organization. Example: environment=production, owner=teamA.

```
az tag create --name environment --value production
```

Q: What is Azure Blueprints?
Blueprints enable you to deploy a repeatable set of Azure resources and policies, including role assignments, templates, and compliance controls—ideal for enterprise environments.

Certification and Learning

Q: Which Azure certification should I start with?
If you're a beginner, start with **AZ-900 (Azure Fundamentals)**. From there, choose a role-based certification based on your career goals: AZ-104 for administrators, AZ-204 for developers, and AZ-305 for architects.

Q: Are there free resources for learning Azure?
Yes! Use Microsoft Learn, which provides free interactive modules and sandbox environments.

Q: How do I renew my Azure certification?
Certifications are valid for one year. You can renew by passing a free online assessment on Microsoft Learn before your expiration date.

Miscellaneous

Q: What's the difference between IaaS, PaaS, and SaaS in Azure?

- **IaaS (Infrastructure as a Service)** – Virtual Machines, Networking

- **PaaS (Platform as a Service)** – App Service, Azure Functions

- **SaaS (Software as a Service)** – Microsoft 365, Power BI

Q: Can I automate everything in Azure?
Nearly everything in Azure can be automated using a combination of:

- REST APIs

- CLI and PowerShell

- Bicep and ARM Templates

- Terraform

- DevOps Pipelines

Q: What tools help with Azure architecture design?
 Use the **Azure Architecture Center**, **Microsoft Learn**, **Well-Architected Framework**, **Azure Advisor**, and **Workbooks** for design guidance.

Summary

This FAQ covers a wide spectrum of topics and is designed to provide immediate, actionable answers for your most pressing Azure questions. Whether you're dealing with architecture, pricing, security, or certification, use this section as a reference point in your day-to-day Azure journey.

Remember:

- Most Azure services are accessible via CLI, SDKs, REST, and the Portal

- Stay up to date using Azure Advisor, updates blog, and documentation

- The community is large—don't hesitate to ask questions and seek help

Bookmark this section and revisit it often as your skills deepen and your Azure usage grows.